School Censorship
21st in the Century

A Guide for Teachers and School Library Media Specialists

John S. Simmons
Professor, English Education and
    Reading
Florida State University
Tallahassee, Florida, USA

Eliza T. Dresang
Associate Professor, School of
    Information Studies
Florida State University
Tallahassee, Florida, USA

INTERNATIONAL
Reading
Association

800 Barksdale Road, PO Box 8139
Newark, Delaware 19714-8139, USA
www.reading.org

The International Reading Association attempts, through its publications, to provide a forum for a wide spectrum of opinions on reading. This policy permits divergent viewpoints without implying the endorsement of the Association.

Director of Publications Joan M. Irwin
Editorial Director, Books and Special Projects Matthew W. Baker
Special Projects Editor Tori Mello Bachman
Permissions Editor Janet S. Parrack
Associate Editor Jeanine K. McGann
Production Editor Shannon Benner
Editorial Assistant Tyanna Collins
Publications Manager Beth Doughty
Production Department Manager Iona Sauscermen
Art Director Boni Nash
Supervisor, Electronic Publishing Anette Schütz-Ruff
Electronic Publishing Specialist Cheryl J. Strum
Electronic Publishing Specialist Lynn Harrison

Project Editor Jeanine K. McGann

Cover Art Will Terry

Library of Congress Cataloging-in-Publication Data
Simmons, John S.
    School censorship in the 21st century : a guide for teachers and school library media specialists / John S. Simmons, Eliza T. Dresang.
        p.   cm.
Includes bibliographical references and indexes.
    ISBN 0-87207-288-6 (alk. paper)
    1. Teaching, Freedom of—United States.   2. Freedom of information—United States.   3. Public schools—United States—Curricula—Censorship.   4. Textbooks—Censorship—United States.   5. School libraries—Censorship—United States.   I. Dresang, Eliza T.   II. Title.
LC72.2 .S56   2001
379.1'55—dc21   2001000008

Contents

Introduction

As part of public school systems, their administrations, and university schools of education and library and information studies during the 20th century, we have collectively spent many decades involved in studying censorship. We have worked to try to understand what motivates it, and we have waged numerous campaigns to combat it. In this book, we will attempt to bring historical perspectives to bear on what censorship in the 21st century will bring. With the voice of past experience, we can offer teachers and librarians a seasoned view on guidelines to deal with the challenges, both old and new, that may arise in the world of 21st century censorship.

In order for teachers and librarians to have a context in which to face the future, we offer a brief historical summary of censorship in the classroom and the library; a bird's eye view of the significant court cases of the past and how they affect the present and future; a synopsis of the development of literature, textbooks, and curriculum throughout the 20th century; and an overview of the long tradition of care in selecting literature exhibited by both librarians and teachers.

In order to provide an adequate context for the several aspects of censorship treated in this book, we have included chapters that describe events that make up the historical backdrop of censorship in U.S. society. These events include the end of the Cold War and the downfall of communism in Europe; the beginning of the Civil Rights movement and the resulting scurrility of children's and young adult literature from the point of view of many marginalized groups; the arrival of the interactivity, connectivity, and access of the digital age in which we now live; the localization of control of school curriculum; and the formation of multiple, active procensorship and anticensorship coalitions.

We examine what has happened with the advent of the Internet and the vast changes it brings to schools, curriculums, students, and access to information. Digitally influenced forms, formats, perspectives, and boundaries have begun to emerge in traditional texts, and the expansion of our world view has brought more multiculturalism to books for young people along with the associated censorship issues. All these new developments have implications for censorship, and some of these findings will come as a surprise to readers.

We offer new and fresh recommendations for the 21st century censorship environment, including a view that involves children and adolescents speaking for themselves more than ever before; an emphasis on the strength of an internal alliance in the school; specific techniques for strengthening the external alliance in the community; and an optimistic view of the future in the midst of seemingly pessimistic circumstances. At the end of chapters for which we have specific classroom or library suggestions, we present "Guidelines for Teachers and Librarians."

As we bring our analysis to an end, the reader will possess a clearer conception of the challenges censorship and censors will present in the 21st century, many tools and suggestions to prepare for these challenges, and a cautiously optimistic view of a future with freer access to information for all.

—John S. Simmons and Eliza T. Dresang

CHAPTER 1

The 21st Century Student

I think the Internet has made me smarter, because it has given me a broader knowledge of things.
> —Joeldine Hyater, age 15 (in Tapscott, 1998, p. 99)

He understood instantly that now he was going downhill. No voice made an explanation. The experience explained itself to him. (Lowry, 1993, p. 81)

Three Scenarios

The following three scenarios, one fictional and two based on real circumstances, set the stage for gaining an understanding of 21st century students. To emphasize the contrast, the fictional piece set in the future is placed between realistic scenarios that represent present and past systems of education in the United States. We, the authors of this book, suggest that if teachers and librarians do not deal successfully with 21st century censorship, the fictional scene may become real, and the real, fictional.

Scenario One—Early 21st Century—Multiage (9-11) Classroom in a Real Community

This scenario is based on the authors' acquaintance with existing student-centered classrooms that may or may not be representative of the majority of U.S. classrooms in the early years of the 21st century.

Nine-year-old Sarah dashes in the door, hastily hangs up her coat, and races to a computer station at the side of the classroom. She activates it with her voice command, keys in her password, and waits impatiently as the images and words appear in vivid color on the screen. She pauses for a moment, now that she has secured a computer upon which to work, torn between checking her e-mail to see if Hans, her friend who has just returned to his home in Holland, has sent her a message or checking with her ThinkQuest Junior group to see what progress they have made on their project overnight. "Only two more weeks before our Flight to Mars Science Fact/Fantasy is due," she thinks, "and lots of text and graphics left to do. At least the research is mainly in place." The other team members (all in different cities) check into their chat room just about now each morning. And, then, there is the Dragonfire MOO (Multi-User Dimension, Object Oriented) she loves to visit, having read several Ann McCaffrey science fantasy novels and become deeply involved in the role-playing game. Not enough time for that now, though. The interaction and digital storytelling in the MOOs take a great deal of thinking. But wait—a news item on her log-in page catches her eye (all classroom computers open to the "Time for Kids" site). "Eight babies born at once"—makes being a twin, as Sarah is, seem lonely. Sarah pauses to read the update, selecting a highlighted area of the article and reading quickly about multiple births and how they happen. Sarah pauses for a moment to reflect on the day she found the first Mars article about the Mars Polar Lander's take-off when she logged on—her interest, shared by her virtual classmates, led her to this Flight to Mars cyberspace project.

Sarah nonchalantly returns to her choice-making among tasks at hand. "Better leave the e-mail until later and look at last year's ThinkQuest winning site with the QuickTime movie," she decides, as that is her particular team responsibility in partnership with the team coach. She quickly finds "Elijah's Page," part of the award-winning Down Syndrome site, and watches the short movie. Sarah also looks briefly at "Martian Internet Goodies," her favorite Mars Web site, and from there links to NASA's daily update on Mars, finding another QuickTime movie to review.

At this point Sarah turns to the discussion group with her teammates. Without so much as saying hello, Carlos rushes to refer his teammates to look again at their first reference, *Discover Mars* (Skursynski, 1998), noting the "cool" 3-D effects and wondering whether the team can duplicate that perspective on the Web in the mini-virtual reality experience and simulation they have planned. "Probably so, but better ask the coach about that," is Sarah's advice. Carlos's job on the team is to select visuals to which their site can link or to create graphics if they do not exist. Eleven-year-old Estela chimes in with her latest find for the science fiction/fantasy Books-on-Mars list. Most of the books she has found (on the Web and in the local library) are written for adults, but are fun to know about and explore. Lixin is equally enthused when he joins his teammates' conversation; he has been in contact with NASA scientists who agreed to a team interview for this project to be recorded and available in RealAudio on their Web site. All four students, from schools in different parts of the United States, hope their site will be useful to others who are interested in space exploration. Any moment the coach, Ms. Brown, will arrive. Good! This busily engaged learning team reviews where it is and sets to work once again.

Scenario Two—The Future—11-Year-Olds' Classroom in a Fictional Community

The following scenario is taken from Lois Lowry's Newbery Award winning book, The Giver *(1993).*

For a contributing citizen to be released from the community was a final decision, a terrible punishment, and an overwhelming statement of failure. Even the children were scolded if they used the term lightly at play, jeering at a teammate who missed a catch or stumbled in a race. Jonas had done it once, had shouted at his best friend, "That's it, Asher! You're released!" He had been taken aside for a brief and serious talk...had hung his head with guilt and embarrassment, and apologized to Asher.

Jonas grinned, remembering the morning that Asher had dashed into the classroom, late as usual, arriving breathlessly in the middle of the chanting of the morning anthem. When the class took their seats at the conclusion of the patriotic hymn, Asher remained standing to make his public apology as was required.

"I apologize for inconveniencing my learning community." Asher ran through the standard apology phrase rapidly, still catching his breath...

"I left home at the correct time but when I was riding along near the hatchery, the crew was separating some salmon. I guess I just got distraught, watching them..."

"We accept your apology, Asher," the Instructor said. He was smiling.

"And I thank you because once again you have provided an opportunity for a lesson in language. 'Distraught' is too strong an adjective to describe salmon-viewing." He turned and wrote 'distraught' on the instructional board. Beside it he wrote 'distracted.' (Lowry, 1993, pp. 2–4)

Scenario Three—19th Century—Multiage (K-8) Classroom in a Real Community

This scenario is based on "National Textbook: The McGuffey Reader," (1991) by independent writer and researcher Neil Weiner http://www.backgroundbriefing.com/mcguffee.html.

Eleven-year-old Thomas sat with his back straight and his feet cold. The rigor, he knew, was good for his mind. He and the 30 other boys in his classroom read silently from their Book 6 of The McGuffey Readers, the national textbook for three quarters of the 19th century (1836–1900), used by four fifths of all children with 20 million copies sold. Thomas had learned in his 6 years with the readers what the teacher expected. The Readers, too, made that very clear. Long ago Thomas realized that he was not to think for himself, but to absorb the thoughts and even the pronunciations of the material presented to him in his classroom. "Rule— Before attempting to read a lesson, the learner should make himself fully acquainted with the subject as treated in that lesson, and endeavor to make the thought, and feeling, and sentiments of the writer his own."

Thomas turned his attention back to absorbing the persona of Benjamin Franklin. Just last week Thomas read aloud to his classroom so his teacher could check for diction—after all, a number of the children came to school speaking broken English or with a peculiar accent. That had to be fixed. Another rule told him to stand as far back from his teacher as possible for her to listen to his speech patterns. He had made the dreadful mistake of pronouncing "his-to-ry" as "his-try" last week. The teacher had required an apology because at his age and stage of education, he certainly should know this word well. Daydreaming a bit, Thomas let his mind slip to a story he had read from an earlier book in the McGuffey Reader series—3 years ago now it seemed, but the story had stuck with him. The tale was about an idle schoolboy who ended up a beggar. Lots of stories were that way: Do good, be good, or the consequences are clear—and not to be desired.

Sighing, Thomas drew his attention back to his reading. He certainly did not want to become a beggar. In fact, reading the passages about the presidents had made him think hard about the possibility of a career in politics like his father and his grandfather before him. He aspired to be wealthy, respected, and a pillar of the community, not like the parents of some of the children in his class. Thomas looked around surreptitiously and wondered what his classmates were thinking—he would not know because once released to the playground, there could be no talk of schoolwork. Nothing interested his friends enough to be discussed outside of class. His thoughts turned briefly to his teacher—unmarried as required by law, dedicating her days and her nights to preparing the lessons, correcting the papers, and enforcing the good behavior that schooling required. He wondered where she had gotten her education, since no girls were in his school—and he had heard from his sisters that few opportunities existed for girls to attend school. It was hardly worth the effort when they had little use for an education—unless they planned to teach, of course. "There must be some kind of special schools for girls to become teachers," Thomas mused.

Should the fictional, tightly controlled scenario from *The Giver* become reality, classrooms would return to an even more bland, limited McGuffey Reader brand of education. In many ways the futurist classroom and the 19th century classroom have much in common: Both limit access to predetermined information and are teacher-centered learning environments. In contrast, the 21st century classroom offers an open, exploratory environment that comes when an expert coach and multiple resources are available to students who become adept, self-motivated learners. Stop a moment and reflect: Which of these scenarios seems more appealing, and which seems more likely to be the norm in the 21st century?

Table 1 brings together the educational environment and characteristics of students in each of these scenarios. Some information is added to that presented in the scenarios to flesh them out. These characteristics must be kept in mind throughout the discussion in this book, as it is not censorship itself that is the paramount concern of educators, but the student who is affected by its presence or absence.

A Closer Look at the 21st Century Learning Environment

The closing decades of the 20th century brought an enormous paradigm shift to society based on a communication revolution. This change in society, due to the ubiquitous microchip, has generated an

Table 1

Characteristics of Possible Educational Scenarios

TOPIC	21st CENTURY (Sarah, Carlos, Estela, Lixin)	FUTURE (Fiction) (Jonas, Asher)	19th CENTURY (Thomas)
Resources/Media	Open access for students to wide variety of resources.	Carefully controlled information sources.	National textbook used for four fifths of all students.
Teachers	Gender not a consideration; partner with students in determining study topics.	Gender not a consideration; person who determines topics to be studied.	Female when only one teacher in school, bound by strict rules of lifestyle, male when a "head teacher" in school; person who determines topics to be studied.
Learners	Actively engaged in learning, absorbing numerous pieces of information that are woven into a broad tapestry of knowledge. Active learners. Deep disagreement about what is appropriate for students to know.	Absorbing the prescribed information chosen by the instructor (not called a teacher). Strict standards for what is appropriate for all persons to know.	Emulation of the "great men" (or selected thoughts of the great men) taught about in McGuffey Readers. Passive learners. Strict standards for what is appropriate for students to know.
Demographics	Variety of ethnic origins. Poverty exists but technology in schools provides a bridge across the gap. No gender differences apparent.	Poverty is nonexistent. Gender is irrelevant. No indication of various ethnicities. Sameness is the ideal.	Overwhelmingly male; only males represented in texts. McGuffey never taught women. He advocated for The Common School but concentrated on economic, not gender or ethnic, inclusion.

(continued)

Table 1 (continued)
Characteristics of Possible Educational Scenarios

TOPIC	21st CENTURY (Sarah, Carlos, Estela, Lixin)	FUTURE (Fiction) (Jonas, Asher)	19th CENTURY (Thomas)
Collaborative Learning	Much learning occurs with collaboration among students.	No emphasis on collaboration, but a great deal of peer pressure for obeying rules.	No emphasis on collaboration. Some older students assist with younger ones.
People as Resources Outside the School	Persons are resources; contacted in real life and through the Internet, people, including parents, are a vital part of the learning process. Home environment influences learning.	Outside speakers brought into the classroom are for the sake of propaganda. Home environment strictly enforces school rules.	None brought into the class-room, but home environment is a factor in inequality of education.
Tests	Products of learning are evaluated rather than discrete items. In other words, understanding and application of what is learned are tested most of the time rather than isolated facts or data. Creativity and curiosity are re-warded as is astute problem solving.	Tests cover the material selected by the instructor (and ultimately by the Council of Elders). Emphasis is on mastering details of preselected material. Curiosity is not encouraged.	Tests cover the material in the readers. Emphasis is on master-ing details of existing subject content.
Short-Term Benefit of Learning	To the team and then to anyone with Internet access.	To the learner only.	To the learner only.

alteration in how people think, know, and work that is as deep-seated and widespread as the modifications brought about by the printing press five centuries earlier. By the early years of the 21st century, microprocessors have entered virtually every realm of daily life. While children wear headsets in an IMAX theater and view 3-D images, monks from the Maha Phruthara Temple use computers to learn about Buddha and his teachings; Keiko, the killer whale, becomes a movie star wearing a computerized monitor that records all aspects of his physiology; and children track the wind's speed and direction in Wales and e-mail it to counterparts around the world (Smolan, 1998). So marked is the impact of this computer chip and related technologies that many refer to the resulting societal environment as the Digital Age. Digital information, as opposed to the previous, more staid analog counterpart, can be processed, transmitted, copied, or changed instantaneously and can be accessed at precisely determined points in a flexible, nonlinear manner.

When the microcomputer, later called the personal computer, arrived in homes and classrooms during the 1980s, it was regarded as a computational device, a desktop stand-alone. Although it is still widely used in this manner, the 1990s brought a new and more important function to this device. It became the gateway to the Internet by which one individual could be connected and could communicate with multiple other persons instantaneously—even in extremely remote parts of the planet and beyond. Computerized signals arrived accurately from as far away as Mars. By the middle of the 1990s, the World Wide Web had entered the consciousness of an exponentially growing portion of the population as a source of information on practically any topic.

In the closing years of the 20th century, the U.S. government, noting the power of access to this connected information, embarked on a successful program to wire every classroom in U.S. schools by the end of the century. A National Center for Education Statistics report issued in 2000 states that "the percentage of public schools connected to the Internet has increased each year from 35 percent in 1994 to 95 percent in 1999" (http://nces.ed.gov/pubsearch/pubsinfo.asp?pubid=2000044). Work toward this goal proceeded with a combined effort of private enterprise and public resources. Microsoft and AT&T, for example, provided computing equipment and software to classrooms while the government required Internet Service Providers to lower their rates for needy schools and classrooms. Schools that qualified benefited from this legislated e-rate. Programs proliferated to train teachers in the technologies that had already become second nature to many of their students. Believing that information held power against tyranny, Nicolas

Negroponte, head of the Media Lab at the Massachusetts Institute of Technology, and his colleagues embarked on a program to bring Internet access to children all over the globe. Apparently many authoritarian regimes agreed with this assessment because the Internet was banned in some countries, such as Saudi Arabia, and owning a modem became a capital offense in others, such as Burma.

With the Internet came the opportunity for every person to become his or her own doctor, lawyer, librarian, stockbroker, real estate agent, and teacher. Recent holiday seasons have brought shoppers to the Internet in droves. The virtual life has become more and more accessible and appealing. Some have resisted this idea of free access to largely unevaluated information, pointing to the danger of inaccurate information and isolated communication. The former complaint was real, and the need grew for information specialists—those who had the skills of the analog-age librarians—to assist with matching users and information. This assistance could be provided behind the scenes with the proper structuring and presentation of information or it could be accessed through personal contact online or face-to-face. Precise, user-directed information matches became instantaneously available. The ability to know everything, however, brought with it dangers of invasion of privacy and nightmares about the reality of "Big Brother," the omniscient head of government in George Orwell's still-relevant novel *1984* (1949). Ironically, the opportunity for the greatest individual freedom brought with it the danger of the greatest government or corporate control. A flurry of legislation in the United States attempted to dissipate this tension between access and abuse.

This is the environment in which the student of the early 21st century is educated. In his book *Growing Up Digital*, Don Tapscott (1998) refers to all persons born in the last two decades of the 20th century as belonging to the Net Generation. Along with all the other changes in the digital world, students and how they learn are changing drastically. Joeldine Hyater, quoted at the beginning of this chapter, is 1 of the 300 students interviewed as background for Tapscott's book. Joeldine does not stand alone in assessing that broader access to information has "made me smarter." Deanna Perry, age 15, disagrees with the "smarter" part, although she understands the impact. She puts it this way:

> I don't believe one should be measured by smartness. Everyone has the mind and skills to accomplish anything. It's just a matter of taking the time to do it and having initiative. Having access to the Internet does not make anyone smarter. It just increases their learning skills if they take the time to utilize the information that is available. (Tapscott, 1998, p. 98)

According to Mike Males in *Framing Youth: Ten Myths About the Next Generation* (1999), the idea that students in general are failing, promulgated in various laments at the end of the 20th century and sometimes attributed to the influences of the Digital Age, is simply a myth. Information is power, and students are using it to become more powerful. However one puts it, the increased, abundant supply of information is available at students' fingertips, and what this means for classrooms, teaching, learning—and censorship—in the 21st century could not be more profound.

The Roots of 21st Century Teaching and Learning

John Locke (1632-1704) and Jean Jacques Rousseau (1712-1778)

How young people learn best has been debated for centuries. The roots of this inquiry go far back in time. Philosophers John Locke in the 17th century and Jean Jacques Rousseau in the 18th century broke from the classic tradition that believed in children's development of faculties through memorization and rhetoric—a notion still prevalent in the 19th century (Cleverly & Phillips, 1986). Locke emphasized learning as a practical activity and dared to suggest that children might read for pleasure rather than for instruction. Rousseau's ideas were authoritarian in a number of ways: The ideal student, Émile, about whom he wrote, could read only one book, *Robinson Crusoe*. Rousseau also put much more emphasis on the goodness of nature and the natural state than does contemporary education. But his thoughts, in part, serve as a basis for the most liberating of education theories. Those closely related to 21st century students are:

- a reduced emphasis on knowing and greater emphasis on acting and doing,
- an environment that encourages the child to depend on his or her own resources, and
- spontaneous child activity, as opposed to predetermined formal instruction.

It is important to keep these points in mind because they dictate a freedom of learning that is not compatible with strict control of content. Both Locke and Rousseau were proponents of a social contract. In its most simplistic terms, this means a contract between the governing body and those governed. In ethical terms, it indicates the government's acknowledgment of certain individual rights with a citizen's exercise of responsibilities, and a citizen's relinquishment of certain individual rights with the responsibility of the government to provide needed protections.

John Dewey (1859-1952)

Every teacher and librarian has heard the name of John Dewey associated with "progressive education." Few may realize how revolutionary Dewey's ideas were and why they are just now, in the 21st century, moving toward being more fully realized than they ever have been in the past. Dewey's educational philosophy was closely akin to that of Rousseau, although they differed in Dewey's view of learning as a social experience with students learning from each other as well as from their teacher/guide. Writing at the same time that the McGuffey Readers were still used in most classrooms, Dewey believed that education begins with experience (rather than with a set body of knowledge) (Dewey, 1899, 1902). The main tenets of Dewey's educational theories are as follows:

- Learning is properly based upon the interests of the child learner.
- A balance must exist between thinking (reflecting) and doing.
- The teacher is a partner or guide, not an authoritarian, learned figure who predetermines lessons and exercises.
- Education is concerned with the "whole child."

A thread of influence from Dewey's thinking appears throughout the 20th century. Few schools by the end of the century attended only to the academic needs of the child. The more controversial aspects of his philosophy, however, were not as widely accepted or implemented in the 20th century and were still considered experimental (or out of favor) in many parts of the United States. Particularly in elementary schools, learning by doing became more acceptable but decreased as students grew older. Basing curriculum on the interests of the child rather than a body of knowledge never gained wide acceptance at any level. Perhaps the most difficult idea to realize has been the role of teacher as colearner rather than as expert. Reviewing the scenario from the 21st century classroom, we note how Ms. Brown relates to the student learners as a "team coach" and not as an authority. This scenario is in accord with the century-old philosophies of John Dewey, a man whose vision of education had to wait until the Digital Age for full realization.

Other Influential Thinkers

It is not expedient to name every educational philosopher whose ideas lie behind the learning of the 21st century student. We note, however, a few additional scholars whose research has had significant impact on student learning at the dawn of the 21st century. First among these is the Swiss psychologist, Jean Piaget (1896–1980), head of the Jean Jacques Rousseau Institute. Piaget studied the systematic development of children and developed an "ages and stages" theory that won widespread acceptance (Piaget & Inhelder, 1969; Singer & Revenson, 1996). His theory was that children must reach a certain level of cognitive readiness before they can incorporate higher levels of reasoning.

Although Piaget's ideas seem to have basic validity, they need careful reconsideration in the Digital Age. We are now able to observe the learning of many more children than was previously possible, and as we observe we find that although Piaget was correct, in general, the "stages" may not be as linearly ordered as once thought. Carol Gilligan of Harvard University objects to Piaget's rigidity and hierarchical scheme. She proposes a less hierarchical model of learning more common to females that brings into question some of Piaget's key findings (Gilligan, 1982).

Lev Vygotsky (1896–1934), a Russian psychologist whose work did not reach the United States until some years after he carried it out, defined a child-adult partnership as the preferred relationship between adult and child in the educational process. Vygotsky advocated for teaching only when the child is ready to learn. He explained that the adult must sense this "proximal zone" when the student is ready to move on to the next learning challenge and needs adult assistance (Vygotsky, 1962). Vygotsky, in short, advocated for the adult to seek the "teachable moment" and to act on it. Vygotsky, like Dewey, believed that children learn through interactions.

Finally, Howard Gardner (1993) laid the groundwork for the learning we see taking place in 21st century classrooms when, in *Frames of Mind: The Theory of Multiple Intelligences*, he identified seven intelligences rather than the one that has been emphasized throughout most of the 20th century. These are verbal, mathematical-logical, spatial (as demonstrated by artists or pilots), kinesthetic (as demonstrated by dancers or athletes), musical, interpersonal, and intrapersonal (akin to self-awareness) intelligences. Gardner gives many examples of how these intelligences can and must be addressed in teaching and learning. They are accommodated much more readily in the classroom of the 21st century than they have been in the classrooms of the past.

Trends in Teaching and Learning

Certain educational movements of the late 20th century that have influenced the 21st century learning environment include cooperative learning, whole language instruction, writing across the curriculum, and multicultural or culturally inclusive education. Cooperative learning, a carefully structured form of group collaboration, has helped to prepare students for the type of teamwork apparent in the ThinkQuest effort, where students have differentiated roles, but all must work together for a common purpose. Likewise, learning to read from "whole literature" rather than from textbook selections has prepared these young people to read widely and understand what they read in context. (Contrary to what some critics assert, the whole language method does not negate the teaching of phonics.) Twenty-first century students will have much writing to do as they prepare projects such as Web sites—writing on a variety of topics that must be incorporated skillfully with other ways to convey information.

Although the subjects of student projects may not be multicultural, the learning group itself will grow increasingly diverse. Projections indicate that by 2060 non-Hispanic whites will make up less than half (49.6%) of the U.S. population (compared with an estimated 71.4% at the turn of the century) (http://www.census.gov/population/proj ections/nation/summary/np-t5-a.txt). Other population projections emphasize the increasing diversity in the U.S. population—each year from 1997 to 2050 more than half of America's population growth will occur among the nation's Hispanic, Asian, and Pacific Islander populations. Both birth and immigration will contribute to this phenomenon. Four of every 10 people added to the U.S. population through net immigration from 1997 through 2050 will be Hispanic, 3 in 10 will be Asian and Pacific Islander, 2 in 10 will be non-Hispanic white, and 1 in 10 will be African American (Spencer, 1996).

Changing Notions About Students' Knowledge and Abilities

It is interesting to note that the more students have been allowed to do and experience, the smarter they seem. Joeldine and Deanna, the teens quoted earlier, disagree on whether they are actually smarter or just seem smarter. Possibly it is some of both. There are two basic points of view about children and adolescents that are legacies of centuries past. One of these viewpoints perceives children as innocent and in need of protection. This is the point of view that existed throughout most of the 20th century, exemplified by the romanticism of the poet William Wordsworth, who authored the following lines from "We Are Seven":

A simple child,
That lightly draws its breath,
And feels life in every limb,
What should it know of death?
(http://homepages.tesco.net/~andy.oddjob/word04.htm)

This image of childish innocence is reinforced through advertisements and sentimental media portrayals to this day.

Another common notion about children is that they are depraved and in need of redemption. Most recent roots of this perspective are also anchored in the past. The teachings of John Wesley, the founder of Methodism, and those of Sigmund Freud, the founder of modern psychoanalytic studies, both looked upon children as needful of salvation—although that salvation was to come in quite different forms. We can see this view perpetrated in contemporary society in the notions of young people who seem to relish violence. (See Males, "Myth: Teens Are Violent Thugs," in *Framing Youth*, 1999, pp. 28–70, for a further discussion of teens and violence.)

Marina Warner, an English novelist and critic of contemporary society, declares these dichotomous views of childhood a major difficulty in a piece titled "Little Angels, Little Monsters" from her *Six Myths of Our Times* (1994):

Many...problems result from the concept that childhood and adult life are separate when they are in effect inextricably intertwined.... Without paying attention to adults and their circumstances, children cannot begin to meet the hopes and expectations of our torn dreams about what a child and childhood should be. (p. 62)

Fortunately, in the early years of the new millennium, a new paradigm for young people is emerging to compete with these long-term notions—a paradigm that lets a child remain a child and yet participate with equality and respect with adults in matters of mutual importance. According to this perspective, children are capable individuals who actively seek connections (Dresang, 1999a). This is a far more optimistic notion that places the child in an active rather than passive role in relation to adults.

We suggest that this new paradigm about children is connected to the emergence of the Digital Age. As computers became more available in schools and libraries, children began to show their natural affinity for them. Seymour Papert (1994) of the Media Lab at Massachusetts

Institute of Technology describes this affinity in *The Children's Machine: Rethinking School in the Age of the Computer.* He also laments that the excitement of learning outside of school often fails to make its way into the classroom. Both Papert and Tapscott note that, for the first time, many children are more capable than adults at something that adults need to know. Sherry Turkle (1995) states, "It is our children who are leading the way, and adults who are anxiously trailing behind" (p. 10). Across the globe, young people are tutoring adults in the use of computers. According to Tapscott, large corps of Finnish youth have been commissioned to bring their computer skills to the adults in Finland (1998). Dresang observes that, "During my last year (1996) as director of library technology in the Madison, Wisconsin school district, with the assistance of state grants, we hired students to serve as both tutors and technology assistants for staff."

Now that technology has revealed children's complex capabilities, some adults speculate that perhaps children are smarter—or at least have the potential to learn and do more at an earlier age—than had previously been supposed. The Dewey ideal of adults working in partnership (rather than in an authority relationship) with young people has become more apparent and possible. Moreover, the voices of children are now increasingly valued as they construct meaning in the classroom setting. In 2000 the International Reading Association featured a section titled "Hot Topic: Classroom Discussion" in its Online Bookstore, which included the following commentary:

> At the turn of the 20th century, U.S. philosopher and educator John Dewey stated that schools need to bring children into contact with other children "in order for there to be the richest social life." He recommended that reading, writing, and oral language be taught in a related way as an outgrowth of a child's social experiences. Today, educators are still struggling with how to put Dewey's ideas into practice. Although schools may provide these types of social environments, research shows that teacher-controlled lessons are still prevalent in classrooms throughout the world. Teachers continue to struggle with how to improve the talk structure of their classrooms and support students as they construct their own learning. (http://newbookstore. reading.org/cgi-bin/OnlineBookstore.storefront/598897735/UserTemplate/3/)

The more students are exposed to learning environments formerly considered inappropriate, the more they can absorb, synthesize, analyze, and apply knowledge. It is amazing to watch preschool children dealing with advanced concepts that Piaget might find surprising. We can conclude that the 21st century child—the child of the Digital Age who has the opportunity to flourish in a "connected" learning environment in the presence of partner-adults—either *is* smarter or at least *seems* smarter than his or her counterpart in previous times.

Some adults might say, "Yes, but this only applies to the privileged, those from an enriched home environment." In fact, observations of young people do not prove this to be true. Eliza Dresang has observed many students—who were not able to access information in a sophisticated manner through less user-friendly print formats—use the computer encyclopedia with its many easy-to-use prompts and enticing format, and subsequently move into the realm of an information-rich environment. She has also noted, through library and classroom observation, that even students without access to computers in their home environment often understand nonlinear, graphically oriented learning tools as a result of their experiences in video arcades. Furthermore, The National Center for Educational Statistics found that 95% of all public school classrooms were wired in 1999 (http://nces.ed.gov/fastfacts/display.asp?id=46), and a recent study by the Kaiser Family Foundation discovered that nearly 7 of 10 children have a computer in their bedroom (http://www.childrens-media.org/medlit/m_rese8.html). In late 2000, the National Telecommunications and Information Administration (NTIA) established a Web site titled "Closing the Digital Divide" (http://www.digitaldivide.gov). This site documents that computers and Internet access are disseminating rapidly into all homes, rich and poor alike, though those with higher incomes are still ahead of the game. The U.S. government has responded to this disparity by putting numerous programs into place, including one called Connecting America's Families, to reduce this economical "digital divide." No child's online capabilities are to be underestimated in this Digital Age, for access to computers will cease to be an issue.

Net Generation Learning and Knowledge-Seeking

Because the Digital Age is so new and because research takes time to conduct, analyze, and disseminate (even in a Web environment), we have only a few studies to which we can turn to assess the learning style of the Net Generation. One of the most recent studies gives us an inkling as to the misguided previous thinking about how children can find and understand information. The researchers discovered that elementary school age children did better on an ill-defined rather than a well-defined task, and that they preferred browsing techniques to systematic, analytic-based strategies (Schacter, Chung, & Dorr, 1998).

What does this tell us? Twenty-first century researchers are delving more deeply into the informal information-seeking behavior of students, information seeking that occurs when students choose the topic of their search rather than having it imposed upon them by an authority (Gross, 1999). Reseachers are considering new paradigms for looking at the information that these students seek, at their search strategies, and at their sense of success (Dresang, 1999b). Some astute educators have already observed what this research has begun to substantiate:

- Young people seek information differently from adults and this may be related to their affinity for hypertextual, nonlinear information. Their information seeking differs in informal situations during which they seek information about something that has captured their interest.

- Young people define a successful search differently from adults. They may be more process oriented than product oriented, and more able to withstand, or even enjoy and seek out, ambiguity and uncertainty. Thus, adults may need to examine what, in fact, determines success and come to some agreement with children as partners.

This suggestion does not differ drastically from what John Dewey suggested about children or what Lev Vygotsky observed. It does, however, differ dramatically from the assumptions that have undergirded much of the curriculum and instruction in North American schools through the end of the 20th century.

A final notion to keep in mind is how learning styles of individual children affect learning in the Digital Age. Again, little research exists in this new environment, but at first glance, the research that has been conducted indicates that children with a variety of learning styles may be drawn to the computer, which provides approaches flexible enough to accommodate these various styles. For example, a White House report on the use of computers found that the time spent on the computer by both boys and girls, at home and at school, does not differ significantly, but that the *nature* of the use differs quite a bit. A March, 1997 *Report to the President on the Use of Technology to Strengthen K–12 Education in the United States* states

> Girls were more likely to use a home computer for school work and for word processing, while boys were nearly twice as likely to play (non-educational) computer-based games...the differential usage patterns observed both at school and within the home raise the question of whether further research might lead to software, content, and user environments that more effectively serve the needs of both. (http://www.whitehouse.gov/WH/EOP/OSTP/NSTC/PCAST/k-12ed.html#7.5)

Characteristics of the 21st Century Student

The young person of the Net Generation who is placed in an environment in which he or she is free to explore interests, in which the access to information resources is unrestricted, and in which there are adults who are willing to act as guides instead of authorities is

- curious, motivated to learn, excited about discovery of new facts and ideas;
- responsive to parameters and policies set by adults because they are developed with respect for his or her capabilities and rights as a learner;
- willing to teach and learn from adult partners;
- oriented toward learning that can be shared meaningfully with others;
- able to reach beyond his or her years and developmental stages when given a properly structured environment or educational experience;
- demographically diverse and blind to gender, ethnic, and socioeconomic differences, except where acknowledging these differences enhances rather than detracts from opportunities;
- computer literate with an affinity for the digital environment;
- adept at teaching others;
- collaborative in nature;
- able to articulate needs and opinions at a very young age;
- interested in the daily news because the student sees him- or herself as part of the "real world," and able to have an influence on it;
- respectful of a wide range of talents, abilities, and interests in others—welcoming of diverse points of view;
- resilient, able to cope with less than ideal circumstances if connected with some adult or peer mentor and given access to needed information;
- capable of synthesizing, analyzing, and evaluating a broad range of information and putting it to use;
- needful of information resources and the skills to use them wisely and productively to solve problems;
- needful (more than ever) of adult support, but *not* adult dictation;

- recognized for his or her own unique intelligence and capabilities and able to use them to the betterment of him- or herself and his or her classmates;

- expecting the full range of First Amendment rights offered all citizens by the U.S. Constitution; and

- interested in connection and collaboration with students far beyond the walls of the school.

So What's Different From Dewey?

The contemporary types of teaching and learning stem from and are based on John Dewey's sparsely realized philosophy about active (or interactive) education. The advantages available for 21st century education that have been missing since Dewey's time include the following:

- Young people have open access to a wide variety of information with which they can pursue their interests and satisfy their information needs.

- Young people have the time to reflect and to think because locating information does not take the hours or days that it did in the past.

Only since the age of the Internet has adequate information been available to allow children actually and fully to pursue their interests with such a high rate of success in locating relevant materials. Dewey's learning by doing—his engaged, active learning—is at long last within the grasp of the regular classroom. In the past, no one teacher or librarian or teacher-librarian team could possibly have prepared an environment in which young (or older) children could find information on virtually any topic. It is now possible. Likewise, students can locate the information they need in a much shorter time, for the emphasis is placed on the "thinking about" rather than the arduous and often futile search. This information-rich environment makes achievement of Dewey's ideal classroom and curriculum possible.

How Does This Relate to Censorship?

Intellectual freedom is the unrestricted access to legally defensible information unfettered by government intervention. Censorship is the attempt to block or suppress that which is considered objectionable even though it is legally defensible and constitutionally protected. Before the printing press was invented and the printed word widely disseminated, censorship of materials for children was not such a large issue. Children were just "around," and they heard and absorbed from adults. However, as knowledge became more codified and organized and put down in written form, children became more isolated from the adult world. Latin grammars (the forerunners of McGuffey's Readers) limited the knowledge to which students were given access.

The attempt to prevent young people from obtaining certain information or knowledge that might be "harmful to minors" has always had loopholes (each of us can think back to our youth, most likely, and remember how we gained information that we were not supposed to have). With the advent of the Internet and the emergence of e-mail, instant messaging, chat rooms, and the World Wide Web, the attempt to block information from minors has become more and more difficult. The open and ready access to communication and information that became apparent near the end of the 20th century stirred some citizens to attempt to censor books and electronic sources because this access ultimately means that adults do not have the power to control children that they had in the past. Authoritarian rulers in countries such as Saudi Arabia and Burma (at this writing) fear the setting loose of information to their populations. In a like manner, but to a less extreme degree, some adults in the United States fear setting loose information to children. Many are engaged in organized battles to maintain tight control of what young people can access. From individual parents who cannot envision the utility of the information environment for their children, to organized groups who attempt to censor, there is a threat to open access to information by children. The remainder of this book will probe more deeply into the whys and hows of these censorship efforts—and make suggestions about how to prevent and deal with the problem.

The tension is terrible. Young learners feel their freedom and are somewhat intoxicated by it. They know the power of experiencing what they want to learn, just as Jonas (*The Giver*, Lowry, 1993) did when he broke free from his repressive society. Some adults, on the other hand, see their power and total control of children's lives slipping away, and they are grasping desperately to hold on to it. These adults are often sincere in their fright at the information to which children are exposed, lacking faith that adult mentors and child learners can work together to achieve a balance of access and understanding.

Throughout this book, regardless of the topic covered, it is important to keep in mind the young 21st century reader-viewer-learner. It is important to understand why it is so essential that teachers and librarians defend the open access to information that this "liberated learner" needs in a manner that builds coalitions with skeptics rather than erects barriers between them and the schools they, in essence, control.

Guidelines for Teachers and Librarians

- Read the chapter summaries of *Growing Up Digital* by Don Tapscott at http://www.growingupdigital.com, or read the entire book. Are you capitalizing on the amazing capabilities of this net savvy generation?

- Read one of the books about classroom discussion published by the International Reading Association, which can be found at http://bookstore.reading.org. Use ideas from these books to provide more opportunities for young people to speak for themselves.

- Compare your own ideas about contemporary young people with "Characteristics of the 21st Century Student" in this chapter. What can you do to encourage these traits?

- Read *The Child and the Curriculum* (1902) by John Dewey, originally published at the turn of the last century. Are his ideas still radical and worthy of consideration?

- Plan a teaching activity that utilizes the open and ready access to communication and information that is afforded by the digital environment; you can do this with students of any age group. Commit to doing this on a regular basis. Talk about its implications with students.

RECOMMENDED WEB SITES

Censorship, Intellectual Freedom, the Internet, and Youth
Recommended for background exploration of issues addressed throughout this book. Annotated links provided by Kay Vandergrift, Associate Dean and Professor, Rutgers School of Communication, Information, and Library Studies.
http://www.scils.rutgers.edu/special/kay/censorship.html

Closing the Digital Divide
A clearinghouse for information from the National Telecommunications and Information Administration about the government's efforts to provide all Americans with access to the Internet and other information technologies that are crucial to their economic growth and personal advancement
http://www.digitaldivide.gov

Dragonsfire MOO
A role-playing site based on science fantasy novels of Anne McCaffrey.
http://www.omnigroup.com/People/Friends/arien/df

Exploring Mars
A Web site billed as "the starting point for exploring Mars on the Internet."
http://www.exploringmars.org

Growing Up Digital
A compendium of excerpts from each chapter of Don Tapscott's book *Growing Up Digital: The Rise of the Net Generation*, as well as a discussion forum for Digital-Age students and links to Web sites created by Net Generation enthusiasts.
http://www.growingupdigital.com

Kids and Media@the New Milliennium
A report by the Kaiser Family Foundation examining media use among a nationally representative sample of more than 3,000 children ages 2–18, including more than 600 who completed detailed media use diaries. The study includes children's use of television, computers, video games, movies, music, and print media.
http://www.childrens-media.org/medlit/m_rese8.html

Martian Internet Goodies
Comprehensive site containing links to various sites with everything you ever wanted to know about Mars.
http://www.kyes-world.com/marsinter.htm

NASAKids
Provides frequent updates from the National Aeronautic and Space Administration (NASA) on scientific topics of interest to students, including detailed status of Mars-related information.
http://kids.msfc.nasa.gov

National Center for Educational Statistics
Information collected in the Fall of 1999 about the extent of Internet access in U.S. public schools and classrooms.
http://nces.ed.gov/pubsearch/pubsinfo.asp?pubid=2000086

Purple Moon
Site by, for, and about active, intelligent Digital-Age girls.
http://www.purple-moon.com

Radical Change
Links to books and Web sites reflecting characteristics of the Digital Age and interactive learning.
http://slis-one.lis.fsu.edu/radicalchange

Report to the President on the Use of Technology to Strengthen K-12 Education in the United States
Findings and recommendations based on a (nonexhaustive) review of the research literature and on written submissions and private White House briefings from academic and industrial researchers, practicing educators, software developers, governmental agencies, and professional and industry organizations involved in various ways with the application of technology to education.
http://www.whitehouse.gov/WH/EOP/OSTP/NSTC/PCAST/k-12ed.html#7.5

ThinkQuest Junior
Annual competition encourages students in grades 4 to 6 to collaborate in developing educational Web sites incorporating innovative uses of Web resources—http://tqjunior.advanced.org includes award-winning Down's Syndrome site,
http://tqjunior.advanced.org/3880/elijahspage.html

Time for Kids
Online news magazine for students through Grade 6.
http://www.pathfinder.com/TFK/

U.S. Census Bureau
"Minority links" providing reference to quick and easy links to the latest data on racial and ethnic populations in the United States.
http://www.census.gov/pubinfo/www/hotlinks.html

"National population projections" giving projections of the resident U.S. population by race and nativity, 1999–2100, in 5-year increments.
http://www.census.gov/population/www/projections/natsum-T5.html

CHAPTER 2

Origins of School Censorship in the United States

To many education professionals, public schools in the United States reflect the society that supports them. Before discussing the presence of censorship in those schools, it is necessary to note some societal factors that relate both directly and indirectly to that presence.

Societal Factors Contributing to Censorship in the United States

From Liberal to Conservative

One such factor is the creeping conservatism that became increasingly evident in the United States during the latter half of the 20th century. It has been over 50 years since Jackie Robinson broke the color line in professional baseball in 1946. It has been over 40 years since the Supreme Court rendered its *Brown vs. Board of Education of Topeka, Kansas* decision, and federal troops forced the integration of Little Rock Central High School in Little Rock, Arkansas. And it has been 30 years since the assassination of Reverend Martin Luther King, Jr. All of the above reflect the struggle for Civil Rights and the backlash expressed by so many once-neutral U.S. citizens. As chemists might remind us: For every action, there is a reaction.

During these years, a wholesale shift among white Southerners from the Democratic to the Republican Party has taken place. Most of the Rocky Mountain and Far West states, minus volatile California, have moved inexorably toward conservatism. Even the once Democratic Northeast/Mid-Atlantic region has become less liberal, and the nation's two largest cities—New York and Los Angeles—are led by Republican mayors: a remote possibility 20 years ago.

The word *liberal*, once a proud emblem worn by millions of adult citizens, is now an epithet that has replaced to a considerable degree the "Commie/Pinko" label thrust on many of those same citizens during the McCarthy era of the 1950s. Other labels, such as "secular humanist," "New Age supporter," "race mixer," and "multiculturalist," among others, have become weapons in the hands of a rising tide of people who firmly believe that only they know what is best for the United States in the new millennium. Such apostles of moral orthodoxy as William Bennett, George Will, Dan Quayle, Linda Chavez, and William F. Buckley have bemoaned the decline in morality among the citizenry in recent years. For these commentators, the Clinton-Lewinsky melodrama of the late 1990s provided ample cannon fodder, and these conservatives have presumed a cause-effect relationship between liberal permissiveness and educational deterioration since World War II.

To those who advocate reason and moderation in dealing with matters of U.S. public policy, W.B. Yeats's poem, "The Second Coming" (1921/1989) sounds as an alarm for the prevailing atmosphere at the end of the 20th century. Yeats's scenario was three-pronged: Powerful rightist forces had seized the cultural and political initiative; the intellectually liberal community posed weak opposition; and the large centrist populace was confused and frightened by the intensity of the attacks on reason and moderation. One of the significant dimensions of conservative zealotry in Yeats's poem was, and is today, the coordinated attack on students' right to read and teachers' right to teach. This attack has grown stronger over the past 20 years and remains present at the dawn of a new century.

Backlash Against Minorities

As indicated earlier, the issue of racial and ethnic progress, especially as related to the quest for equal status by African Americans, has had a significant effect on the rightward drift of white citizens in the past 50 years. Resistance to several chapters of the Civil Rights Act (1964) and the Voting Rights Act (1965) has continued in countless communities to the present day. The "Southern Strategy" evolved by Richard Nixon, John Mitchell, and Harry Dent produced various kinds of overt and clandestine acts of defiance in the mid-1960s. The essence of this strategy was the assertion that the entire Civil Rights movement, with its creation of unfair advantages for minority citizens, had come about through the statements and actions of Democratic Party initiatives. Thus, it appeared that the Republican Party stood for stability in the (white) Southern community and against radical change. These maneuvers, as practiced by politicians and even law enforcement agencies, are still evident today. The result of all the above has been distrust, equivocation, and animosity among the races.

In this ongoing struggle, neither side has behaved in an exemplary manner. Earlier black activists such as Eldridge Cleaver, Huey Newton, and Bobby Seale, as well as groups such as the Weathermen and the Black Panthers created fear among white citizens throughout the United States—fear that has aided and abetted racist whites who have hammered away at the "I told you so" theme. In more recent times, such prominent African American figures as the Reverend Al Sharpton and Louis Farrakhan have fanned those flames, and the media spotlight on the questionable actions of high-profile athletes such as Mike Tyson, Latrelle Sprewell, and Michael Irvin has not helped the cause of racial harmony, but instead has contributed to the backlash noted earlier. In school curricula and library offerings, this backlash has been manifested in demands that many valuable writings of African American authors such as Frederick Douglass, Richard Wright, Gwendolyn Brooks, and Langston Hughes be challenged, often without regard to the contexts in which such works have been presented.

Athletics Versus Academics

Another reality that has aided in polarizing U.S. society is the current sports mania extant in all corners of the country. From all-consumed Little League fathers to the antisocial acts of highly visible professional athletes, the veneration of physical prowess over intellectual achievement is evident. Rather than compile a long list of corroborating incidents, a quote from H.G. Bissinger's best-selling 1991 text, *Friday Night Lights*, a nonfiction chronicle of high school football in certain Texas communities, will suffice:

> There was one teacher at Carter who didn't pay homage to the Carter Cowboys.
>
> His name was Will Bates and he looked like his name, rotund, sallow-looking, with the exact mannerisms that one might expect from a man who had dedicated his life to the teaching of math and industrial arts. He seemed intent on not turning his classroom into a mill where everyone passed regardless of how much or how little they knew. He had a notoriously high failure rate, which of course made him the anathema of Carter High School.
>
> Will Bates was Gary Edwards's teacher in Algebra II, which seemed amazing given the fact that Edwards was a Carter Cowboy and Bates was a hard-nosed grader who made no bones about flunking kids.
>
> Bates tried to follow the school policy guidelines for grades in daily participation and homework. But that proved tricky in Gary Edwards's case when he missed class one day so he could watch game film in the coaches' office. Should he receive a zero for class participation that day? Or should the grade for class participation be waived because the absence was a valid one?

Edwards clearly struggled in Algebra II. He got a 40 on the first weekly test, and then a 60, and then another 60, and then a 35.... At the rate he was going, he would no longer be eligible for football once he received his grade for the six-week period. He wasn't making a 70. (pp. 297–298)

The resultant uproar—a courtroom drama focusing on whether or not Gary Edwards would be permitted to play in a critical playoff game— clearly demonstrates the magnitude to which athletics have taken precedence over academics in the United States:

> Peering out into the crowd in the hearing room, one contingent of which was black and from the city of Dallas and another contingent of which was white and from the suburbs, Commissioner Kirby couldn't help but wonder if the priorities of the public had gone slightly mad.
>
> American education was faltering and Texas was no shining exception. The state ranked thirty-fifth in the nation in expenditures per pupil for public education. Its average SAT scores ranked forty-fifth in the nation. Earlier in the year, a landmark $11 billion lawsuit that would determine how local school districts were funded by the state had played to an empty courtroom. Here, with the issue of whether the Carter Cowboys would stay in the playoffs or be replaced by the Plano East Panthers, the place was packed and frothing....
>
> Kirby patiently listened to the testimony and ruled that Gary Edwards had flunked Algebra II and was ineligible to participate in football under the rule of no-pass, no-play. An hour later, the University Interscholastic League, which sanctioned high school sports in the state, kicked Carter out of the playoffs and replaced it with Plano East. Supporters of Plano East cheered and said that justice had been done.
>
> But lawyers for Carter and the Dallas school district weren't about to quit. With the kind of frantic behavior that is usually associated with trying to stay the execution of a death row inmate, they rushed to the Travis County Courthouse in Austin and asked district Court Judge Paul Davis to grant a temporary restraining order delaying the playoff game until the Court had had an opportunity to consider all the issues in the case. Among their legal arguments, the lawyers said that depriving the Carter Cowboys from competing in the playoffs would cause irreparable harm.
>
> With ninety minutes left before the game, Davis granted the order. (pp. 302–303)

If you multiply behaviors such as those described in these excerpts, adding rule evasions and pressures on teachers (from middle schools to major universities) to dilute vigorous reading requirements and inflate grades, you gain insight into the magnitude of this problem: A student population, and a U.S. citizenship, that places little value on education will not be willing or able to defend the right to read against the arguments of censors.

Intolerance and Hypocrisy

There is also the widespread issue of moral hypocrisy and intolerance that virtually all observers notice, on all points of the national compass. A quick summary of several other factors contributing to the increasingly murky climate in U.S. society are as follows:

Cheating—From school transgressions on assigned projects to standardized tests to income tax evasion, embezzlement, and other "white collar" crimes.

Homophobia—Attacks on the activities and careers of gays, lesbians, and bisexuals. The categorical assumption is that diverse sexual preferences are reflective of moral deterioration.

Grade inflation—The notion that, because high grades in high schools, colleges, and professional schools are the means of finding prestigious, lucrative employment opportunities, grades given by instructors that fall below the "A" level are questionable, if not unacceptable.

Evolving espousal of narrow religious standards—During the past 30 years, the significant decline in the membership of main-line Protestant churches is contrasted with substantial increases in the ranks of fundamentalist Christian churches, certain radical Muslim sects, Mormon-affiliated churches, and pre-Vatican II Catholic parishes.

Condemnation of the poor, especially those who represent minority groups—Some have waged a vigorous assault on the entire welfare system regardless of recipients' needs, in a sense blaming the victims for their poverty.

General feeling of uneasiness, frustration, and fear—This is manifested by an insurgence of job insecurity caused by corporate takeovers or downsizing, the widening gap between "haves" and "have nots," road rage, hate crimes against minorities, condemnation of HIV/AIDS sufferers, the growth of militia groups in reaction to "big government," and other neuroses.

The Spread of Censorship

One reaction to the overall profile developed here has been a great escalation in complaints and challenges lodged by individual citizens and organized groups against the use of a wide range of materials and teaching strategies in schools. The incidence of school censorship episodes is nationwide and focused on virtually all content areas—especially English language arts, social studies, science, health/safety, and art/music appreciation. Occurrences have been noted in urban, suburban, and rural settings and have included virtually all socioeconomic groups. The would-be censors are concerned with materials acquired for media centers and libraries, as well as in courses of study. They have criticized all-school reading programs and materials and strategies utilized in school guidance and counseling agencies. In California, protests about textbook content have caused the governor to reject a sophisticated, carefully crafted, and research-based statewide writing assessment program created by nationally esteemed literacy specialists that cost millions of dollars (see Chapter 4, page 73). Censorship is widespread and unpredictable in nature. Data gathered by such organizations as the American Civil Liberties Union, the National Coalition Against Censorship, the International Reading Association, People for the American Way, the National Council of Teachers of English, and the American Library Association—to name the more prominent agencies—indicate that no state, school system, teacher, or librarian is "safe" from its intrusion. As we enter the 21st century, censorship is a virtual malignancy.

One likely reason for the difficulty in finding a viable solution to the persistent problem of widespread censorship in U.S. schools is that it pits two basic rights against each other. The first of these is the First Amendment to the U.S. Constitution: "Congress shall make no law respecting an establishment of religion or prohibiting the free exercise thereof; or abridging the freedom of speech, or of the press, or the right of the people peaceably to assemble, and to petition the government for a redress of grievances." In this frequently litigated Amendment, a person's right to freedom of expression is granted. Few citizens' rights have been tested more than this one. Recent U.S. Supreme Court cases involving allegedly unacceptable pornography in the publications of Larry Flynt and the right of citizens to protest by burning the American flag are prominent testimony to conflicts in the belief in this constitutional provision—often challenged by opponents through charges of slander and libel. Spokespersons for a wide range of controversial causes have sought protection under this Amendment, and many more will follow until our system of government ceases to flourish.

In conflict with the right to freedom of expression stands the uniquely American commitment to local control of the hundreds of school district systems, large and small, currently in operation in all 50 states. Apologists for the United States "way of life" frequently cite as a plus the fact that there is no Minister of Education and no central authoritative educational body holding power over all U.S. schools—unlike the systems in place in most European countries. However, this results in the fact that in School District X, a locally elected five-member school board can, on a 3 to 2 vote, rule inappropriate for classroom study or library inclusion a work of literature frequently taught and widely acclaimed in other school districts in that state and all other states. Thus, the assignment of Mark Twain's *The Adventures of Huckleberry Finn* may be required reading in high schools in District A, may be an item on schoolwide tests in neighboring District B, may be optional reading in classes taught in District C, may be totally forbidden in neighboring District D, and may be the subject of ongoing debate or provisionally allowed in District E. Any or all of these edicts can change after each school board election. In any event, advocates of both the right to free expression and the right to local control of school districts have clashed throughout most of American history—a conflict that is illustrated in chapters that follow.

Types of Censorship

In light of all of the above, an overview of the many faces of censorship, as those faces manifest themselves today, is appropriate. Some are time-honored and familiar; others are of a more recent vintage. They are as follows:

Classic/Traditional Censorship

Classic censorship is the type with which many teachers, librarians, administrators, and teacher educators are well acquainted, and which follows a predictable path:

- First, the teacher assigns Text A to the class.
- Students bring the text home; they may even (although infrequently) discuss it with their parents.
- With or without this dialogue, parents become alarmed. Some mention the text to friends, fellow workers, and/or neighbors, many of whom become concerned about the text's appropriateness, possibly adding the prepositional phrase, "with our taxpayers' money."
- Someone, usually an angry parent, launches a complaint to the offending teacher, to the building principal, to the district superintendent, or to a particular school board member.
- Finally, actions take place and decisions are made—through an ad hoc committee, through parent-school officials' dialogue, through summary elimination of the text, or through litigation.

As reported by the National School Board Association, the American Library Association, and People for the American Way, these incidents are occuring in large numbers throughout the United States. Moreover, all these groups claim that the numbers of challenges reported constitutes about 15–20% of the total actual number of challenges.

Proactive Censorship

Some concerned citizens go to the source of the problem (as they view it) and raise objections to the publishing houses in the textbook production phase of the industry. Challenges of this nature are varied: In the 1950s, a large U.S. text book publisher was asked by officials of a large state education agency to remove material from its junior high U.S. history text books containing complimentary treatments of Langston Hughes and Eleanor Roosevelt. Later, in the same state, officials condemned the inclusion of John Hersey's *Hiroshima* (1946) in a high school literature series. In the 1990s, science text publishers were urged to deemphasize evolution as a study topic in their biology publications. *All* works of such well-established authors as John Steinbeck and Norman Mailer have been peremptorily removed from some literature anthologies because citizens have raised objections to the overall character or political positions of those authors.

Publishers of school textbooks are, after all, concerned primarily with making money. When their products are under attack by groups of citizens, they have two choices: (1) remove the offensive elements, or (2) defend those elements against the voiced complaints. More often than not, they choose the former course of action. This decision is particularly true when the publishers are bidding their wares in "adoption" states. These U.S. states use a formal text adoption assessment procedure, usually conducted by a committee comprised of classroom teachers, journalists, district and state education officials, and "everyday citizens." A company landing a statewide adoption sees its books placed on a (usually) short list from which districts must choose if they want to use state funds in making such purchases. At present, such states number 27 and include 3 of the 4 most populous ones: California, Texas, and Florida.

Because the competition for large textbook adoptions is intense, the competitors are extremely sensitive to any criticism leveled against their products, especially those raised by prominent citizens. Probably the best known among such challengers are Mel and Norma Gabler, an older, marginally educated Texas couple. For about 40 years, they have waged a relentless, highly publicized struggle against materials they judge to be unpatriotic, un-Christian, or otherwise objectionable.

In the late 1980s, a high ranking official of the Texas Education Agency, Alton Bowen, was quoted as stating, "Their ideas about educational materials are what [students'] parents want" ("The Gablers," 1979, p. 76). Such influence has led Ed Jenkinson, a retired Indiana University professor and longtime crusader for students' right to read and teachers' right to teach, to comment publicly that the Gablers are "the two most powerful people in education today" ("The Gablers," 1979, p. 76). This claim may be somewhat exaggerated, and the influence of the couple waned during the 1990s, but they have been a force to be reckoned with and, more importantly, have caused copycat individuals and groups to emerge in several U.S. states.

Abridgment and Adaptation

Closely related to proactive censorship, the abridgment and adaptation strategy has been widely used for a long time. As bidding time nears, it is not uncommon for textbook editors to be assigned the task of slowly leafing through their newest product for the incidences of *hell, damn, bastard,* and other such objectionable language. Also on the list is any explicit description of sexual intimacy. The process of removing such language or dalliances from a text has become a common practice in the last 50 years.

All such erasure is done discreetly, even clandestinely. With a text still in the private domain, there is always the threat of litigation, either from the author(s) or the publishing house that holds copyright. With texts now in the public domain (i.e., texts published before 1920), the editors are prone to take considerably greater license. Thus it was that in the fall of 1983, two senior high school students, one from Vienna, Virginia, and the other from Minneapolis, Minnesota, made coincidental, surprising discoveries. In comparing their school literature anthologies with family owned editions of the Shakespeare plays *Romeo and Juliet* and *Hamlet,* they discovered that some 200 lines had been excised from the former text and 105 from the latter. In both instances, the excisions were lines focusing on intimate relations, albeit in Shakespearean language. This realization was subsequently noted in *The Boston Globe, The New York Times, The Washington Post,* and *The Minneapolis Star Tribune,* as well as several other well-known U.S. newspapers. It also was mentioned in *Time* and *Newsweek.* In November 1984, the National Council of Teachers of English, at its annual convention in Detroit, passed with ringing support a resolution condemning abridgment and/or adaptation of any literary text to be published for use in the classroom. The publishing company involved, one of the largest houses in the textbook industry, admitted its culpability. It did not, however, offer any apology for its decision, nor did it restore the lines that had been omitted. With the dramatic increase in literature that reflects the controversial, contemporary multicultural environment of the United States, there is little reason to believe that this censorship practice is going to be eliminated or reduced in big textbook publishing houses.

Student Journalism

The three previous types of censorship had to do with students' assigned reading tasks and the degrees to which they were found unacceptable by some members of the community. A persistent problem of a different nature involves the limits placed on students' written expression—some by outraged citizens, but more by school building administrators and/or district officials. This censorship reflects a certain irony in U.S. schooling: From their earliest years as public school students, young people are taught about freedom of expression in general and the significance of a free press in particular. In a landmark decision of the U.S. Supreme Court, handed down in the *Tinker vs. Des Moines* decision in 1967, Justice Abe Fortas, writing for the majority, stated, "Students do not shed their constitutional rights to freedom of speech or expression at the schoolhouse gate" (Simmons, 1992, p. 311). Just 11 years later, however, a very different corps of judges effectively took away that right in a case involving a student newspaper produced by the staff of a high school in Hazelwood, Missouri.

After the student editors had accepted a piece on attitudes toward HIV/AIDS sufferers and a second one on the effects of parental divorce on teenagers—two essays approved by the faculty advisor—the school principal caused both pieces to be removed from the newspaper. As the culmination of a 6-year legal battle, Justice Byron White voiced the majority opinion in *Hazelwood Schools v. Kuhlmeier* when he wrote, "A school need not tolerate student speech that is inconsistent with its educational mission.... School officials may impose reasonable restrictions on the speech of students, teachers, and other members of the school community" (Simmons, 1992, p. 311). A longstanding conflict pitting students' First Amendment rights against the right of communities to rule on curricular issues was settled in that decision. It has not ended the controversy, however. In virtually every issue of the *Newsletter on Intellectual Freedom*, published twice annually by the American Library Association, cases involving such disputes are recorded. Since the Hazelwood decision, however, administrators have felt more secure in their restriction of students' journalistic prerogatives.

Student Creative Writing

Although there are fewer literary magazines than journalistic publications in U.S. schools, they are still produced fairly often, especially in large urban and suburban high schools. Generally the more high-quality the creative publications produced, the more widespread their visibility. Thus, it follows that some of the more affluent high schools in the suburban school districts of Westchester and Nassau counties in New York; Cook County, Illinois; Miami-Dade County, Florida; and Simi Valley, California have been the settings of complaints by parents and other county residents about obscene, offensive, and undesirable stories, essays, and poems published in such school magazines. While students are often punished to some degree for these unpalatable publications, the blame is usually laid at the feet of the faculty advisor.

A case in point, though from a college publication, provides a pertinent example of this clash involving the censorship of creative writing. The Spring 1968 edition of Florida State University's annual creative writing publication, *Smoke Signals*, had accepted a short story titled "The Pig Knife," written by an African American undergraduate who had recently returned from a combat tour in Vietnam. Not surprisingly, the story had to do with a recently returned, black GI and his struggles to reassimilate himself into the civilian population. The setting was an East Coast inner city, and the street talk was suffused with profane and obscene epithets. An editorial board composed of three faculty members and two students reviewed the piece and voted 4 to 1 to endorse its publication. The one dissenter, a senior faculty member, went directly to the university president's office, related the incident, and urged him to quash the entire issue.

The president agreed, the magazine was removed, and the campus erupted with angry dissent. The local newspaper sided with the president's decision and admonished students and faculty to back off. In partial response, the university faculty senate voted in emergency session to censure the president, who immediately resigned, drawing another angry reaction from the Governor, the state legislature, and the Board of Regents. The latter body urged the president to rescind his resignation, which he reluctantly did. The sense of decorum on the Florida State University campus was effectively destroyed by these events. For the next 8 months, chaos reigned. Then the president again resigned, and an aura of martial law settled over the campus—all over a story submitted by a student to a school literary magazine.

Self-Censorship

One of the consistent findings of American Library Association (ALA) investigators is that approximately 30% of censorship complaints and challenges in the United States each year come from school administrators, faculty, and staff (Simmons, 1990, p. 117). The focal point of these actions may be literary material, sex education tracts, "left-leaning" materials distributed in social studies classes, scientific studies of evolution, journal writing that gets personal, and self-assessment or introspective activities conducted by teachers or guidance counselors. Whatever the case, the cry raised by colleagues in a given school is substantial. One rather representative act worthy of note is the decision made by an English Department head of a small North Florida high school. When new editions of English Literature anthologies arrive at her office, she routinely takes a razor blade and removes certain works. Among such eviscerated selections are Chaucer's "Miller's Tale," Jonathan Swift's essay, "A Modest Proposal," Yeats's poem, "The Second Coming," and Nadine Gordimer's story, "The Train from Rhodesia." As the old *Pogo* comic strip would have it, "We have met the enemy, and he is us."

Reflection Points

If the contention with which this chapter began—that schools are truly a reflection of society—is true, then it would be appropriate to close with some questions asking for serious social and political reflection about the direction that the culture of the United States is taking. Most of the questions below relate to U.S. society as a whole, and have implications for the degree to which students and teachers are free to pursue knowledge in whatever direction their searches lead them:

1. To what extent do our children and young people have the right to read and the freedom to express themselves in this era of creeping conservatism?

2. Can there ever be a true reconciliation between the access of First Amendment rights and local control of the school curricula and learning methods?

3. Will the American people ever accept the spirit of separation between Church and State as it relates to the management of all phases of our public schools?

4. Is it possible for thoughtful, unbiased, and fair-minded people to create and ascribe to a canon of taste to be shared with society in general and manifested in public school curricular choices in particular?

5. Can viable school-community relations, based on mutual trust and respect, ever be established? If so, what is the best way to proceed?

6. Where and when should honest, unequivocal, meaningful preparation for adulthood in this society begin in our schooling strategies? What topics should be stressed? What topics should be approached with caution? What topics should be categorically avoided?

7. When can "school language" and "real world language" be effectively reconciled without curricular leaders being accused of an "anything goes" approach to that language development?

8. How can advocates of a school curriculum based on factual knowledge only resolve their differences with those who value the teaching of critical thinking, values clarification, and multicultural awareness?

9. Will political correctness continue to influence public discourse and overall school management? Where and how will mutually acceptable limits be established?

10. In this new century, can the diverse citizens of the United States even begin to seek a consensus on the other nine questions above?

RECOMMENDED WEB SITES

American Civil Liberties Union
http://www.aclu.org

American Library Association
http://www.ala.org

See also:
Newsletter on Intellectual Freedom
http://www.ala.org/alaorg/oif/nif_inf.html

Brown vs. Board of Education of Topeka, Kansas
http://brownvboard.org/research/opinions/347us483.htm
http://brownvboard.org/research/handbook/handbook.htm
http://brownvboard.org/research/opinions/opinions.htm

Black Panthers
http://www.cs.oberlin.edu/students/pjaques/etext/acoli-hist-bpp.html

International Reading Association
http://www.reading.org

Hazelwood Schools v. Kuhlmeier
http://www.bc.edu/bc_org/avp/cas/comm/free_speech/hazelwood.html

Mel and Norma Gabler
http://www.textbookreviews.org

National Coalition Against Censorship
http://www.ncac.org

National Council of Teachers of English
http://www.ncte.org

People for the American Way
http://www.pfaw.org

Tinker vs. Des Moines Independent Community School District
http://infoeagle.bc.edu/bc_org/avp/cas/comm/free_speech/tinker.html

CHAPTER 3

A 21st Century Media Specialist-Teacher-Student Alliance

A school library is the place where "students must always remain free to inquire, to study and to evaluate, to gain new maturity and understanding.... to test or expand upon ideas presented to [them] in or out of the classroom." (*Island Trees v. Pico*, 1982, pp. 868–869)

The claims of educational unsuitability and control of values are more likely to carry weight in the "compulsory environment of the classroom." (*Island Trees v. Pico*, 1982, p. 869)

Protecting Access to Information

The courtroom was silent in anticipation. A proverbial dropped pin could have been heard. United States District Judge G.T. Van Bebber began to read his opinion in *Stevana Case v. Unified School Dist. No. 233* (D. Kansas, 1995): "After careful consideration of the evidence and arguments in this case, the court concludes that defendants unconstitutionally removed *Annie on My Mind* from the school libraries" (Meyer, 1996, p. 22). Judge Van Bebber's orders were clear: Nancy Garden's novel about two high school girls who fall in love was to be placed back in circulation and was to "be made available according to the usual terms and conditions prescribed for the use of library materials in the district" (p. 25). And so ended 2 years of controversy in the Oalthe (Kansas) School District.

The media specialist in this censorship case was Loretta Wood. When Nancy Garden was asked how long she was on the witness stand, she responded by saying,

I don't know exactly, but it was not very long. It was around half an hour. Maybe a little longer, maybe a little shorter, but it was nothing in comparison to Loretta Wood, who was on the stand forever. She was our star witness. She was really under fire there for a long, long time and did, apparently, an absolutely beautiful job. (Meyer, 1996, p. 25)

Loretta Wood reflected on the case, saying, "I hope that people will continue to follow their professional expertise and not run scared and quit selecting the books we truly believe young adults should be reading" (p. 25). Garden's experience with this case prompted her to write a new novel, *The Year They Burned the Books* (1999), that explored the censorship of classroom curriculum, student journalism, and library books by a school official from the point of view of the young adults involved. In Garden's fictional account, as in the real life drama, the anticensorship forces prevailed. As an addendum, Garden was the 2000 recipient of the Robert Downs Intellectual Freedom Award, awarded annually by the Graduate School of Library and Information Science at the University of Illinois at Urbana-Champaign. The award is granted to those who have resisted censorship or efforts to abridge the freedom of individuals to read or view materials of their choice.

Far north of Kansas in Alaska, Anne Symons, former President of the American Library Association (ALA) and a librarian at Douglas High School in Juneau, Alaska, related a censorship incident in her school district involving a picture book with male partners titled *Daddy's Roommate* (Willhoite, 1990). The book had been retained from the shelves by a 7–1 vote of the school board. Nonetheless, the battle to keep it was intense. Symons explained some of the reasons for the successful resistance of this censorship attempt:

> The librarians were well organized and selected one librarian to be the "leader." They attended all public meetings as a group.... The librarians used the challenge as an opportunity to get people involved. This included parents, ministers, and representatives of local organizations with strong ties to intellectual freedom and high school students. Teachers and students seized this opportunity to use the First Amendment as a part of assignments. Students testified at hearings, and they initiated a resolution with their state student government organization. (Symons & Harmon, 1995, pp. 100–101)

A third anecdote puts these two cases in perspective, reminding us why these books were placed in school libraries despite the possible controversy they might provoke. According to a phone conversation conducted by Eliza Dresang with a librarian at West High School in Madison, Wisconsin, in the fall of 1995, this librarian claimed to have been checking over the new books when she happened to leave a new nonfiction tome with the word "homosexuality" boldly displayed on its cover lying on a public table. Drawn to another task, she returned to find the book had vanished without being checked out. Resigned to the loss of the book, several weeks later she was surprised to find it back where she had left it. Stuck inside the cover was a note that read, "I am sorry I took this book without checking it out. I had to have the information, but I was too embarrassed to let anyone know" (personal communication, Fall, 1995). This is what the judges in the *Island Trees v. Pico* case meant when they said a school library is a place where "students must always remain free to inquire, to study and to evaluate, to gain new maturity and understanding...to test or expand upon ideas presented to [them] in or out of the classroom" (1982, 868–869). This free access to ideas is part of the freedom of expression that Loretta Wood and the librarians in Juneau defended.

Classroom Versus Library Cases of Censorship

Both teachers and librarians need to recognize the different standard that the courts have applied to freedom of expression in the classroom as opposed to that in the library. Of the cases discussed in this volume (see especially Chapter 8), only a few cases center on censorship controversy in the school library; most are related to censorship of classroom resources or student actions. Note that the aforementioned Pico was a student who, along with several other students, challenged the right of the school board to remove books from the school library. Perhaps students have turned to the media center for information that is not available within the confines of the classroom because cases to censor classroom materials have succeeded more often than those aimed at the media center—and complaints have been more common. Teachers and librarians must recognize how this judicial tendency to regard the library media center as more appropriate than the classroom for free exploration of ideas relates to the vocal 21st century student, changing instructional practices in the classroom (see Chapter 1), the changing role of the 21st century school library media center, and to a beneficial coalition among these players. How will the school media center of the 21st century allow teachers, librarians, and students to capitalize on these factors in combating censorship? In response to this question, we examine the characteristics of that media center, and of the 21st century media specialist who manages it, in order to understand the powerful potential for an in-school alliance.

The 21st Century School Library Media Center

The model school library media center of the 21st century parallels and supports the type of student-centered, resource-rich classroom learning in which Sarah, Carlos, Estela, and Lixin were engaged (see Chapter 1, p. 4). *Information Power: Building Partnerships for Learning*

(1998), a set of national guidelines for school media programs developed by the American Association for School Librarians and the Association for Educational Communication and Technology, details this type of media program. The library media center in the 21st century does not serve merely as a support to the learning community as it once did, but rather it is now a catalyst for change and an integral part of that community. Later in this book (see Chapters 9 and 10), we will see how this internal learning community spreads far beyond the walls of the school to build coalitions and combat censorship, but we must first look at the background laid for that coalition-building within the school itself.

A Student-Centered Library Media Program

The first national standards for school media programs were created in 1918 by the National Education Association and adopted in 1920 by the American Library Association. (See "School Library Media Standards and Guidelines: A Review of Their Significance and Impact" [Gann, 1998] for an excellent historical review of school library media standards through 1988.) Every decade or so since then, new standards have been issued. Prior to 1960, the focus was on quantitative measurement, whether school libraries should be under the jurisdiction of the school or the public library, and what materials should be included in a school library. Many of us can remember the days when the school library was a place where we went to "check out a book," but very quietly so the librarian would not whisper "Shhhh." If we do not remember, we are familiar enough with the stereotype that lingers even today. For instance, during the 2000 presidential campaign, the following anecdote appeared in a *New York Times* article regarding candidate George W. Bush's wife Laura, a former elementary school librarian: "Years ago, Mr. Bush occasionally joked in public speeches that his wife had a librarian's narrow concept of oratory, and it amounted to a single syllable: 'Shhhh!' Mrs. Bush was not amused" (Bruni, 2000). In recent years, more than 35 million children around the world have become acquainted with Madame Pince, the librarian in the Harry Potter books who consistently "shushes" the students.

Although a librarian's responsibilities have remained mired in this stereotype, since the 1960s the emphasis in the national standards has begun to focus on the media specialist as a coteacher who plans and teaches in a variety of forms and formats in conjunction with the classroom teacher. In 1975, the national standards brought attention to the local media center as only one component in a network of resources—for the first time the library was seen as a component in a system. In

1988, the "guidelines" (now the preferred term) became almost entirely qualitative rather than quantitative, with the only numerical stipulation being that there should be one full-time media certified specialist and an aide in any school library (Gann, 1998). These guidelines focused on the multiple roles of the media specialist, incorporating old paradigms and translating them into new perspectives. In 1998, the national school media guidelines specified desired student outcomes for the first time, centering on creating an environment that produces information-literate students above all else. This new category of literacy, *information literacy*, centers on the ability of a student to find and use information.

Radical New Roles

A close reading of the 1998 guidelines shows that the media specialist, in his or her multiple roles, serves not only as a link between resources and users (teachers and students), but as a leader in building a learning community (American Association of School Librarians/ Association for Educational Communications and Technology, 1998). An understanding of the more sophisticated and multifaceted role of the media specialist is essential in order to understand how the learning community can work together against censorship. This understanding must be gained not only by teachers and administrators but also by librarians themselves, who, like teachers, must keep up with the technology that has leapt into their laps. What are these radical new roles? Actually, a description of the 21st century media specialist goes beyond roles to an intersection between roles and themes. The themes of the media center are collaboration, leadership, and technology. The roles of the media specialist are teacher, instructional partner, information specialist, and program administrator. Table 2 illustrates how these themes and roles intersect to support the 21st century school.

By scrutinizing this table, a media specialist can see what a challenging but exciting job these guidelines define, while teachers and administrators can see, perhaps from a new perspective, what a valuable person the media specialist is as a full participant in the instructional team. This is a far cry from the person in the isolated, quiet book room of the past.

However, new (or returning) media specialists in graduate programs are routinely introduced to this relatively radical new way of thinking about their role, while new teachers and administrators rarely encounter it in their professional preparation. Furthermore, media specialists must take classroom-related education courses, while teachers usually need not take media-centered education courses. Forward-

Table 2
The 21st Century Media Specialist

ROLE/THEME INTERSECT	COLLABORATION	LEADERSHIP	TECHNOLOGY
Teacher	Collaborates with students and other members of the learning community to analyze learning and information needs, to locate and use resources that meet those needs, and to understand and communicate the information the resources provide.	Serves as curricular leader on instructional team and constantly updates personal skills and knowledge in order to work effectively with teachers, administrators, and other staff to expand their general understanding and to develop specific sophisticated skills in information literacy, including uses of information technology.	Is knowledgeable about current research and is skilled in applying that which calls on students to access, evaluate, and use information from multiple sources in order to learn, to think, and to create and apply new knowledge.
Instructional Partner	Works with individual teachers in the critical areas of designing authentic learning tasks and assessments and integrating information and communication abilities required to meet subject matter standards.	Takes leading role in developing policies, practices, and curricula that guide students to develop a full range of information and communication abilities.	Joins with teachers to identify links across student information needs, curricular content, learning outcomes, and a wide variety of print, nonprint, and electronic information resources.

(continued)

Table 2 (continued)
The 21st Century Media Specialist

ROLE/THEME INTERSECT	COLLABORATION	LEADERSHIP	TECHNOLOGY
Information Specialist	Brings awareness of information issues into collaborative relationships with teachers, administrators, students, and others.	Provides leadership and expertise in acquiring and evaluating information resources in all formats.	Masters sophisticated electronic resources and maintains a constant focus on the nature, quality, and ethical uses of information available in these and in more traditional tools.
Program Administrator	Works collaboratively with members of the learning community to define the policies of the library media program and to guide and direct all activities related to it.	Serves as an advocate for the library media program and provides the knowledge, vision, and leadership to steer it creatively and energetically through the 21st century.	Demonstrates proficiency in the management of staff, budgets, equipment, and facilities so that students can make effective use of information and information technology.

Adapted from *Information Power: Building Partnerships for Learning* (1998), pp. 4–5. Note: The explicit links made in this table do not appear in this form in the original text.

looking teachers and administrators are introduced to the concepts portrayed in the table when they meet one of these indoctrinated media specialists on the job—but that is not the most efficient way to build this potentially strong collaborative network. If the guidelines in this book are to work, a stronger partnership and a more widespread understanding between librarian graduate programs and classroom teacher education must also spread through academia.

Emerging Standards for Information Literacy and Classroom Content

Information Literacy Standards and the Media Specialist

Gone are the days when the following statements about libraries and librarians were true:

- the worth of the library is measured solely on "inputs"—how many books or how much technology exists per pupil;
- circulation of materials or other "output" measures have prime importance;
- classroom teachers think of the media center only as "somewhere to check out a book";
- media specialists teach library skills in isolation from the rest of the school curriculum;
- teachers think the best way their students can learn to use information sources is to have weekly lessons in library skills; and
- principals support this poor use of an expensive resource.

While it remains important to have adequate resources and to have resources that are used wisely, the learning outcome or the satisfaction of a need for information is now the ultimate objective. The standards now articulated are those for student outcomes, and the media specialist strives to fulfill the collaborative roles mentioned in Table 2. These roles are of increasing importance, as research conducted by Keith Curry Lance (1993, 1994) has shown: Regardless of students' backgrounds, well-funded libraries and full-time media specialists are highly correlated with high student academic achievement. The desired end result is articulated in nine "information literacy standards for student learning" under three umbrella topics:

- information literacy

- independent learning
- social responsibility, or positive contribution to the learning community

(American Association of School Librarians/Association for Educational Communication and Technology, 1998, p. 8).

For each of the nine standards, there are several indicators, carefully chosen to demonstrate the level of competency that the student has achieved. Let us think back to Sarah, Carlos, Estela, and Lixin completing their "Flight to Mars Science Fact/Fantasy" project (Chapter 1, pp. 3–4), and apply the nine information literacy standards (in question form) to see how well their classwork matches the outcomes sought through the media center standards:

Information literacy—
- Do students access information efficiently and effectively?
- Do they evaluate information critically and competently?
- Do they use information accurately and creatively?

Independent learning—
- Do students pursue information related to personal interest?
- Do they appreciate literature and other creative expressions of information?
- Do they strive for excellence in information seeking and knowledge generation?

Social responsibility—
- Do students recognize the importance of information to a democratic society?
- Do they practice ethical behavior in regard to information and information technology?
- Do they participate effectively in groups to pursue and generate information?

(American Association of School Librarians/Association for Educational Communication and Technology, 1998, 8–9)

Scanning back through the text of Chapter 1, it appears that the young people in the first classroom meet most if not all of the standards for information literacy. They are learning efficiently and effectively, and they are researching, evaluating, and producing information both individually and as a group. All of these information-related competencies are important for 21st century learners—they are essential, but they are not enough.

Classroom Content Standards and the Classroom Teacher

The movement for standards in classroom content subjects can be traced to the publication of *A Nation at Risk* in 1983. Certainly for the last two decades of the 20th century, there was a great deal of activity in this area. Individuals at the Mid-Continent Research and Evaluation Laboratory (McREL) in Aurora, Colorado, worked for more than 7 years to produce a compendium of standards from different content fields. Kendall and Marzano's *Content Knowledge: A Compendium of Standards and Benchmarks for K-12 Education* (1997) can be found at the McREL Web site (http://www.mcrel.org/resources). This compendium is intended to assist local entities in developing their own content standards. Why are standards so important? According to McREL, "standards serve to clarify and raise expectations, and standards provide a common set of expectations" (http://www.mcrel.org/standards-benchmarks/docs/chapter1.html). At this same Web page, a chart of the history of standards development in various disciplines gives an overview of the wide array of content knowledge that faces the classroom teacher. The National Council for Teachers of English and the International Reading Association, for example, jointly published *Standards for the English Language Arts* in 1996.

The Dilemma for Classroom Teachers

A recent McREL survey of classroom teachers found there are too many standards and not enough time to accomplish them; an accompanying report offers some suggestions to teachers for coping with this problem (Florian, 1999). Here is another place where tension exists—this time about what the 21st century classroom curriculum will contain and what the teacher is accountable for in the process of student learning.

In addition to setting up standards for teachers, there are various methods by which the content of the classroom is controlled. In the society surrounding the school, community voices often insist that teachers teach core knowledge. They turn to pundits such as E.D. Hirsch, whose 1987 book *Cultural Literacy: What Every American Needs to Know* has become the basis for the curriculum in various states around the United States. Sometimes state boards of education have a close hold on curriculum content—in Texas, California, and North Carolina, for example—through textbook selection processes. Other states, such as Wisconsin, have curriculum standards but no control through statewide textbook or resource adoptions. One way in which states have recently begun to control classroom curriculum is through inclusion or exclusion of subjects on state achievement tests that determine individual and school rewards based on student success.

In 2000 the nation's attention focused on a red hot state board of education race in Kansas between candidates who supported the previous board's decision to remove questions on evolution from state tests (effectively, argued many, removing it as a topic from the classroom) and those who wanted it reinstated. In an August 2000 election, the antievolution foes were ousted from the Kansas State Board of Education, but the fact that the question continues to be raised in this century is a statement in and of itself. In Florida, a statewide revision of the teacher education program in 2000 shifted the focus from methods of teaching to subject content—seemingly a step into the past, but clearly linked to "what students need to know." The chilling effect of national and local censorship on what are deemed "controversial materials" is a form of control. Some U.S. courts have ruled that schools exist to inculcate young people with fundamental values of the society (*Ambach v. Norwick*, 1979).

With textbooks, testing, and core values weighing on them, classroom teachers and those who set national standards in subject content areas realize that information literacy in the 21st century must not be lost in the cacophony of voices that demand specific subject content. Yet classroom teachers are caught in the middle of constant controversy—on the one hand, they must determine what subject content to teach, under enormous pressure to teach that which is to be tested as well as that which extends and enriches; on the other hand, they are driven to produce students who are skillful users of the seemingly uncontrollable amount of information with which they are faced in the Digital Age. The 21st century has not lessened the tension nor made it any easier to dispel; it has only become worse with the rapid communication of a digital era. Where the 21st century teacher stands, then, is in the crossfire of a myriad of competing demands, teaching young people who are growing up saturated with ideas from an information-rich environment.

The Blurring of the Classroom/Media Center Lines

The media specialist has traditionally been thought of only marginally as a teacher and rarely as an instructional partner. In the 21st century, this is no longer an accurate view. There are, however, differences in emphasis and in time spent in these roles. The classroom teacher is held accountable for subject content and for the skills embedded in subject matter, such as reading, math, and geography skills. The library media specialist is held accountable for the information literacy of students and for leadership in several other areas that affect the entire school (see Table 2, pp. 44–45). We might deduce that the classroom and the media center are so different in purpose and content and that the teacher and the media specialist are governed by such different expectations, that never the twain shall meet. But that is only the most superficial picture. In fact, the lines between the 21st century media center and the 21st century classroom, and the professionals responsible for each, will only continue to blur as the Internet moves more pervasively into both classrooms and media centers. These two educational units in a single learning community are closer in philosophy, purpose, and content than ever before, and the professionals in them are better equipped to work as a collaborative instructional team.

A publication that was discussed earlier provides a preliminary guide to how this can happen. The first two chapters of *Information Power: Building Partnerships for Learning* (1998), have been published as a separate booklet for media specialists to share with teachers. In these chapters, the match between the classroom curriculum and the information literacy goals of the media center are made abundantly clear, and pave the way for powerful classroom/media center alliances. Each information literacy standard is correlated with both possible classroom curriculum units and with an example from several subject content standards in the McREL compendium. What becomes clear when the Information Literacy Standards for Student Learning are matched with the McREL standards is that information literacy permeates content standards from every content area, many of which are similar to those associated with information literacy in *Information Power*. Librarians learned long ago that teaching either simple or sophisticated information skills in isolation from classroom instruction is not productive. Every fruitful curriculum conference between media specialists and teachers has the underlying theme of how information literacy and classroom content can be brought together in one integrated lesson.

In a reversal of the roles experienced by the media specialist, the classroom teacher has traditionally been thought of only marginally as an information specialist and rarely as a program administrator. This is no longer an accurate view either. While the classroom teacher usually has the most in-depth training and experience with teaching and instruction, the media specialist has the most in-depth training and experience with information provision and program administration. When the Internet first became available in the classroom during the mid-1990s, some classroom teachers mistakenly thought they no longer needed the media specialist to continue in the role of information specialist. The truth soon became clear, however—the evaluative insights into material evaluation, selection, acquisition, organization, and dissemination remained a specialty of the media professional. The everyday reality of the changes in curriculum—such as whole language and resource-based teaching, and the penetration of the Internet and LAN software into the classroom—has forced the classroom teacher to gain expertise in these areas. But the wholesale selection of a myriad of resources that extend beyond the walls of the building calls for the traditional expertise of the media specialist.

Now the physical location of the resources is everywhere. The idea of a media center is no longer merely a place; it is a program. The actual location of the resources is not as important as the responsibility that is attached to them. When the teacher becomes a guide-on-the-side rather than a purveyor of content, the classroom resembles more closely the flexible access media center—with a number of learning activities occurring simultaneously and the need for proper coordination and administration paramount.

The bottom line is that the classroom professional has traditionally taken care of the teaching while the media specialist has traditionally supported instruction, with the provision of information resources and the administration of the media program. Now each professional must take significant responsibility for each of these roles, while retaining the depth of expertise in their traditional areas of responsibility.

These classroom/media center mergers and intersections offer the means for coplanned and coexecuted authentic student learning experiences. They provide a way to resolve some of the tension that tears at the classroom teacher by providing a teaching partnership. They provide a means for the media specialist to teach information literacy without the senselessness of teaching it in a content vacuum. And specifically for our interest in offering guidelines for teachers and librarians, this overlap in desired student outcome points directly to a potential means to resolve some of the issues of censorship. For in such an open and information-accessible environment, these issues are sure to arise.

The Student's Place in This Merger

Students of the 21st century move easily between media center and classroom. For students, the blurring of roles and responsibilities makes sense, for it all has to do with learning. Students learn differently not because of which adult does what, but because of their place in the learning process. The old picture had the teacher in the center, the student as receiver, and the librarian as a small supporter on the side. The new 21st century picture draws an equal partnership among teachers, media specialists, and students. Each player is on a team, and each has both a general and a specialized role. In this modern scenario the students are not the only ones who learn.

A Media Specialist-Teacher-Student Alliance

Media Specialists. Twenty first century *media specialists* wear the hats of teacher, instructional partner, information specialist, and media center manager in relation to collaboration, leadership, and technology in the school's learning community. They may find past stereotypes hard to dispel, but nonetheless they are moving into full partnership as members of their school's instructional team. They understand their position of leadership in building a learning community, and they take that responsibility seriously. They have always had special relationships with students who love to read—now that relationship can be extended to every student in the school. The media specialist has been and continues to be committed ideologically to unfettered access to information, and he or she incorporates these principles as part of teaching information literacy.

Teachers. Twenty first century *teachers* function as teachers, instructional partners, information specialists, and classroom managers. It is easy for them to get so involved in these various roles that they fail to realize that the media professionals in the building are also teachers with a set of desired learner outcomes—outcomes that can be most productively taught when integrated with classroom curriculum content. Perhaps they are not fully aware that media specialists' goals can overlap with classroom processes and skill goals, or that they can learn to rely on this extra teacher for reducing what they must teach. Teachers are just learning how to serve in the information specialist role that has long been the untouchable and expected territory of the media specialist. The classroom teacher adheres to and believes in "the student's right to read," but has found that there is an undesirable level of scrutiny and control on classroom and curriculum content.

Students. Twenty first century *students* are technologically savvy, independent learners, as well as learners who work well with others.

Their interests are as widespread as the Internet and as deep as the most scholarly book. They become information literate while studying subject content. They have become accustomed to speaking for themselves and to making intergenerational connections around the world. Learning can be stifling or stimulating—with more opportunities for the latter than ever before. The 21st century student assumes open access to information even though others in the school environment do not always agree.

How can teachers begin to truly work together with media specialists and students, and what relevance does this have to the guidelines for dealing with censorship in the 21st century?

Principals: One More Partner in the Mix

For a strong alliance to work, it must have the support of the building principal. The principal must be aware of all the chances being taken and must accept them as healthy in the school environment. Principals often are the first people in the building to become aware of changes and to embrace them as appropriate and good. Unfortunately this is not always the case, and sometimes much individual persuasion and teaching by example must be done. To this end, the library media specialists of the state of Alabama distributed a document to principals titled *Literacy Partners–A Principal's Guide to an Effective Library Media Program for the 21st Century* (Alabama Department of Education's Office of Technology Initiatives, 2000). For this 21st century paradigm to work, principals must play a strong part, and media specialists and teachers must encourage them to get involved.

Strong Arguments for an Alliance

Reasons for the media specialist-classroom teacher-student (and principal) alliance lie in the results of extensive research by Dianne McAfee Hopkins of the University of Wisconsin School of Library and Information Studies, who has studied censorship during the 20th century and the strategies that were effective in combating it. Hopkins has conducted both state (Wisconsin) and national research into how to combat censorship, and she is regarded as the leading expert on the status of censorship in school media centers—as evidenced by her selection as the author of the chapter for school librarians in the American Library Association's *Intellectual Freedom Manual* (1996). (See http://www.ala.org/alaorg/oif/intellectualfreedommanual.html)

Hopkins's research builds on the work of researchers such as Charles Busha (1972), Mary Woodworth (1976), and Judith Serebnick (1979), but she extends and clarifies the findings in light of the best

20th century thinking. Two seemingly contradictory and somewhat star-tling factors have come out of her research: (1) More than 30% of cen-sorship challenges come from school personnel, with the majority of these coming from the building principal, and (2) Challenged materi-als were retained more frequently when the anticensorship effort was supported by principal, teacher, and library media specialist. Hopkins conducted a U.S. national study including more than 6,000 partici-pants, and drew conclusions from her data using correlation and re-gression statistical analysis. From the conceptual model that she created before the research, Hopkins found that a number of factors present in the alliance suggested in this chapter influenced retention of materi-als. Among these was the school environment, which was interpreted as overall internal support of the librarian during the challenge. Other factors that Hopkins found that supported retention after a challenge were the community environment (external support during the chal-lenge), the existence and use of a district selection policy during the challenge, and the nature of the challenge (originating from an external as opposed to an internal source of censorship) (Hopkins, 1992, 1993).

Hopkins also found that the internal relationships of the library me-dia specialist prior to the challenge affected the outcome of the chal-lenge, with positive relationships correlated with support and then retention. This reinforces the idea of the suggested alliance. Despite the strong correlation that is suggested between internal and external sup-port and retention, however, Hopkins found that 88.4% of the librarians in her study sought no outside assistance, and only about half sought internal assistance (Hopkins, 1998). In other words, there is still a need for all school personnel, including the media specialist, to be aware of the need for a strong alliance. Hopkins's research supports the idea that the groundwork must be laid for an alliance before the censor arrives— it is far too late to assemble this coalition when a crisis has occurred. The librarian as information specialist must move to the forefront to ini-tiate and guide the development of policies and procedures that in collaboration with the teachers and the principal will cover all re-sources—classroom and media center alike.

Students as Silent Partners

The conclusions from the 20th century must be studied and brought forward to the 21st, but a key ingredient is missing from much of 20th century research. That key missing ingredient is the student. The two landmark court cases cited at the beginning of this chapter are most commonly referred to by students' names—Pico and Stevana—both teenage plaintiffs in the actions filed. Seven students fought the school board in the *Island Trees v. Pico* case. Stevana Case and several other students and parents were the plaintiffs in the case involving the attempted removal of *Annie on My Mind* from school media centers in Kansas. After the superintendent announced that the book would be removed from library media center collections, Oalthe East High School senior Stevana Case—honor student, National Merit semifinalist, and president of the student government—presented a unanimous resolution of the Oalthe East study body condemning censorship and calling for the return of *Annie on My Mind* to the library media center collection (Meyer, 1996). Students were at the forefront of the action, yet when opinions were asked and statistics were collected, it was the adults rather than the students whose voices were heard. Students became the proactive, silent partner.

In all walks of 21st century life students' voices are heard, increasingly taking action in their own lives. Major leadership organizations are urging learner control. Idealistic and committed students are already at the table, but their place needs to be acknowledged, applauded, and pursued and many more students need to be involved.

Strengthening the Alliance

By joining hands to defend First Amendment rights, citizens of a school are much more likely to defeat challenges. Because many challenges can originate internally and internal challenges are the most likely to succeed, having all internal partners strongly committed to the same effort is one of the best defenses against censorship attempts. Teachers, librarians, and students can engage in mutual learning projects that assure that all parties (including the principal) have an accurate understanding of the First and Fourteenth Amendments and their core place in a democratic society. Even elementary school students, who once were considered too young to understand such complex content, have moved forward in the digital world to show that they can understand far more than they have been given credit for. Both media specialists and teachers have responsibility for teaching the legal and ethical principles that support democracy—our Constitutional rights. A benchmark for the McREL History Standards K–4 describes students who "understand the basic principles of American democracy... freedom of speech and religion" (Kendall & Marzano, 1997), while the American Association of School Librarians' list of "The Nine Information Literacy Standards for Student Learning" (in *Information Power*, 1998) puts a high premium on "the importance of information to a democratic society" (http://www.ala.org/aasl/ip_nine.html).

Experiencing Censorship Through Literature for Youth

The fictional book by Betty Miles, *Maudie and Me and the Dirty Book* (1980) is indicated by the publisher as appropriate for grades 3–6 and could be used by teachers or media specialists to give their students an experience of the effects of censorship. In this book, the 11-year-old protagonist, Kate, reads a book to first graders. Her choice is *The Birthday Dog*, which prompts the children to inquire how puppies are born. Parents object, and the principal steps in and puts a halt to the reading project. As a result, Kate, her friends, and very young readers learn about censorship first-hand. Very young children know what it means to be denied information on a topic that is personally important. The meaning of the First Amendment and how it is sometimes abridged in schools makes sense to youth when it is presented in a familiar context such as through this book.

A popular book with high school students that addresses one of the most censored books of the 20th century, Mark Twain's *Huckleberry Finn*, is *The Day They Came to Arrest the Book* by Nat Hentoff (1982). In fiction, as is often the case in factual instances, the students are the heroes of this anticensorship protest. (More on the lightning rod effect of *Huckleberry Finn* will be discussed in Chapter 5.) Many stories with censorship as a theme have been published for youth in the past 15 years. At the end of this chapter, a list of fiction and nonfiction selections for children and adolescents surrounding the theme of censorship appears. It is a resource to be used by teachers and media specialists as part of partnering with youth in the anticensorship effort.

Students are the heroes and heroines of many actual censorship cases. What better way for students to understand the courageous stand they may someday have to take than reading about others who have come before? John Gold wrote an entire book titled *The Board of Education vs. Pico* (1995) for young people grades 6–8 about the case discussed earlier. Obviously he thought it appropriate for young readers, and not too complex for them to understand. Two additional books to help with educating the alliance are Kathleen Krull's *A Kids' Guide to America's Bill of Rights: Curfews, Censorship, and the 100-Pound Giant* (1999) and *Make Yourself Heard: Teen Power Politics* (2000) by Sara Jane Boyers. (See Figure 1 for a list of books about censorship for young people.)

Capitalizing on the 21st Century Learning Environment

For only one decade in the 20th century, 1972–1982, did the courts focus on cases involving school libraries. In *Minarcini v. Strongsville*

Figure 1
Books for Youth Related to Censorship
and Intellectual Freedom

Blume, Judy. *Places I Never Meant to Be: Original Stories by Censored Writers.* New York: Simon & Schuster, 1999. (Fiction/Nonfiction)

Outstanding YA writers Norma Fox Mazer, Julius Lester, Rachel Vail, Katherine Paterson, Jacqueline Woodson, Harry Mazer, Walter Dean Myers, Susan Beth Pfeffer, David Klass, Paul Zindel, Chris Lynch, and Norma Klein write with great teen appeal. Following each story is a personal comment about censorship by the author. Proceeds go to the National Coalition Against Censorship.

Facklam, Margery. *The Trouble With Mothers.* New York: Houghton Mifflin, 1992. (Grades 6–8, Fiction)

The trouble with the author-mother of eighth grader Luke Troy is that some of the community considers her novels pornographic.

Garden, Nancy. *The Year They Burned the Books.* New York: Farrar, Strauss & Giroux, 1999. (Fiction based on true story)

The school's new policy to distribute condoms coincides with the election of a new, highly conservative school board member. The issue is a newspaper editorial—to publish or not to publish. Gay issues subtheme.

Gold, John Coppersmith. *Board of Education v. Pico.* New York: Twentieth Century Books, 1995. (Grades 6–8, Nonfiction)

Mentioned several times in this book, the precedent-setting *Island Trees Board of Education v. Pico* shows to young people the central role they can play in many censorship challenges.

Greenberg, Keith. *Adolescent Rights: Are Young People Equal Under the Law?* New York: Twentieth Century Books, 1995. (Grades 6–10, Nonfiction)

A strong proponent of adolescent rights, this book uses historical context and contemporary point of view to relate to the theme of this chapter—bringing youth into the anticensorship alliance.

Hentoff, Nat. *The Day They Came to Arrest the Book.* New York: Dell, 1982. (Grades 6–10, Fiction)

The highly complex issue of censorship related to fair treatment of race discussed in Chapter 5 plays itself out in this story of teens' involvement in a challenge to the teaching of *The Adventures of Huckleberry Finn* in a high school classroom.

Herda, D.J. *New York Times v. United States: National Security and Censorship.* Berkeley Heights, NJ, 1994. (Grades 6–8, Nonfiction)

Although not set in a school, this landmark case about freedom of the press can bring lively discussion in a classroom.

Krull, Kathleen. *A Kids' Guide to America's Bill of Rights: Curfews, Censorship, and the 100-Pound Giant.* New York: Avon Books, 1999. (Nonfiction)

(continued)

An entertaining, accurate account of the first 14 amendments to the U.S. Constitution is guaranteed to raise the consciousness of students and provide great encouragement for the recommended proactive stance. Far more lively than most others on the topic.

Lasky, Kathryn. *Memoirs of a Bookbat.* New York: Harcourt, 1994. (Grades 7–9, Fiction)

More parent trouble—this time fundamentalist Christians who launch a censorship promotion while their avid-reader teen daughter flees in protest.

Meyer, Carolyn. *Drummers of Jericho.* New York: Harcourt, 1995. (Grades 7–10, Fiction)

A Jewish girl in a small western town stands up for her convictions (with the help of her father and the ACLU) that the school marching band, to which she belongs, should not make the formation of a cross.

Miles, Betty. *Maudie and Me and the Dirty Book.* New York: Knopf, 1980. (Grades 3–6, Fiction)

Reading a book, *The Birthday Dog*, to the first grade seemed simple enough to 11-year-old Kate—until parents complain to the principal because the young children ask about how puppies are born. Kate and her friends learn about censorship from experience.

Pascoe, Elaine. *Freedom of Expression: The Right to Speak Out in America.* Brookfield, CT: Millbrook, 1992. (Grades 5–8, Nonfiction)

Illustrated with political cartoons and photographs, this history of the First Amendment speaks directly to its youthful audience.

Peck, Richard. *The Last Safe Place on Earth.* New York: Delacorte, 1995. (Grades 6–10, Fiction)

The suburbs are the last safe place on earth, but when religious fanaticism in the neighborhood and censorship in the school library enter the picture for teenager Todd, the last safe place doesn't seem so safe anymore.

Sherrow, Victoria. *Censorship in Schools.* Berkeley Heights, NJ: Enslow, 1996. (Grades 6–10, Nonfiction)

After giving a brief, straightforward historical overview of censorship, the author divides the remaining chapters by issue.

Steins, Richard. *Censorship: How Does It Conflict with Freedom?* New York: Holt, 1995. (Grades 6–9, Nonfiction)

This book details censorship in an historical context.

Thompson, Julian. *The Trials of Molly Sheldon.* New York: Holt, 1995. (Grades 7–10, Fiction)

First the books in her father's bookstore are attacked by censors, and then Molly herself becomes the object of a witch hunt.

(continued)

Figure 1 (continued)
Books for Youth Related to Censorship
and Intellectual Freedom

Tolan, Stehanie S. *Save Halloween!*. New York: Morrow, 1993. (Grades 5–8, Fiction)

> Johanna, a middle schooler, has never celebrated Halloween because of her family's religious convictions, which she now begins to question just as her uncle comes to town to show the evil of the holiday. The main character is better realized than in some of the other fiction books on the list.

Zeinert, Karen. *Free Speech: From Newspapers to Music*. Berkeley Heights, NJ: Enslow, 1993. (Grades 7–10, Nonfiction)

> The historical context of censorship battles relating to newspapers, books, magazines, music lyrics, movies, radio, and television are expressed in teen-friendly terms.

(1976), the court stated, "A library is a mighty resource in the marketplace of ideas.... It is a forum for silent speech." In *The Right to Read v. Chelsea* case (1978), which focused on a poem written by a 15-year-old girl in the anthology *Male and Female Under 18* (Larrick & Merriam, 1973), a district judge said, "What is at stake here is the right to read and be exposed to controversial thoughts and language...a valuable right subject to First Amendment protection.... The most effective antidote to the poison of mindless orthodoxy is ready access to a broad sweep of ideas and philosophies. There is no danger in such exposure." Decisions regarding libraries sometimes favored students' right to read *and* sometimes school board authority until the *Island Trees v. Pico* case in 1982. Although this case did not technically set a precedent, the fact that it set limitations on a school board's right to remove books from the library seemed to have the same "chilling effect" on censorship that censorship sometimes has on the selection of materials. Between 1972 and 1982 there were several major rulings on challenges in school libraries. The only case in court since 1982 regarding the removal of a book from a school library is *Stevana Case v. Unified School Dist. No. 233* (1995) mentioned earlier. The anticensorship alliance can capitalize on this knowledge in selecting the resources from which to teach.

With teachers, librarians, and students as instructional partners, and with the 21st century classroom incorporating a multitude of materials, a diversity of resources can be made available to students. In the year 2000, e-book readers appeared on the scene, and immediately e-books found their way into a number of schools. In the fall of 2000, IDG books and iUniverse became pioneers in the provision of "books by chapter and verse," or parts of books on demand. The Internet provides a dazzling depth and breadth of resources (including the delivery of the aforementioned books). Resources that might at one time have been merely supplemental to the "main text" move to the center of curriculum in the 21st century classroom. The job of the censor in this digital environment becomes increasingly difficult because students have the opportunity to choose their resources for reading and research from an almost limitless array. The desperation with which some censorship groups are acting in the early 21st century, described throughout this book, possibly stems from the realization that the hole is in the dike, the horse is out of the barn—that their chance for controlling young minds is virtually over. What censors are really trying to control is ideas—and it is ideas that are constitutionally protected. When those ideas appear in so many different venues, many of them overseen by the school media specialist on the instructional team, they become extremely difficult to suppress.

What Makes This New Alliance So Strong?

The digital age has encouraged adult-youth partnerships, particularly when the youth know more than adults who are working with them, such as in the area of technology. One of the most encouraging aspects of the increasing local control of school districts delineated in Chapter 2 is that local students care about their schools and their own rights, and when they speak loudly, and in chorus with supportive adults, often they will be heard.

What makes this alliance of adults, students, and administrators so strong? The answer can be found in one of the most popular books by the author Dr. Seuss, titled *Horton Hears a Who*. Try as they may, the Whos of Whoville cannot make Horton hear—until the one absent Who appears—and then together the whole village is heard. In other words, encouraging all stakeholders within a school to understand and act on their constitutional rights may bring the one voice missing to make all the other voices heard. It is the simple truism: United we stand and divided we fall.

Guidelines for Teachers and Librarians

- Read Pat Scales's article "Studying the First Amendment" and adapt her suggestions to your school's media center and classroom environments.

- Link the concepts of a democratic society with free access to information. Provide opportunities for students to discuss what would happen if these guarantees did not exist.

- Post the text of the First Amendment in classrooms and in the media center accompanied by the question, What does this mean for you? Also post the Library Bill of Rights and The Students' Right to Read.

- Reenact one of the famous "trials" that involve censorship in a school setting.

- Set up a role play for students about a challenged classroom or media resource, or set up a debate in the media center and invite other classes to attend.

- Read aloud a book with a censorship theme (see list in Figure 1). Discuss its tie to the First Amendment. Or ask students to choose a fiction or nonfiction book from the list, and hold a class discussion when they have finished reading it.

- Assign an essay on "What my school should do if a censor comes...."

- Introduce the concept of intellectual freedom and discuss with students what it means.

RECOMMENDED WEB SITES

Board of Education, Island Trees Union Free School District v. Pico, 457 U.S. 853, 102 S. Ct. 2799 (1982)
http://www.tourolaw.edu/patch/Pico
For a brief summary, see **http://www.fleurdelis.com/pico.htm**

Collaborative Activities to Teach Information Literacy Skills Through Classroom Content
http://www.alsde.edu/26/Librarians/KindergartenSocialStudies.htm

Hazelwood School District v. Kuhlmeier 484 U.S. 260, 108 S. Ct. 562 (1988)
http://www.tourolaw.edu/patch/Hazelwood
For a brief summary see **http://www.fleurdelis.com/hazelwd.htm**

IDG (ebooks)
http://www.idg.com/www/idg/sections.nsf/IMS98/HTML/search.html

Information Power: Because Student Achievement is the Bottom Line
An American Association of School Libraries Web site with links to the "Nine information literacy standards for student learning," excerpts from most chapters in *Information Power: Building Partnerships for Learning*, and full text of background readings suggested in *Information Power*.
http://www.ala.org/aasl/ip_implementation.html

Intellectual Freedom Awards
An American Library Association (ALA) Web site with links to several national intellectual freedom awards given by the Intellectual Freedom Round Table of ALA, other ALA units (with lists of winners) and other organizations.
http://www.ala.org/alaorg/oif/ifawards.html

International Reading Association
http://www.reading.org

Standards for the English Language Arts
http://newbookstore.reading.org/cgi-bin/OnlineBookstore.storefront/ 2086415999/Product/View/889-553

Literacy Partners—A Principal's Guide to an Effective Library Media Program for the 21st Century.
http://www.alsde.edu/26/librarians/LiteracyPartners.pdf

Mid-continent Research for Education and Learning (McREL)
Subject content standards, research reports, dimensions of learning, and other essential information for K–12 educators.
http://www.mcrel.org

Tinker v. Des Moines Independent Community School District 393 U.S. 503, 89 S. Ct. 733 (1969).
http://www.tourolaw.edu/patch/Tinker
http://www.fleurdelis.com/tinker.htm

U.S. Bill of Rights
http://www.law.cornell.edu/constitution/constitution.billofrights.html

CHAPTER 4

Prime Targets

Humanists are aggressive and evangelistic. They are adept at tearing down traditional faith, even if it means permitting the occult to enter the classroom. They are skilled at pouring their anti-God dogmas into the void.

—Mel and Norma Gabler, 1985

E nglish or reading educators who have been working in schools for a long time are often confronted by new classroom teachers with hard questions. One of the more frequent ones goes something like this: "How can I make sure that the books I assign will be safe from censorship challenges?" Given our utter lack of possession of magical powers, we have to reply candidly that no book is truly "safe," and the complaints about materials assigned in classes or procured for school libraries are virtually unpredictable in terms of theme, content, or author.

This predicament has never been more evident than it is at the present time. Everything we assign as reading material is vulnerable, given the fact that people do not just read words; they read different meanings into those words. A rather recent example of this hazardous state of affairs can be illustrated by one of the promises of Michael Farris in his 1994 campaign for gubernatorial office in the state of Virginia, USA. Mr. Farris, then Republican lieutenant governor, deplored the presence of objectionable materials in Virginia schools, especially at the elementary level. Particularly, he wanted three objectionable texts out and would lead the charge against them were he elected chief executive. The three titles were *Cinderella, The Wizard of Oz* (both print and film versions), and *Rumplestiltskin.* Mr. Farris lost the election to his Democratic opponent 54% to 46% in the midst of a statewide Republican landslide. Conservative religious groups, which had provided him with considerable financial support, were disappointed. There may be no cause-and-effect relationship between Mr. Farris's censorship stance and his loss, but the result at the polls must have been a relief to a large number of elementary school teachers and principals in that state.

Topics and Themes Under Attack

The targets of censorship are many and varied, and have increased significantly over the past 20 years. Some of the more traditional ones have been augmented by such curricular movements as "real literature," multiculturalism, personal writing, and political correctness. An important development of a slightly longer tenure is the direction that has been taken by young adult fiction. Over the last two decades, this genre has moved steadily toward more contemporary and realistic settings, characters, themes, and cultural happenings. (Chapter 6 will delve deeper into young adult fiction.) What follows is an annotated listing of the most prominent topics and themes under attack at the end of the 20th century.

Profane, Obscene, and Otherwise Objectionable Language

A 14-year review of censorship challenges titled *Attacks on the Freedom to Learn* (People for the American Way, 1996), reveals that language consistently holds the lead position as the most frequent cause for complaints. Thus, the challenges to Salinger's *Catcher in the Rye* (1948)—arguably the most censored book in public secondary schools in the last half-century—continue due to the use of the "f-word" (six times, by actual count), which offends parents, citizens, clergy, and even school staff, across the United States. Books with a much lower incidence of bad words, however, continue to raise criticism. In one Florida community, *My Friend Flicka* (O'Hara, 1941) was taken off all secondary school shelves because of one "damn" and two "bitch" uses—the latter in reference to a female dog. In another Deep South community, *Life with Father* (Lindsay & Crouse, 1948) was removed because the author went beyond "damn" to "Goddamn" in a speech made by the play's protagonist, Clarence Day.

The rise in popularity of multiethnic and multiracial authors and texts over the past 20 years has added new dimensions to this problem. As a means of creating an authentic image of their lifestyles and environmental situations, African, Hispanic, and Native American authors have often employed profanity and obscenity in their characters' dialogue. Thus, in recent years the works of Richard Wright, Alice Childress, James Baldwin, Maya Angelou, and Toni Morrison have been contested in middle schools, high schools, and even community junior colleges. Jewish authors such as Saul Bellow, Bernard Malamud, and Philip Roth have had their fiction removed from classrooms for various grievances, including objectionable language.

The rise of the political correctness movement has led to increasing incidences of challenges to any work that contains even the most minimal inclusion of racial, ethnic, or religious slurs. Thus the word *nigger*, so often found in traditionally taught and respected novels, short stories, plays, poems, essays, and biographies, has been the subject of school-community confrontations nationwide. The classic Mark Twain novel, *The Adventures of Huckleberry Finn* (1884), rose to a place near the top of the most-censored lists in the 1990s. The incidental use of the same word is one of many reasons why Steinbeck's *Of Mice and Men* continues to rank among the three most challenged literary works introduced in secondary school classes. In the young adult (YA) novel category, such celebrated texts as Robert Cormier's *The Chocolate War*, Alice Childress's *A Hero Ain't Nothin But a Sandwich*, Judy Blume's *Blubber*, and the anonymously authored *Go Ask Alice* have suffered the same fate.

Critics of "progressive" curricular inclusions have objected to any student writing in which profanity is allowed, even in the case of semiprivate journal entries. Even more intensively criticized have been those sociolinguistic texts that describe cultural pluralism in general and relativistic usage dialect study, semantics analyses, and even lexicography introduction. In fact, modern dictionaries have been under attack for at least the last 40 years because of their inclusion of "dirty" words. James Moffett's (1988) *Storm in the Mountains: A Case Study of Censorship, Conflict, and Consciousness* provides a detailed—and profoundly disturbing—chronicle of the violent, bloody uprising in Kanawha County, West Virginia, in 1969. The cause of this fanatical confrontation between the education establishment and the community was the introduction of a new sociolinguistic text into secondary school classrooms. The opposition, mounted by the largely rural, uneducated populace, to these "sinister, one-world, Godless" ideas stands as testimony to the results of curricular innovation when it apparently clashes with basic community values.

Finally, those novels and plays that feature characters who use a minority dialect are also prone to attack because of the bad grammatical models they offer young people.

It is safe to claim, then, that objectionable language is still the leading cause of censorship episodes in our country. Moreover, in recent years the scope of concerns over what can be found "objectionable" in language has expanded. Such concerns have led to extreme reticence and caution among language arts teachers who once introduced certain texts to their students with enthusiasm and pride.

Explicit Depiction of Sexual Activity

Second to objectionable language as the cause of censorship challenges is the inclusion of descriptions of sexual encounters, until recently limited to those of a heterosexual nature. Many texts that are otherwise popular with teachers and students alike have been banned, avoided, or bowdlerized to permit their use in the classroom. Already cited for its objectionable language, *Catcher in the Rye* has also been condemned for the general, albeit marginal, sexual episodes within its narrative. One in particular—the apparent advance made to the novel's male protagonist by a former, and still trusted, prep school teacher—has drawn significant protest from parents and others. Likewise, *The Chocolate War* (Cormier, 1974) contains incidents of male masturbation, adding to its vulnerability to challenge. Objections have been raised about classroom use of the futuristic *Brave New World* by Aldous Huxley and *1984* by George Orwell because of the incidental sexual episodes in each text (among other reasons). Over the past two decades, the intense and longstanding opposition to certain novels of Judy Blume has led to the elevation of that young adult fiction author to the top of the most censored young adult writers lists. Her novel *Forever* (1982), with its four explicit descriptions of sexual intercourse between a teenage couple, ranks high among the most censored novels in the United States.

The neopuritanical preoccupations still evident in U.S. culture have produced a succession of challenges that seem extraordinary in the 21st century. This is a society that, after all, has rejected such words as "pregnant" in films as recently as 1953 (*The Moon Is Blue*); has permitted only the expurgated version of D.H. Lawrence's novel, *Lady Chatterly's Lover*, in 1960; and still chafed at the use of "son-of-a-bitch" in a film in 1966 (*Who's Afraid of Virginia Woolf?*). The struggle to keep such "smut" out of public school classrooms and libraries may be considered a kind of rear guard action by the defenders of virtue and chastity as this century begins. Although it is hard to argue with the opponents of sexual overkill, it must seem paradoxical, if not laughable, to the streetwise teenagers of today to see books being removed from classrooms because they describe a full-bosomed female or an incident of nocturnal emissions of semen. After all, outside the classroom students casually encounter *Playboy*, *Playgirl*, and *Penthouse*; X-rated films; sadomasochistic video games; and the Internet—all theirs for the asking. Given the fact that serious discourse on real human problems is conspicuous by its absence, school programs of study may take on an Alice-in-Wonderland aura to many of these young people.

Critical "Anti-American" Materials

Throughout the 20th century, extremist patriots have consistently attacked assigned materials that they deem to be unpatriotic. Together with profanity and sexuality, "Anti-American" materials comprise the third axis of the "Big Three" in the world of school censorship. The concept of patriotism espoused by sincere, well-intentioned, would-be book censors has taken on some distinctive hues—orthodox political or economic conservatism and white Anglo-Saxon Protestantism are the two most prominent ones. Five of the more longstanding defenders of these positions are the Daughters of the American Revolution; the American Legion; the Daughters of the Confederacy; the Veterans of Foreign Wars; and the Cold War progeny, the John Birch Society. All of these groups have, from time to time, raised objections to texts and other media presentations when those school offerings did not meet their criteria for putting "our way of life" in a "proper" (positive) perspective. Thus Upton Sinclair's early 20th century potboiler, *The Jungle*, was deemed to be inadequately supportive of capitalistic initiatives; Maxwell Anderson's verse play, *Winterset*, painted an unnecessarily sympathetic portrait of the executed Massachusetts anarchists Sacco and Vanzetti; and Sinclair Lewis's novel *Babbit* unjustly characterized life in the Midwest heartland. John Steinbeck's *Grapes of Wrath*, with its realistic portrayal of the trials of a Great Depression-era family of migrant workers, is another novel that has been accused of being critical of the free enterprise "American way."

Several texts and films depict the actions and motives of the "Great Wars" in less than patriotic tones. To some defenders of such sentiments, Erich María Remarque's novels *All Quiet on the Western Front* (World War I) and *A Time to Love and a Time to Die* (World War II) had the audacity to scrutinize the problems, hopes, and fears of young German soldiers. John Hersey's *Hiroshima* agonized over the human slaughter and misery caused by the first nuclear attack on Japan in 1945. Joseph Heller's *Catch 22* drew an unacceptably crude and irreverent caricature of life in the U.S. Army; and Kurt Vonnegut's *Slaughterhouse Five* drew unflattering attention to the Allied air raids of the civilian, culturally rich, and largely undefended city of Dresden in early 1945. More recently, novels and films such as *Platoon, Full Metal Jacket, Apocalypse Now*, and *The Deer Hunter* took aim at the Vietnam conflict to the dismay and outrage of veterans and supporters of that war. Certain young adult novels written by Robert Cormier have even been accused of deploring the work of the CIA (*I Am the Cheese*) and the antiterrorist tactics of the U.S. Army Security Agency (*After the First Death*). The "my country, right or wrong" stance of a small but vocal segment of the U.S. population has made for challenges to these and many other selections introduced in English and social studies classes in the 20th century. As this volume is written, there is reason to believe that these challenges will continue into the 21st century.

New Age Selections

Once called "Secular Humanism" by activist book banners, the "New Age" label covers a variety of materials and classroom activities. The range of challenges related to New Age curricular approaches stretches from Kindergarten through Grade 12, although it has been concentrated in recent years on the early grades. Attacks on literary materials, response tasks, creative classroom activities, and a whole host of media center acquisitions have been mounted in many U.S. states, particularly in California where such attacks have been supported by a "concerned" governor and certain factions in the legislature or assembly. Probably the most visible material to be attacked under this rubric has been the Harcourt Brace elementary level reading/language series, *Impressions* (1984), which will be considered later in this chapter.

To its critics, New Age covers a panoply of questionable learning events. Among them are non-Christian texts, satirical pieces on orthodox religious and civic institutions and practices, criticism of "Family Values," rock music, transcendental meditation, magnetic imaging, sex education, texts containing morbid or depressing themes, self-assessment activities, and others. Within this potpourri, studies of Greek, Celtic, Norse, and other non-Christian mythologies have received particular attention and criticism. This negative attention has also been paid to virtually any material that features aspects of Asian or Islamic religious and spiritual content. Vulnerable, too, have been any materials or class discussions related to contraception, pre- and extramarital sex, HIV/AIDS and other sexually transmitted diseases, teenage pregnancy (as a health issue), self-esteem strategies, gay and lesbian relations, and abortion. Whether these topics are introduced in the classroom through texts, periodicals, guest speakers, films, videos, or any other medium, they will frequently draw an angry response from the community. The dramatic rise in challenges to so-called New Age materials increased dramatically in the 1990s and now rivals the previously described "Big Three" as a cause of censorship events.

Satanism, Witchcraft, the Occult, and Extraterrestrials

In a sense, this collective target could be considered part of the New Age topic, but in the 1990s it established its own distinctive identity and emerged in a variety of garbs. Near or at the top of this list has been the wholesale assault by community groups on any school-based activity that relates to Halloween. Some schools have renamed the celebration "The Fall Festival" and have downplayed the witch, goblin, and skeleton paraphernalia that stood so long as features of children's celebrations. Pumpkins generally have remained, as has candy, as long as the shapes are not too suggestive. Other schools have abandoned the annual celebration entirely, forbidding any bulletin board or other building decorations, along with the wearing of masks and costumes, the telling or reading of pertinent stories, and, of course, assembly programs. Principals tell concerned citizens that what happens after school and off the premises on Halloween is the business of the children and their parents. Thus the event lives on in trick-or-treat onslaughts, but not on school grounds.

In literary terms, the works of Shel Silverstein, Roald Dahl, Alvin Schwartz, and Katherine Paterson, to name some of the more prominent authors, have been removed from countless elementary and middle school classrooms and libraries. A recent addition to that list is the Harry Potter books by J.K. Rowling, to be discussed at length in Chapter 6. Scary films and videos have met the same fate. At the senior high school level, the texts of Nathaniel Hawthorne, Edgar Allen Poe, Washington Irving, Samuel Taylor Coleridge, William Blake, and more recently, Robert Cormier, have come under a new scrutiny.

The Image of Minorities

African American, Hispanic, Asian, Native American, handicapped, and feminist groups have raised objections to their portrayal in literature—even that literature that is written by a member of one of these minorities. A truly representative catalog of texts that have been challenged under this rubric could not reasonably be provided in this chapter, but some of the more prominent works and authors are as follows:

The Adventures of Huckleberry Finn—The use of the word *nigger* and the characterization of Jim have spurred opposition to this classic by Mark Twain. Ironically, some attackers are offended by the sympathetic treatment of the friendship between a white Huck and a black Jim; others by the mere presence of *nigger* throughout the novel.

To Kill a Mockingbird (by Harper Lee)—Once again, the opposition comes from two groups—whites taking issue with the "redneck" stereotypes; blacks opposed to the pathetic image of Tom Robinson.

Cannery Row, Tortilla Flat, The Pearl—to some Hispanic spokespersons, these and other Steinbeck novels portray Mexicans in an unflattering light.

Any text by Flannery O'Connor—The "redneck" image in just about all her novels and short stories is evident, often grotesque, and consistently unflattering.

The novels of Sandra Cisneros—For large numbers of Hispanic readers, students, and community leaders, the picture this rising young novelist paints of underprivileged, Hispanic life in U.S. urban settings is a bit too frank, too coarse, and generally unacceptable in polite company.

The novels of Zora Neale Hurston—Hurston is an African American author best known for her highly acclaimed novel *Their Eyes Were Watching God*. We can add to this list many of the works by Alice Childress, James Baldwin, Toni Morrison, Alice Walker, Richard Wright, and August Wilson. Most of these writers include profanity, descriptions of overt sexual incidents, and portrayals of stereotypic African American characters in their works—all of which can be the source of complaints.

Any text that places females in a stereotyped, "traditional," or compromising position—This list is probably inexhaustible and has grown, in terms of cataloging such sexist works, over the past 30 years of feminist analyses. In actuality, female literary figures from Eve on are suspect in the eyes of committed feminist spokespersons. A quick look at a 1990 list of the most widely taught full-length texts may provide some perspective. Compiled in a federally sponsored, longitudinal study completed at the State University of New York at Albany by Arthur Applebee and Susan Langer (1989), the list is as follows:

The Adventures of Huckleberry Finn, by Mark Twain
Romeo and Juliet, by William Shakespeare
Macbeth, by William Shakespeare
Hamlet, by William Shakespeare
To Kill a Mockingbird, by Harper Lee
The Scarlet Letter, by Nathaniel Hawthorne
Lord of the Flies, by William Golding
The Pearl, by John Steinbeck
Of Mice and Men, by John Steinbeck
The Great Gatsby, by F. Scott Fitzgerald

(Applebee, 1989)

Few of the female characters in these 10 most-widely taught texts are portrayed positively. Assess the characters of Juliet, Lady Macbeth, Gertrude or Ophelia, and Daisy Buchanan. With the possible—and tainted—example of Hester Prynne, it is hard to say much for these female characters. This concern has provided plenty of ammunition for those who feel that the public school literature curriculum has been too long dominated by dead, white, European American male authors who have featured dead, white, European American male protagonists in their works (O'Hara-Connell, 1994).

Violence, Sadism, and Rape

The inclusion of brutality in works of literature provides another opportunity for would-be book censors. Look at all the bloody happenings in the *Iliad*, the *Odyssey*, *Beowulf*, *El Cid*, most of Shakespeare's works, and just about all novels, stories, poems, and plays about war—especially those written in the last 100 years. Recent young adult fiction authors that include violence in their novels include Robert Cormier, S.E. Hinton, Lois Duncan, and Gary Paulsen. To please the many citizens who would like to see less violence in the texts studied in schools, the novels of Charles Dickens would have to be removed. So would almost anything written by Norman Mailer, Ernest Hemingway, Jack London, or Richard Wright. The fact is that the incidents of cruelty and violence described in these works pales by comparison with the popular films of Jean Claude Van Damme, Arnold Schwarzenegger, Steven Segal, Chuck Norris, Bruce Willis, and Clint Eastwood, and many late-night television dramas and crime shows. These all represent violence and brutality to a far greater degree than that in the aforementioned novels. These cinematic offerings, however, are not purchased with taxpayer dollars, as the book censors remind us.

A Censorship Scorecard

From 1982 to 1996, People for the American Way (PFAW), under the leadership of Norman Lear, kept a scorecard on state-by-state incidences of censorship challenges. These have been recorded in the now-curtailed annual report, *Attacks on the Freedom to Learn*. In the final issue, 1995–1996, PFAW provided national censorship data. Below are three "Top Ten" lists found in that publication: 14-year summaries of the most frequently challenged literary texts, classroom materials, and authors.

Most Frequently Challenged Books, 1982–1996

Of Mice and Men, John Steinbeck

The Catcher in the Rye, J.D. Salinger

The Chocolate War, Robert Cormier

I Know Why the Caged Bird Sings, Maya Angelou

Scary Stories to Tell in the Dark, Alvin Schwartz

The Adventures of Huckleberry Finn, Mark Twain

More Scary Stories to Tell in the Dark, Alvin Schwartz

Go Ask Alice, Anonymous

Bridge to Terabithia, Katherine Paterson

The Witches, Roald Dahl

A few others that made the annual list on one occasion or another: Shel Silverstein's *A Light in the Attic*, Alice Walker's *The Color Purple*, Judith Guest's *Ordinary People*, Lois Lowry's *The Giver*, Madeleine L'Engle's *A Wrinkle in Time*, and four Judy Blume novels—*Forever*, *Blubber*, *Deenie*, and *Then Again, Maybe I Won't*.

Consider now the classroom materials that have suffered the most challenges:

Most Frequently Challenged Materials, 1982–1996

Impressions [textbook series]

Pumsy in Pursuit of Excellence [self-esteem program]

Quest [self-esteem program]

Developing Understanding of Self and Others [self-esteem program]

Rolling Stone [magazine]

Romeo and Juliet [film]

YM [magazine]

Schindler's List [film]

Michigan Model for Comprehensive School Health Education

Junior Great Book Series [reading texts]

And, finally, there are the authors themselves:

Most Frequently Challenged Authors, 1982–1996

Judy Blume

Alvin Schwartz

Stephen King

John Steinbeck

Robert Cormier

J.D. Salinger

Roald Dahl

Maya Angelou
Mark Twain
Katherine Paterson

(PFAW, 1996, pp. 303–306)

The 10 authors noted here were remarkably consistent in their presence on 14 years' worth of annual lists. More recently, the names Shel Silverstein, Alice Childress, Madeleine L'Engle, and Judith Guest probably could be added as well.

A Closer Look at Censored Materials

Before bringing this chapter to a close, it is pertinent to give a bit more detail about a few of the noteworthy materials that have become prime targets in recent years.

A Series Under Fire

The Impressions Reading/Language Arts series is a bona fide victim of circumstances. In 1989, the California legislature took the forward-looking step of making a substitution on its adopted list of school materials. That body replaced the time-honored basal reader series—with its highly limited vocabulary, its ultra-sanitized, dumbed-down reading passages, and its mind-numbing classroom activities—with what they called "Real Literature." Education critics, especially those who were supportive of the then-popular Cultural Literacy movement, applauded. By "Real Literature," the legislators meant fairy tales, nursery rhymes, legends, myths, and folktales from a wide spectrum of cultures. In their search for appropriate publications that would include these elements, they came across Impressions. This popular series for grades K–6 was developed by Holt, Rinehart and Winston of Canada Limited, at that time a subsidiary of Harcourt Brace Jovanovich.

A literature-based series, Impressions contains 822 selections in 15 books, including biographies, short stories, nonfiction, folklore, and excerpts from novels, plays, and other literary genres. Criteria for literary selections included quality of authorship, strength of theme or message, interest and appeal to children, reading level, appropriate treatment of sensitive issues, and effectiveness as a stepping stone to language learning. The series includes stories by 70 award-winning authors, including Martin Luther King, Jr., C.S. Lewis, Laura Ingalls Wilder, A.A. Milne, Arnold Lobel, Betsy Byars, Scott O'Dell, Jane Yolen, and Dr. Seuss. Moreover, it incorporates the "whole language" philosophy, a method of teaching reading and language arts that originated in New Zealand

and is now the predominant approach in that country as well as Australia and Canada—three countries that have some of the highest literacy rates in the world. Developed by a team of highly respected educators, Impressions also provides teachers with considerable instructional material to use along with the text.

The initial response to the series in California was one of widespread and enthusiastic approval. Other states usually pay close attention to what California does in matters pertaining to education, and many also adopted Impressions for use in their own beginning reading programs. It was not until after this initial response, however, that bodies of citizens in California and elsewhere took a closer look at the contents of the series and, in community after community, raised objections to their schools' governing authorities.

Those familiar with the earlier discussion of topics and themes under attack in this chapter should not be surprised at the specific charges leveled at the Impressions series from numerous communities in all regions of the United States. One of the most frequently repeated was that witchcraft, sorcery, and magical events proliferated in the literary selections at all (K–6) grade levels. To several of these critics, these topics smacked of New Age philosophy, a term that showed up frequently in the challenges. A sizable group of parents claimed that their children were not old or mature enough to cope with many of the stories and that they were traumatized by them to the point where they experienced nightmares after classroom exposure. Closely related to these complaints were the charges that many stories were redolent of violence and bloodthirsty episodes, which also reflected sadism and human cruelty. Corollary charges of thinly disguised sexual incidents, including rape, were frequently added.

Another major complaint made by protesters was of the spiritual dimensions of the series. The oft-repeated charge was made that decidedly un-Christian supreme beings and deities appeared in the stories. The utter lack of Christian anthropomorphic protagonists concerned many objectors, as did the humanistic aspects of the mythological deities; that they could consort with humans, that they were subject to human frailties, and that they seemed unapologetic for much of their behavior were troubling facts to many. The "wanderings" of the chief Greek god, Zeus, were broadly unacceptable to an equally large number of concerned citizens. Finally, many parents felt that the series was not enhancing the reading skills of their children. Those making that claim yearned for a return to the good old days of preprimers, primers, and basal readers, all undergirded by large amounts of phonics training. Where those feelings persist, the term *whole language* has become a negative epithet to be placed alongside of "liberal" and "secular humanist."

During the 1990s, community opposition to the implementation of Impressions in a large number of U.S. elementary schools led to formal initiatives against school boards demanding the wholesale removal of those materials with deliberate speed. These petitions were most frequently filed in California. As this chapter is being written, challenges have been successful in roughly half of the requests to remove the Impressions series from schools (PFAW, 1995).

Steinbeck's Challenged Classic

A brief review of three often-challenged novels will bring the "prime targets" discussion to a close. These novels have been chosen because they represent the conflict between literary quality and objectionable subject matter, a common censorship battlefield. First among these is John Steinbeck's *Of Mice and Men* (1937/1993). Readers may recall that this novel ranked first among challenged literary selections over the period 1982–1996 (see list on p. 72). This novel is also the work of one of six U.S. authors who have won the coveted Nobel Prize for Literature. In the United States, where allowed, it has been a frequently assigned text at several grade levels, particularly Grade 11, where it stands as an American literary classic. Because it is short and action-packed, it has been consistently popular with teenage students on both sides of the Atlantic.

Of Mice and Men depicts a sensitive treatment of life on the underside of early-to-mid 20th century U.S. society. The friendship between Lenny and George is touching, especially because of its tragic ending. Life among the bunk house residents provides a graphic portrait of underprivileged, uneducated men who are struggling to survive and echoing the haunting theme of loneliness. Candy, the crippled bunk house custodian, is a study in pathos, as is the outcast, African American ranch hand, Crooks. The combination of outer action and sensitive characterization have, for over a half-century, made this text a natural for teenagers' reading and study.

This novel does not, however, get into the hands of U.S. students in a large number of instances. Its profane, sexual, and sadistic elements have already been noted in this chapter. More recently, African American groups have objected to the racial stigmatization of Crooks, and the use of the word *nigger*, which his fellow workers often use in discussing him. Also, more recently, those who oppose the book's treatment of both the physically and mentally challenged have attacked the novel; Candy is physically challenged, and Lenny has limited mental capacities. For those seeking a likely target, *Of Mice and Men* has often filled the bill. Beyond the text itself, there is the political position established by its author. Several years ago, a watchdog group of Texans petitioned the State Education Agency to ban all Steinbeck fiction because of the author's radical positions on several political issues. That petition was denied.

Paterson's Magic Kingdom

The novels of Katherine Paterson, a celebrated young adult fiction author, have been attacked frequently over the past two decades. Of these, the text most often challenged has been *Bridge to Terabithia* (1978), a novel centered around two innocent children in their early teenage years—a friendship that is unarguably chaste. Without other school companions and situated far from any urban culture, these characters create their own magical kingdom, which becomes their refuge of choice. Tragically, the female protagonist, Leslie, dies in an accident, and her friend Jess is left to deal with the momentous struggle of loss.

A highly sensitive, nonviolent story, *Bridge to Terabithia* has won several awards for excellence in recent years. On the surface, it is not burdened by either profanity or descriptions—even intimations—of sexual intimacy. Moreover, it has no connection with unpatriotic subthemes. Why, then, the frequent complaints? Simmons (1998) offered a possible reason in an Assembly on Literature for Adolescents (ALAN) Review essay:

> I came to the ultimate conclusion that two elements within the novel, one underdeveloped, the other of fundamental importance, may be largely responsible for the complaints and challenges that have been lodged against it. The minor one: Leslie displays inherent kindness, generosity, maturity, and *joie de vivre*, all despite the fact that she does not participate in traditional, i.e., Christian religious activity. When it is revealed late in the novel that she's never been to church, some readers, or more probably the parents of those readers, may have been shocked and thus galvanized into protest.... Their fundamental and angry question: How could a kid get to be so good without Jesus? Their answer: She couldn't. Their conclusion: Bad role model.
>
> My inference of the major objectionable element in this novel is its wholesale embracing of the imaginative world as created by Jess and Leslie. When the two children discover their remote location and dress it in the garb of a fairy tale Kingdom, they place the *human* imagination in a role of central importance in their lives. Many of the chief protesters from the Christian Fundamentalist Right want none of that, especially in schools that their hard earned tax dollars support.... The creation of imaginary worlds, so appealing to young people, seems to be anathema to the angry observers from that gentry.... It seems ironic indeed that even as they condemn imaginative class-

room activities, so many of these self-righteous, ultra-suspicious parents save their money in the cookie jar to underwrite their kids' vacation to the Magic Kingdom of Orlando's Disney World. (p. 23)

Whether the proposed thesis is or is not correct, the fact remains that this novel—highly popular with both early adolescent readers and many of their teachers—has often been the object of challenges, and more than half of these challenges have resulted in its removal from the classroom.

Lowry's Dystopia

One final mini-case study involves popular response to Lois Lowry's Young Adult novel, *The Giver* (1993). This story of a futuristic society rose to second place in the "most challenged" literary texts list in 1995–1996 (PFAW, 1996). *The Giver* is the subtly fantasized story of a young man named Jonas who has been chosen to be the leader of a society in which all family ties, goals, mores, and interactions are determined by The Committee of Elders. When the committee decides that a small, infirm child who has been placed with Jonas's family must be liquidated, the young man chooses to forsake his future position and flee with the child—a decision that ends in tragedy for both.

Again, it is necessary to probe a bit in order to find reasons for the quick, intense objection to this novel's presence in secondary school classrooms or libraries. There is little objectionable language. Boy-girl relations are furtive and timid, at best. There is no taunting of anybody's patriotism, or any unflattering portrayal of a minority. There is no Satanic or "magic" subtheme. A closer look reveals probable cause, however—a well-crafted, frightening satire of family values and of the ideal society, vaguely reminiscent of Aldous Huxley's famous—and often maligned—futuristic novel *Brave New World*. Complaints about *The Giver* have appeared in several state-by-state summaries of censorship including *Attacks on the Freedom to Learn* (PFAW, 1996) and the ALA's *Newsletter on Intellectual Freedom* (Krug, 1995). Few literary selections have "enjoyed" such immediate reaction.

The controversy over the three Young Adult novels just discussed is typical of many of the arguments that have traditionally been made against works of quality by potential censors. Issues such as sex, bad language, and violence have always raised the censors' hackles, while multiculturalism and "New Age" materials have developed into major new targets in the ongoing struggle. In Chapter 5, these prime targets will be updated to reflect new complexities, such as the many sides of multiculturalism, that have emerged in the last quarter of the 20th century and the beginning of the new millennium.

RECOMMENDED WEB SITES

The American Family Association
http://www.afa.net

American Legion
http://www.legion-aux.org

The Christian Coalition
http://www.cc.org

Daughters of the American Revolution
http://www.dar.org

Daughters of the Confederacy
http://www.hqudc.org

Family Research Council
http://www.frc.org

Focus on the Family
http://fotf.org
http://www.family.org

John Birch Society
http://www.jbs.org

People for the American Way
http://www.pfaw.org

Veterans of Foreign Wars
http://www.vfw.org/home.shtml

Emerging Concerns

Chapter 4 focused on censorship targets that have been the concern of various groups and individuals over a long period of time. Societies are dynamic entities, however, and at different times in U.S. cultural history, citizens have turned to attack new, different, and often surprising targets. In the final quarter of the 20th century, a number of these new targets emerged. How these new targets came to be the focus of citizens' ire can be illustrated by taking a short journey through the history of the culture that produced them.

A Short History of Hatred in U.S. Cultural History

Let us go back in time to the early 1970s. The United States was then awash in conflict, anger, and confusion. The Vietnam War dragged on—with scenes of death, suffering, and civil strife appearing nightly on the six o'clock news. Richard Nixon was denouncing protesters as thugs and doggedly pursuing peace with honor. The violent deaths of Rev. Martin Luther King, Jr. and Robert Kennedy had catalyzed racial violence, especially in large cities. In the fall of 1973, an Arab oil embargo brought the most powerful nation in the free world to its knees. Insurgent groups such as Students for a Democratic Society caused disruptions on college campuses nationwide. The drug culture was growing rapidly, and the Hip Movement was in full swing. Religious leaders were advocating civil disobedience. The states hardly seemed united.

Through all this turmoil, there was substantial evidence of a backlash from Middle America. Before Watergate destroyed his presidency, Richard Nixon coined the phrase "the Silent Majority." Toward the end of that turbulent decade, the millions of U.S. citizens who feared and opposed the chaotic conditions began to flex their muscles. As certain older groups became more vocal (The American Legion) and new groups staked out their reactionary positions (The Moral Majority, Eagle Forum), the voices of orthodoxy grew in volume. Theirs was a confrontational, angry message: "Preserve the American Way of Life, as we know and cherish it. Drive out these loud, smelly, bearded, profane infidels!"

Psychologists have claimed for a very long time that people need something to hate, and such hatred is enhanced when it becomes anthropomorphic—embodied in the smiling face of Saddam Hussein or the hysterically gesticulating Ayatolla Khomeini. This propensity can be noted in 20th century U.S. society beginning with the Great Depression, when fearful, un- and underemployed citizens voiced their antagonism to the Red Menace. Although never a truly decisive factor in U.S. politics, the aura spread by the Communist Party provided a galvanizing force for those who had a visceral fear that the capitalist system was on the ropes. Portraits of Lenin and Trotsky were vilified. Party members became the objects of suspicion and hostility.

With the advent of World War II, the threat of communism gave way to that of the Axis expansionists, whose avowed goals and incredibly ruthless tactics gave U.S. citizens and free people everywhere plenty to fear and despise. The new objects of hatred were portraits of Adolph Hitler, Benito Mussolini, and Hideki Tojo. With the fall of those powers, the unconditional surrender of their armed forces, and the trials against the genocidal leaders, that interlude came to an end and the hatred of communism returned. The brutal, megalomaniacal tactics of Josef Stalin and the beginnings of the Cold War with the former Soviet Union were enough to restore the image of the Communist bogeyman back to the number one position on the U.S. geopolitical hit list. The aggressive behavior of China, especially when it intervened in the Korean War, added fuel to the fire.

For 50 years, the Communist threat provided the foe against which U.S. citizens railed. The threat, both overt and clandestine, seemed omnipresent, and suspicion ran rampant. That suspicion was exacerbated by the initiatives of demagogues such as Senator Joseph McCarthy, and the entire House Un-American Activities Committee, with the help of many congressional colleagues. These witch hunters gained a high-profile assistant in J. Edgar Hoover, who helped direct the anti-Bolshevik campaign. Hoover's relentless pursuit of Rev. Martin Luther King, Jr. linked communist subversion with the Civil Rights movement, implying that the tactics of such crusaders were redolent of deceit, subterfuge, and mendacity. While the witch hunters held the spotlight, the Red Menace loomed frightening indeed to ordinary citizens.

The fear/hatred element of modern existence was eloquently dramatized by the citizens of Oceania in George Orwell's novel *1984*. Written in 1948 in the wake of Hitler's Germany and the rise of a totalitarian Soviet Union, the novel cataloged the manipulation of citizens' emotions by the leaders of that fictitious nation. The object of the people's hatred was O'Brien, whose grim, menacing face was displayed throughout each community, and whose cruelties were reported on regularly produced, state-sponsored television programs. (Television, a relatively new phenomenon to the American people, was skillfully and ominously exploited as an instrument of propaganda in Orwell's text.) Every day, the people of Oceania observed an intense experience called "The Two Minutes Hate," during which enemy leaders, belligerents, and atrocities preoccupied them. Through this interlude, the people exorcised their hostility, aimed as it was, at O'Brien and his bloodthirsty hordes.

This Orwellian hatred of communism and the Soviet Union by many U.S. citizens continued unabated until 1989—the year the Berlin Wall came down. This populist insurrection obliterated Soviet communism in the countries of Eastern Europe and was followed quickly by the downfall of the Soviet Union, leaving its member groups in a state of chaos. The end of the Cold War created a somewhat troublesome byproduct, however: It left millions of U.S. citizens with no Evil Empire to hate.

So the search began for a new group to target. One likely group was the new generation of African Americans—those young, often outspoken black people who while moving up in the professions, the political realm, the corporate ladder, and the world of academe, constantly clamored for more. Another was the increasing numbers of immigrants from non-European origins, who demanded citizenship, status, and a piece of the American dream. Still another was the "liberals," described earlier in this text as those who thought differently from the mainstream. Many of these people were intellectuals who displayed (in the eyes of their detractors) aloofness from and contempt for ordinary people, and who, like Plato's bad poets, had such persuasive powers as to make the worse appear the better cause. There were also the out-of-the-closet gays and lesbians, whose "alternative lifestyles" made them immoral and undesirable to many U.S. citizens. The advent of the AIDS crisis in the 1980s was seen as a sign of judgment from God against homosexuals to many of these haters.

U.S. Teachers—A History of Mistrust

More obliquely, even subconsciously resented—rather than necessarily hated—were the public school teachers who lived and taught in the United States. In 1958, the now-deceased English educator Mary Tingle concluded a study of images of the teacher in 20 works of U.S.

literature from the 19th and 20th centuries. Her research revealed that teachers were viewed as less virile or feminine than other people, more meekly accepting of their modest socioeconomic situation, and less industrious than most. Moreover, the men were often viewed as homosexual and/or suicidal, and the women were resigned to a life of spinsterhood. Most important, in the context of this hypothesis, teachers were not viewed as valued or important members of the community. To some of those who no longer had the communists to vilify, teachers became a subtler target.

To many U.S. citizens, public school teachers were a race apart. They were the classmates who typically got the best grades in school. They stayed out of trouble, were teachers' pets, and went on to college. For the most part, they also sought their own company and eschewed the opportunity to be "one of the boys/girls." When they completed degrees, received certification, and became public school employees, they settled into their communities—often back in their old hometown.

The citizens of those communities, i.e., the taxpayers, were basically in charge now. They elected school board members and, in dwindling numbers, elected a district superintendent. They also had the vote on bond issues, which determined school repair, new curricular and extracurricular offerings, and teacher salaries. By participating in the decision-making actions of their public schools, this latter group had a chance to put these teachers in their place. They voted down bond issues; questioned grading, groupings, and disciplinary policies/decisions ("not my kid!"); opposed collective bargaining and union-style representation for teachers; voiced suspicion of any teacher benefits; and displayed bumper stickers that claimed, "My kid beat up your honor student." It is no wonder that, urged on by the pressure groups that have arisen over the past 20 years, these citizens have raised the question of dirty, controversial, or suggestive teaching materials during that same time frame. To use modern argot, the parents and citizens informed the teachers, "Gotcha!"

The Growth of Modern Censorship Targets

Beyond this often subtle adversarial attitude toward educators, today's U.S. citizens have found a number of more obvious targets of opposition. Many of them have been clustered under the label New Age, which replaced the "secular humanist" label of the 1980s. New Age proponents—with their alleged support of psychedelic scenery; rock, rap, and soul music; contemporary multicultural literature; and unorthodox teaching strategies were repugnant to more conservative, traditional citizens. To older members of the mainstream, they were nothing more than the Beatniks of the 1950s and the Hippies of the 1960s and 1970s, albeit in different clothing and hairstyles. Furthermore, while the earlier "radical" groups concentrated on young adults, the New Agers also influenced elementary school children with their scary stories and their modified transcendental meditation classroom activities.

Briefly, the more recent targets for censorship challenges, which now come from both left- and right-wing sources include the following:

Multicultural additions to literature anthologies, as well as single text adoptions —The significant reduction of Eurocentric texts and authors has taken place nationally but has been particularly evident in areas where large numbers of minority citizens have established residence. In early 1998, considerable publicity was generated by the leadership of the San Francisco public schools, who replaced their traditional high school literature anthologies with texts by and about minorities. Their explanation for this change: 8 of every 11 high school students in the city were non-Caucasian.

School journalism—Since the landmark 1988 U.S. Supreme Court case *Hazelwood School District v. Kuhlmeier* (fully described on p. 146), school principals throughout the United States have been scouring student newspapers with the proverbial fine-tooth comb. They have been concerned with editions that contain op-ed pieces on substance abuse, gangs, inappropriate parental behavior, objectionable school rules, and gay or lesbian affairs, to name a few of the more prominent topics.

The attack on the Humanities in the classroom—With the 1994 Republican takeover of both houses of Congress, some outspoken adversaries of providing funds for both the National Endowment for the Arts (NEA) and the National Endowment for the Humanities (NEH) found themselves in leadership positions. The aggressive behavior of Senator Jesse Helms, House Speaker Newt Gingrich, and others put both those agencies, as well as the Public Broadcasting System, at risk of extinction. Although that has not happened as yet, funding for all three of the bulwarks of public involvement in culture and the arts has been reduced significantly. This has been particularly evident in the drop in support for young artists, sculptors, musicians, and imaginative writers. Using the controversial Robert Mapplethorpe photograph exhibit of 1990 as a cause célèbre, politicians' attacks have been mounted against any artistic expressions that feature nudity, sexual postures, varieties of contemporary music, and certain minority literature endeavors. The capability of the NEH to bring cultural programs to regional nooks and crannies has been lessened. The overtones of racism in such repressive constraints are unmistakable.

Opposition to study of or involvement in gay-lesbian issues—Attuned to demonstrations against Gay-Lesbian Week celebrations at public libraries and the ongoing attack on Disney World's permissive attitude on this topic, many school systems have cringed at the possibility of being taken to task for any consideration of gay/lesbian matters in their classrooms, media centers, or assembly halls. The denunciation of (a) class discussions on homosexual topics, (b) freewriting tasks that "promote" such subjects, or (c) literary texts that raise the issue symbolically has had its effect, particularly on principals who responded by using the *Hazelwood* decision to abolish a range of objectionable materials and activities. Now that principals can decide what is and is not consistent with the educational mission of their schools, their range of toleration has narrowed and gay/lesbian curricular inclusions have been among the first to go.

The Dictionary—For many decades, and most pointedly since the 1961 publication of *Webster's Third New Collegiate Dictionary*, this essential classroom reference tool has been under fire both from the left and the right. During the time of the initial controversy, Webster's chief editor, Philip Gove, offered what was to some a most radical pronouncement: The dictionary was a *describer*, not a *prescriber* of the American English lexicon (1961, i). This statement led to philosophical dialogue that sometimes rose to levels of hysteria. The debate then revolved around the appropriateness of including words that described sexual activities, bodily excretions, and the like. More recently, the range of censorable content has expanded, and other words found in contemporary dictionaries have come under fire. In 1997, African American pressure groups drew national attention by leading the charge against the inclusion of certain derogatory racial terms. Although other racial and ethnic minority groups, as well as some feminists, have joined in this protest, lexicographers, to date, have resisted these demands.

Ongoing opposition to certain test instruments—The past 20 years or so have witnessed a dramatic increase in organized complaints and challenges to various school testing instruments, whether psychological in nature (personal preference inventories) or academic (absence of Latinate grammar element of writing/language achievement tests). Under the cloak of parental concern, challengers have continued to demand that orthodox beliefs and theses dominate the testing landscape.

Standardized test results tied to school and teacher evaluation—The manner in which standardized tests control the curriculum might be called "backdoor censorship." In the late 1990s and early 2000s, a number of state legislatures passed laws that tied the performance of students on standardized tests such as the Iowa Test of Basic Skills to a "grade" for the school and to teacher evaluation. Among these states are Florida, Georgia, Kansas, Virginia, Texas, and Delaware. Often there are standards of learning issued by each state's department of education that tie the curriculum to the material to be tested.

The impact of this practice on school curriculum was brought to a head in Kansas in the spring of 2000, when the State Board of Education voted to remove the teaching of evolution from the state tests. (This case is discussed in more detail in Chapter 6.) In the next election, only candidates who opposed this act (four) were elected to the Board, bringing hope that the old standards will be restored. As one news editor from *The Washington Post* stated, "this creates a real disincentive for local school boards and individual teachers to spend much time on the subject" (Editorial, 1999, p. A14).

In addition to affecting what is taught in the classroom, inclusion or exclusion in state standards influence what school media specialists purchase for their collections. For example, librarians in one school district stated that they did not purchase the picture book about African American astronomer and mathematician Benjamin Bannaker's grandmother, *Molly Bannaky* by Alice McGill, because Bannaker is not in the state standards of learning curriculum guides. Therefore, they concluded, the book would not circulate—a measurement still used in the district where these librarians work.

The practice of setting state content standards that are reflected on state standardized tests, an increasingly common practice, may be a more dangerous form of censorship than the more overt challenges that occur, for a response to direct challenges is easier to formulate than one that requires changes to a standardized test or state curriculum (or requires helping teachers and librarians discover strategies to cope with the issues of time and testing). It is not easy to convince the public that holding teachers accountable for learning through specific content testing is not necessarily good.

The trend toward relying on standardized test scores to prove achievement is perhaps part of the trend to find someone or something to hate or blame that was discussed earlier in this chapter. Local schools, including school boards, administrators, and teachers, are clearly an object of mistrust. If these parties were competent, the reasoning might go, then children would be learning, and the need to dole out punishment for poor performance on standardized tests would not be necessary. As is discussed below, the focus on improving test scores may be a cover for something else that is too complex for state legislators to fix quickly.

Electronic reading programs—The widespread advent of computers brought several electronic reading programs into the classroom during the 1990s. One of the most widely used is published by Advantage Learning Systems and is called the *Accelerated Reader* (http://www.advlearn.com/ar). Books are assigned a reading level, and children select books from their level, take tests on the books, and in turn get various kinds of intangible and tangible rewards. Betty Carter of the Texas Women's University has written a scathing attack on these programs and the damper they have put on reading for pleasure (1996, 2000). The rigid use of these programs results in a kind of censorship in that librarians report not being able to purchase or promote books that are not on the Accelerated Reader-approved list. Teachers likewise look to the list for required reading for students.

Again the issue of control through standards set by an institution or organization external to a school comes into the picture, and the results on achievement of this external standardization of approach or content is mixed. A 5-year longitudinal study was conducted by Cherryville, North Carolina, teacher Janie Peak and Mark Dewalt, an assistant professor (Hart & Dunnevant, in press). This team followed students using the Accelerated Reader from third through eighth grade. These students showed no gain on the California Achievement Test Reading Scores in the beginning, but did improve by the end of 5 years. Other shorter term research studies have not found gains on achievement tests, in student motivation, or in student use of the library media center. The jury is still out on the impact of these reading programs, but from the point of view of this study, they now constitute somewhat of a national parameter on books that students read.

The Complexities of 21st Century Multiculturalism

In the digital world, complexity reigns. Perhaps as David Macaulay, author of the children's picture book *Black and White* (1990), says "It is essential to see, not merely to look" (Macaulay, 1991). In Macaulay's book, nothing is black and white (obvious), but rather many shades of grey (ambiguous). A more in-depth analysis of one of the emerging areas of concern presented earlier serves as an exemplar of the difficulty in determining who is censoring whom about what. The issue of multiculturalism in classroom and library resources presents many layers to contemplate. The term *multicultural* is used here in a broad sense to include all kinds of diversity—racial, gender, sexual orientation, age, ability or disability, or any other feature of a subset of the overall U.S. population that has resulted in its exclusion, stereotyping, or discrimination. As we shall see, the value of multiculturalism in curriculum, texts, and books for children often lies in the eye of the beholder.

Crayon Color Controversy

Something as simple as the crayon, used by children across the United States for many years, serves as an example of the growing demand for sensitivity to differences in the U.S. population. In the spring of 1999, a newspaper brandished the following headline: "Crayola Changes Stripes." The article reported,

> Sometimes a few simple strokes can hint at the sweep of history—strokes of a crayon, say. Only twice in 96 years had Crayola changed a color's name, rechristening "Prussian blue" as "midnight blue" in 1958 because people had lost track of exactly what Prussia was, and changing "flesh" to "peach" in 1962, recognizing that flesh is a many-colored thing. Now it will relabel "Indian red" to wipe out any associations with Native Americans. (Herring, 1999, p. 2)

In July 1999, Indian Red was changed to Chestnut. When Eliza Dresang e-mailed the Crayola company from their Web site (http://www.crayola.com) to seek their version of why they changed the name, she received this answer in an unsigned e-mail: "In response to the feedback of consumers and educators who believed that some children wrongly perceived that this color was intended to represent the skin color of Native Americans" (personal communication, July 1999). If changes in society and societal attitudes can affect crayons, they certainly can affect items of greater magnitude, such as textbooks, trade (library) books, and curriculum. Was the removal of Prussian Blue, Flesh, and Indian Red crayons sensitive, sincere, or politically correct? Was it a change to make up for a past mistake or a response to censorship? We need to look beyond crayons at these issues to understand the complexities of a double-bind form of censorship that grew out of the push to bring more accurate representation of marginalized populations into the classroom and library.

Marginalized Populations: The Road to Inclusion

People of color. One author who included minority characters in her work long before others was Florence C. Means. In *Shuttered Windows*

(1938), she portrayed a 16-year-old African American female who leaves her Midwest home to spend a summer visiting relatives in a small South Carolina community. The indignities suffered by the protagonist, Harriet Freeman, represent one of the earliest racism themes propounded by a young adult author—and perhaps the first teenage African American female main character in the genre. Means followed with books about Japanese Americans forced into relocation camps in World War II, about Navajo teens, and about young Hispanic Americans. Jesse Jackson (1908–1983) also wrote at a time when no other African Americans had novels for young people published by mainstream presses. He intended for his novels—*Call Me Charley* (1940), followed by two sequels—to heighten awareness of the problems facing African Americans. There were other African Americans writing for children, but they were few and far between.

The first major impetus to include marginalized populations in mainstream texts and library books for children came from the realization in the general public that these populations had been excluded. It took the Civil Rights movement of the 1960s for this circumstance to be noticed in a way that would have an impact. Until Nancy Larrick's article "The All-White World of Children's Books" appeared in the *Saturday Review* in 1965, the publishing world had not stopped to take stock of this lack of representation. Larrick found that only four fifths of 1% of the 5,000 children's books published from 1962–1964 included *any* mention of contemporary black people. Three decades later, African American author Toni Morrison documented in *Playing in the Dark: Whiteness and the Literary Imagination* (1992) that for much of literary history, the use of dark people in literature was as a foil for the white people in the story. One book widely read by youth and taught in many schools that was used as an example was Twain's *The Adventures of Huckleberry Finn*, one of the top 10 most challenged books of the 1990s.

In 1982, Rudine Sims Bishop's groundbreaking book *Shadow and Substance: Afro-American Experience in Contemporary Children's Literature* pointed out that as books began to emerge with African American characters, they were written first from a "social consciousness" point of view (the white child's conscience), then as "melting pot" books, and, finally, as offerings conscious of the African American culture. In the mid-1980s, the Cooperative Children's Book Center (CCBC) in Madison, Wisconsin, started to trace the development of multicultural literature, and to record statistics about it as part of their commitment to equity and excellence in literature.

From their annual report initiated in the mid-1980s, *CCBC Choices*, we know that books by authors and illustrators of color still make up an extremely small percentage of the total number of books published annually. For example, in 1999 only 81 of the 4500–5000 new children's books published were created by black artists or illustrators and 26 by Latino authors and illustrators....Even when books with, for example, Latino themes (as opposed to books created by Latinos/Latinas), are included in the statistics, only 64 were published in 1999, with 41 on American Indian themes and topics, and 61 about Asians and Asian Americans. (Horning, Kruse, & Schliesman, 2000, pp. 12–15)

The estimated percentage of books reflecting multicultural themes and peoples of the United States falls considerably below the 28.6% of the population that is projected by the U.S. Census Bureau to be other than white, non-Hispanic at the beginning of the 21st century (http://www.census.gov/population/projections/nation/summary/np-t5-a.txt).

Some hopeful signs are emerging, however. In *Multicultural Literature for Children and Young Adults* (1997), the librarians of the CCBC annotate the best of the multicultural literature that has been written for children (Kruse, Horning, & Schleismann). Barreras, Dressman, and Thompson's *Kaleisdoscope: A Multicultural Booklist for Grades K–8* (1997) also documents outstanding books by and about African American youth. Bibliographies documenting recommended books by and about young Latino/Latina Americans, Native Americans, and Asian Americans are also appearing at the end of the 20th century.

The female sex. The book *And Jill Came Tumbling After: Sexism in American Education* (Stacey, Bereaud, & Daniels, 1974) includes articles on children's books, textbooks, and curriculum. It points to the omission of girl characters—or at best their placement in a secondary, supportive role for the males who are the adventurous protagonists. Teachers and librarians are urged to seek out books with strong female characters and to avoid books that portray girls in traditional or passive roles. Redress sought by those concerned with the role of females has brought relatively swift change, as documented in Kathleen Odean's book *Great Books for Girls: More Than 600 Books to Inspire Today's Girls and Tomorrow's Women* (1997), in which she includes only those books that have female protagonists who "defy stereotypes" (p. 2). (Odean followed this in 1998 with *Great Books for Boys: More Than 600 Books for Boys 2–14.*) In the past decade, more attention has turned to the plight of males in children's books—seen as stereotypic from another point of view.

Physically challenged individuals. Stereotyping and marginalizing "handicapped" characters in children's literature has also been documented. Karen Harris and Barbara Baskin wrote *Notes From a Different Drummer: A Guide to Juvenile Literature Portraying the Handicapped* (1977) and *More Notes From a Different Drummer: A Guide to Juvenile Fiction Portraying the Disabled* (1984); the latter is still in print. The first volume contains a historical overview that demonstrates the same thesis that Toni Morrison offered in her book about African Americans: Handicapped characters historically have been included in literature as mere foils for nonhandicapped characters, or worse, as bumbling idiots (for example, the visually impaired Mr. Magoo). Positive, full-bodied portrayals of physically challenged individuals were almost nonexistent in children's literature until the mid-1970s.

Homosexuals. Gay and lesbian culture was another of the multicultural representations that had not found its way into books for young people until after the social upheavals of the 1960s. Christine Jenkins has written two articles chronicling the history of gay and lesbians in books for youth, the last of which includes an analysis based on a feminist schemata (Jenkins, 1993, 1998).

Jenkins's 1993 study is comprehensive: It lists and annotates every young people's book with gay and lesbian characters and themes published between 1969 and 1992. Her descriptive, statistical analyses include a demographic view of the characters—by gender (males predominate), race (white), and by occupation (the arts appear frequently). Contemporary gay characters are not as likely to meet an unpleasant fate as they were in books published in 1969, but the number of books published annually and the secondary roles of most gay and lesbian characters has not changed a great deal. Only a small handful of books depict gay characters as the protagonist, and very few portray lesbians. Jenkins did find some progress in her 1998 study in the amount of cultural specificity and community that authors have permitted gay and lesbian characters. But her study shows that there are still fewer instances of gay and lesbian characters portrayed in a culturally integrated, distinctive manner than there are of female or African American characters.

From the late 1960s until the late 1980s, the Council on Interracial Books for Children (CIBC) published essays that pointed out the omissions and stereotypic inclusions of these various marginalized groups. New books were reviewed from this socially conscious point of view. Classroom curriculum was also scrutinized and lesson plans that promoted inclusion were spelled out. In 1980, the CIBC published

Guidelines for Selecting Bias-Free Textbooks and Storybooks that included a checklist for evaluating children's books; in 1981, the CIBC published *Unlearning Asian Stereotypes*. The CIBC also sponsored an award from 1967 to 1979 for the best new author of color each year. The winners of these awards read like a Who's Who of children's literature: Walter Dean Myers (two of whose recent books are discussed extensively in Chapter 6) got his start in this contest, as did Sharon Bell Mathis, Mildred D. Taylor, Virginia Driving Hawk Sneve, and Minfong Ho. An artist's showcase in each issue brought to the attention of art directors in publishing houses such subsequent luminaries as Donald Crews, Pat Cummings, and Leo and Dianne Dillon. Many found the consciousness-raising of the CIBC envigorating; others found it dampening and likened it to censorship. The battle had begun.

While few would argue that marginalized populations are represented in as complete and multifaceted a manner as the mainstream population, their entry into literature for children and young adults—however small the number—has stirred sometimes bitter and angry controversy and has raised questions that were not posed in the past. Does excluding books with stereotypic portrayals of a member of a marginalized group amount to censorship? How accurate do fiction books have to be when portraying these characters? Who determines accuracy? Who is qualified to write about these characters? Here the fine line between censorship and selection becomes even more faint—and the battles drawn around it even more bitter.

Rocks in the Road to Inclusion

The social context in which the march to inclusion of marginalized groups has occurred has always had a large influence on children's books. The same battles that have taken place in the larger society and in adult literature have been reflected, and have intensified, in literature for children and young adults. In a way it is healthy that books for children and young adults are no longer held to a different standard than adult literature or ignored in the turmoil of the times. But it makes the road to inclusion difficult—and brings perplexity and complexity to critics, publishers, authors, and parents.

Initially the censorship battles focused on one or two well-known literary pieces—Helen Bannerman's *Little Black Sambo* for children and Mark Twain's *The Adventures of Huckleberry Finn* for young adults. *Little Black Sambo* became a cause celebre for those who were angry about the stereotypical representation of African Americans in children's books. Originally published in 1899, *Little Black Sambo* was written for Bannerman's children. The book was set in India, where this

British family lived at the time, but the name "Sambo" already had a derogatory ring in the United States—it was a demeaning term applied by white slave owners to their slaves in the southern United States. Moreover, if the illustrations were meant to show Indians, the physical features looked suspiciously close to those of Africans. The book sold in the United States without controversy for many years, and it was read and loved by both whites and blacks. But in the raised consciousness of the 1960s, *Little Black Sambo* became a symbol of all that frustrated marginalized ethnic groups and their mainstream supporters about the failing of children's literature to represent positively all components of the population.

In 1976 Phyllis Yuill wrote an analysis of the phenomenon titled *Little Black Sambo: A Closer Look—A History of Helen Bannerman's* The Story of Little Black Sambo *and Its Popularity/Controversy in the United States.* Initially those who rushed to remove this book from the library shelf and classroom desk did not see the underlying issues of censorship that surrounded their actions. In 1998, distinguished African American author Julius Lester and illustrator Jerry Pinkney "recaptured" the story of Little Black Sambo and retold it in *Sam and the Tigers.* That same year, Fred Marcellino reillustrated Bannerman's *Little Black Sambo*, leaving the text intact but changing the characters' names to their Indian equivalents—Little Black Sambo became Little Babaji. These publications brought the Bannerman book back to the forefront. *Little Black Sambo* signaled the start of the complexities that began to arise in late 20th century censorship—but the story had only just begun.

The Adventures of Huckleberry Finn, one of the most frequently challenged books of the past century, was initially considered unsuitable for youth because of its rough language. It was banned in Concord, Massachusetts, in 1885, because "officials at the Concord Public Library thought it was 'rough, coarse and inelegant...the whole book being more suited to the slums than to intelligent, respectable people'" (Zwick, 1997). Twenty years later, when Tom Sawyer and Huckleberry Finn were removed, it was because the boys' actions raised ire. Library officials explained that they provided bad examples to the youth of the day (Zwick, 1997). But starting in the 1950s, as awareness of racism in U.S. society entered the collective conscience of Americans with the advent of the Civil Rights era, *Huckleberry Finn* was criticized for Twain's portrayal of "Nigger Jim"—in the 1990s, the Pennsylvania chapter of the NAACP characterized the mandated teaching of the book as a hate crime (Zwick, 1998a). In 1994, Kathy Monteiro, a high school teacher in Tempe, Arizona, started a campaign to have *Huckleberry Finn* removed from her school's required reading list on the basis that it, in the words of her lawyer, "created, exacerbated and contributed to a hostile work environment" at the school (Zwick, 1998b). Although the court ruled against banning the book based on its content, the court's opinion in the case is viewed by Monteiro and her lawyer as a victory because it also ruled that schools can be held liable if they do not address complaints of a racially hostile environment. This is the first time that a federal appeals court has ruled that schools can be held financially liable for a racially hostile environment in the same way employers are held liable for allowing a sexually hostile environment to persist in the workplace.

The point of view that *Huckleberry Finn* is directly or indirectly harmful to minors so infuriated intellectual freedom advocate Nat Hentoff that he wrote a book for young adults on the subject: *The Day They Came to Arrest the Book: A Novel* (1982). Hentoff followed this with a work that explicates the complexity of the matter titled *Free Speech for Me—But Not for Thee: How the American Left and Right Relentlessly Censor Each Other* (1992). One reviewer commented on this book by stating that

> [Hentoff] especially criticizes "civil libertarians" who use the First Amendment as protection of things they like and then ignore it when trying to ban what they hate (racist writing, sexual harassment, etc.). Rather than set up left-wing straw men to knock down, Hentoff details stories of how the left censors, while acknowledging that the right censors as well. But since conservatives admit their intentions they are not as dangerous as the duplicitous people on the Left. Hentoff seeks truth in everything, and this book is his finest. ("Hentoff seeks the truth," 1999)

Ralph Wiley, a prominent African American critic of race relations, has written a movie script for *Huckleberry Finn* that he hopes will be produced by filmmaker Spike Lee, with whom he has coauthored two books. According to Zwick, "Wiley's script sticks close to Twain's text but the stage directions provide new insights by telling us what the characters are thinking and feeling. Instead of relying on Huck's interpretation as narrator of the novel, Wiley gives us his interpretation of what Twain meant in each scene" (Zwick, 2000). Portions of Wiley's script are posted on the Internet with permission for classroom production (Wiley, 1997).

In January 2000 the PBS series *Culture Shock* aired a segment about Huckleberry Finn titled *Born to Trouble: The Adventures of Huckleberry Finn* (Janows & Lee, 2000). The accompanying teacher's guide, *Huck Finn in Context* (Carr & Forchion, 1999), is useful for exploring the various issues with or without the film (see recommended Web resources). More than a century after its publication, this book—considered a masterpiece by many and a travesty by others—remains an object of controversy and incites regular instances of attempted removal.

Political Correctness: Another Rock in the Road

The issue of what has become known as "political correctness" soon cast its long shadow into the world of children's books. It reached fever pitch by the early to mid-1990s—and since has receded somewhat in favor of even more complex controversy in the multicultural arena. In 1994, Eliza Dresang asked undergraduate and graduate students in her Multicultural Literature for Youth class at the University of Wisconsin to collect at least 20 newspaper (articles and political cartoons), radio, and television media examples of the use of the term "politically correct." At the end of the semester, the students had to write an essay giving their definition of political correctness drawn from the various media pieces they had collected. They then had to analyze whether this was a term used by the political left, the political right, or an unknown. The students were amazed at the many different ways in which the term was applied, and how it was used by both sides of the political spectrum.

Sometimes the term was used by, or applied in a complimentary manner to, those who were sincerely interested in the inclusion of marginalized groups, and not just children's books. However, more often it was used as a term of humor or ridicule to put down those who would bring the marginalized into the mainstream. Dresang's students observed how complex the situation was, because some of those on the political right were using the term to censor those who advocated inclusion. By making political correctness seem like something excessive, bizarre, or laughable—including women in leadership positions, or minorities in adequate numbers, or persons with disabilities as main characters in literature—a sort of censorship of this redressing of past ills set in. It became clear how complex the situation was when some book reviewers or critics went overboard in their criticism of books that included marginalized groups in stories that, while not racially derogatory, did not always show them in the most flattering light. Virginia Hamilton's Newbery Honor book *Sweet Whispers, Brother Rush* (1982), for example, drew disapproval from some critics because the African American mother left her teenage children attended only by a housekeeper while she went away for days at a time to earn money to sustain them. On the other hand, the ridiculing of any attempts to bring accurate inclusion and more multicultural numbers into the "all-white world of children's books" was unfair and had an obvious political agenda. Dresang's students were amazed at the depth of the analysis they had to do to try to understand political correctness and its relationship to very different perspectives on the censorship of multicultural literature for children and young adults.

Mean and hurtful rocks were hurled from both sides of the road. For example, in a 1991 article titled "The Tragedy of Multiculturalism," Irving Kristol wrote, "Though the educational establishment would rather die than admit it, multiculturalism is a desperate—and self-defeating—strategy for coping with the educational deficiencies and associated social pathologies of young blacks" (http://www.aidsinfobbs. org/articles/wallstj/91/201). Those, for many, are fighting words at best, and an attempt at censorship at the worst. Also in 1991, John Leo criticized New York State's "new and improved report on multicultural social-science education," in an article titled "Multicultural Follies," which subsequently forced the New York Public Schools into a situation of withdrawing a textbook series chosen for inclusion of marginalized groups. Leo claimed that, "Despite all the racism, most surveys I have seen seem to show high levels of patriotism among black Americans" (Leo, p. 12). This is an example of the chilling effect the critics of inclusion had. Joel Taxel responded with a 1994 article in *The New Advocate* titled "Political Correctness, Cultural Politics, and Writing for Young People," in which he pointed to the censorship that had occurred with the widespread attempts to include previously marginalized groups.

Emerging Concerns About Multiculturalism in the Classroom

As the 21st century dawned, the debate had moved beyond the "politically correct" versus "politically incorrect" discussion to focus on very real concerns in the world of literature for children and young adults—issues that continue to raise the question of what is critical analysis and what is censorship. This continuous debate is one to which 21st century teachers and librarians must attend. It incorporates some aspects of the politically correct point of view but does so from a more informed, analytical, and less politically motivated stance. The voices in this debate, as it pertains to books for young people, are all deeply socially conscious. Neither side intends to censor, but the danger still lurks and the issues are not easy to reconcile or resolve. A subset of this debate might be labeled the "art" versus "authenticity" point of view.

Among the more sophisticated spokespersons on the deeper issues of multiculturalism, each with his or her own point of view, are

Hazel Rochman, Marc Aronson, Mingshui Cai, and Violet Harris. In her book *Against Borders: Promoting Books for a Multicultural World* (1993), and in a 1995 article based on this book, Hazel Rochman takes the stance that it would be insulting to say that a book is good just because it is multicultural. Rochman states, "Underlying much of the debate [about multicultural inclusion] is the demand that each book must do it all.... We start to recommend books because they give us the 'right' role models, depending on what's considered 'right' in the current political climate" (1995, p. 148). In her article on multiculturalism, Rochman quotes author Walter Dean Myers, who was once criticized for having so many African Americans playing basketball in his books for youth (a stereotype say these critics). According to Rochman, Myers replies, "Every book I write can't take on the whole African American experience. He likes basketball, lots of African American kids like basketball, and this one book is about that world" (Rochman, p. 148). Rochman's point is for inclusiveness across the body of literature for youth—but tolerance for individual portrayals, recognizing they must be offset by other points of view.

Marc Aronson, in "A Mess of Stories" (1995) and "No Rennaissance Without Openness: A Philosophy of American Multiculturalism" (1996), describes 21st century U.S. society with depth and accuracy. Aronson points out that each "pure" cultural event is, in fact, composed of a "mess of stories": "I am calling," he says, "for the intellectual honesty that recognizes the complexity of culture" (1995, p. 164). To demonstrate what he means about a cultural "mess of stories," Aronson traces the history of the song "Children, Go Where I Send Thee," based on the assumption that this song is a part of African American culture. He follows the song's evolution through Ozark versions; a 1625 interpretation in the British Museum; and Latin, German, French, Provençal, and Spanish versions, until he discovers that its most likely ancestor is a song sung during the Jewish Passover, "Had Gadya." One song incorporates many perspectives and many voices (Aronson, 1995). Aronson passionately supports inclusiveness, but like Rochman, does not see that as the job of any individual work of children's literature, which must be judged on its literary merit, not its matching of social ideals.

Others may agree, but may not think that the marginalized peoples in our societies have established their own authentic base firmly enough to gain the respect of the mainstream population. Part of the debate has focused on "what is authentic?" and "who can write about whom?" Dresang tackled this topic in a short piece titled "What Is Authenticity?" which suggests that there are three ways to determine authenticity: extensive experience of the culture, in-depth studying of the culture, and being of the culture (http://www.scils.rutgers.edu/special/kay/authentic.html). The first two factors are essential; the third is usually desirable and adds insurance to the first two, but is not absolutely necessary. Violet Harris, editor of *The New Advocate*, and researcher Mingshui Cai both offer some of the reasons that cultural authenticity must be a concern in the world of children's literature.

Harris addresses the topic of authenticity from a variety of perspectives. She admonishes that one has to realize that "for hundreds of years, European Americans have written about African Americans; with few exceptions, the works were one-note variations of the same refrain. Notably, the authors produced Sambo...contented slaves such as Amos Fortune, unnamed sharecroppers as in *Sounder* (1969) (Harris, 1996, p. 109). The question is not so much, Harris says, the authority of one race to write about another. "Rather the authorial arrogance of some European American authors who demand the freedom to write about whatever they wish without subjecting their work to critical scrutiny" (p. 113). She muses, "how many authors are likely to have an understanding of the 'Other' that does not stem from media stereotypes, pseudo-science, or well-intentioned, paternalistic writers?" (p. 116). Harris notes the hesistancy of publishers to allow authors of color, even those of the stature of Virginia Hamilton, to write outside their own experience. She concludes that questions about authenticity, insider/outsider views, and authorial freedom remain unsolved. Harris reveals in her writing an honesty, openness, and willingness to change her opinion as she learns more, which is rare among many of those who address this sensitive topic.

Mingshui Cai notes that children often know about people of other cultures from picture books before actually encountering those cultures in life, and that initial impressions often last. In a study of 73 picture books Cai found in a small Midwest community library, he concluded that

> while biased stereotypical portraits have not been eliminated, cultural inauthenticity is the main flaw many books exhibited in both the content of the texts and the details of the illustrations. To transmit accurate information and to maintain the integrity of the culture, authors and illustrators are obligated to undertake earnest research in that culture. Imagination alone cannot help them to cross the cultural gaps. (Cai, 1994, p. 188)

A virtue of Cai's writing is that he gives in-depth examples of what is and is not authentic about the portrayal of Chinese culture, giving the reader a better grasp of the difference that authenticity can make.

Native American author and storyteller Joseph Bruchac raises the question of language in children's books. He says that "respect for and understanding of other cultures also means respecting and understanding other languages, for language carries much, if not most, of the richness of any culture" (Bruchac, 1995, p. 161). This is another major issue of authenticity, and more bilingual texts for children appear each year.

These emerging concerns have focused on ethnicity, but the same kinds of commentary exist (with perhaps less visibility in the world of children's books) about gender, issues of sexual orientation, and representation of disability. This discussion has hardly scratched the surface of the multicultural debate that swirls in our 21st century society; a debate that extends beyond books for children and young adults to other media, and to the society at large. Until society resolves its problems, literature will not either.

In her book *Radical Change: Books for Youth in a Digital Age* (1999) Dresang talks about multiculturalism in the 21st century and how an important factor is not only to look for inclusion, but for diversity within the diversity. When a marginalized group first enters the literature, often a "positive portrayal" rather than a human portrayal of the group is considered necessary. Although this is understandable as a form of redress against the stereotypes of the past, it is no longer the best way to look at inclusion. Each group needs to have its unique voice represented in literature—but that unique voice needs to reflect all the complexities of the human condition.

Guidelines for Teachers and Librarians

- Engage children in discussion of the three different versions of *Little Black Sambo* mentioned in this chapter. Introduce the concept of stereotypes. Ask them to give examples. Is eliminating stereotypes a form of censorship? When is it? When is it not? Would responding to a parent complaint about a stereotype be censorship?

- Introduce high school students to the complexities of political correctness. Ask them to find references to the term in the popular media. See if there is any relationship to censorship.

- Discuss Hermione, the principal female character in J.K. Rowling's Harry Potter books. Is she a good or bad role model? How does she compare to Harry? To girls in real life? To girls in other novels? Is this kind of discussion a form of censorship? Why or why not?

- Find all the books in the media center that portray youth with disabilities. How many are there? Read them and discuss them with your class. Compare these books to Mr. Magoo and Captain Hook stereotypes.

- Discuss the issue of standardized testing and electronic reading programs with students. Are they a form of censorship?

RECOMMENDED WEB SITES

The Américas Award
Source for outstanding books reflecting Hispanic culture and selected for potential for classroom use. Given every year since 1993 by The Consortium of Latin American Studies Programs (CLASP) at the University of Wisconsin-Milwaukee.
http://www.uwm.edu/Dept/CLACS/outreach_americas.html

American Legion
http://www.legion-aux.org

Cooperative Children's Book Center, School of Education, University of Wisconsin–Madison
The Web site of a noncirculating reference examination, study, and research library for adults with an interest in children's and young adult literature whose staff has been involved in the examination and documentation of multicultural literature for many years. Included on the Web site are "Thirty multicultural books that every child should know," "Recommended picture books featuring interracial families," and a review of a new Book of the Week throughout the year.
http://www.soemadison.wisc.edu/ccbc

The Coretta Scott King Award
Source for outstanding books by African American authors and illustrators. Given every year since 1970 (author) and 1974 (illustrator) by the Social Responsibilities Round Table of the American Library Association.
http://www.ala.org/srrt/csking/cskawin.html

The Eagle Forum
http://www.eagleforum.org

Huck Finn in Context: A Teaching Guide
A detailed teaching guide with essays and many links to Web resources.
http://www.pbs.org/wgbh/cultureshock/teachers/huck/index.html

Mark Twain with Jim Zwick
Links to more than 700 sites about Mark Twain and his works. Zwick has written a number of well-done interpretive articles. Opinions on as many facets of the controversy as Zwick can find online are included.
http://marktwain.about.com/arts/marktwain/mbody.htm

The Pura Belpré Award
Source for outstanding books by Latino/Latina authors and illustrators. Given every other year since 1996 by the Association for Library Service to Children of the American Library Association and REFORMA, National Association to Promote Library and Information Services to the Spanish Speaking.
http://www.ala.org/alsc/belpre.html

CHAPTER 6

No Longer Safe—Children's and Young Adult Literature

I believe in any person's right to read whatever she or he chooses. It astonishes me that there are people who believe that by simply avoiding a discussion of sex, for instance, or cruelty, that they can protect the children in their community from any experience of these things. (Rachel Vail, 1999, p. 60)

I know when a book is challenged, I will not be the one who suffers. It will be the teacher or librarian who is called upon to defend what I have written who must stand in the line of fire. They are true heroes to me—the guardians of the constitutional freedoms which make this country great. I admire them more than I can say. If we lose their witness, we will have lost democracy itself. (Katherine Paterson, 1999, p. 70)

It's easy enough to censor an article, a newspaper, even an idea. But no matter how hard you try, you cannot censor a mind or an imagination. You can never censor the future. (Susan Beth Pfeffer, 1999, p. 126)

Literature for the 21st Century Young Adult

"The best time to cry is at night, when the lights are out and someone is being beaten up and screaming for help." This is the opening sentence of the young adult novel *Monster* (1999), the story of 16-year-old Steve Harmon, who is on trial for his alleged involvement in a robbery/murder. The author is Walter Dean Myers, honored for his work with the 2000 Printz award, which is given to the best book for young adults published in the preceding year. *Monster* was also a finalist for the National Book Award for Youth. Young adult literature expert Patty Campbell says the following about *Monster*:

Every decade or so a book comes along that epitomizes what has gone before and points the way to what is to come. In young adult literature *Catcher in the Rye* was such a milestone book, and *The Outsiders*, and *The Chocolate War*. And now Walter Dean Myers' stunning new novel, *Monster*, deserves landmark status on both these counts. (1999, p. 769)

What does *Monster* contribute to young adult literature that points the way to come? Campbell continues,

> Looking backward, it is the peak achievement of a brilliant career that has paralleled the development of the genre in its own growth, and, looking forward, it is a perfect example of the revolutionary new literary direction Eliza Dresang has described in her ground-breaking critical study, *Radical Change: Books for Youth in a Digital Age....* Dresang bases her theories on the idea that in our digital age widespread exposure to electronic media...has changed the way we gather and process information, the patterns of our thinking.... Literature, and especially literature written for young people, is beginning to reflect this metamorphosis in ways Dresang terms "Radical Change." (1999, p. 769)

Just as children and their learning and living environments have been changing, so have their resources—books as well as digital resources. The interactivity, connectivity, and access of the digital world is reflected in books by what might be called "handheld hypertext" and "digital design." *Monster* reflects these changes in its nonlinear, Digital-Age form and format. The story is told with many quick cuts back and forth in time and place, rather than in a linear strand that moves in a classic plot pattern. The words become pictures that convey visual as well as verbal meaning. How does this work? Myers uses two types of interspersed narrative—and each type has its own typeface and its own color of paper.

The thoughts inside Steve's head as he stands trial appear in his own handwriting—a kind of journal originating in his mind, recording, thinking, and pondering about what he sees going on around him. But although the reader is privy to Steve Harmon's innermost thoughts, Harmon never reveals the whole story—he never tells all he knows. Before the incident, Steve was involved in a filmmaking project at his high school. Remembering this, he starts a movie script in his head—visually separated from the journal because it appears in typeface, rather than handwriting, and on white, rather than gray, paper. The typeface does not stay stable in size, however. The word MONSTER appears in large letters from time to time, but it is slashed out. Photographs, unusual in a young adult novel, add to the graphic nature of the text.

The nonlinearity is not limited to these two narratives, and the story unfolds in what Dresang (1999) refers to as "multilayered text." Within the film script there are flashbacks to Steve's life before the crime—with bits and pieces of conversations and small episodes from the past arranged in a nonsequential fashion. It is left to readers to fit all these pieces into a more holistic picture—just as those same readers have to do with all the everyday information in their own lives.

But that is not the end of reader involvement. Not only do readers have the opportunity to participate in arranging the story (as in hypertextual reading), but throughout the story tension builds as readers become jurors and take on the task of declaring innocence or guilt. Is Steve Harmon a monster or is he not?

Another characteristic of Digital Age literature for youth rests in the ability of the young protagonist to speak for himself—or at least appear to speak for himself—rather than through an adult narrator. Dresang (1999) identifies numerous types of voices in literature for youth that were absent or uncommon in the past. Steve's voice as an African American teenager accused of murder, telling his story through journal and film, stands out as unique even in the tradition of realistic novels for young adults. Just as youth have gained their voices on the Internet, Steve develops his own voice in this book.

We have examined two types of radical change apparent in *Monster*—changing forms and formats and changing perspectives. A third type of change appears in the book as well: Previously established boundaries are broken down. Characters, settings, and subjects have a sharp edge that challenges assumptions about young adult literature. Maia Mertz and David England (1983) identified common features of young adult novels, which include

- characters who reap the consequences of their actions,
- characters who resolve their problems in a satisfactory way, and
- characters who are highly independent.

Monster negates all three of these characteristics as well as other common expectations of books for youth, as follows:

- At the end of the book, the jury acquits Steve, but his lawyer turns away from him, and Steve wonders if he is, indeed, a "monster." So we do not know if Steve is reaping the consequences of his actions (in the punitive sense). Because Steve never tells us in his journal or his film script whether he is guilty or not (or if he does, one has to extrapolate from very subtle hints), we are left wondering whether the jury has done justice. In fact, a reader may be glad that Steve does not reap the consequences of his actions (if he was indeed guilty). Although the ending is not definitive, readers may find it satisfactory because Steve has a chance to try again. Campbell characterizes it, despite its topic, as "a work of great freshness and emotional and moral power" (1999, p. 769). Maybe there are consequences, but they are not the straightforward ones we might look for.

- Many would say, despite his deep thinking, that Steve does not resolve the problem for himself nor does Myers resolve it in a definitive manner for readers.

- Certainly Steve is not highly independent—he is at the mercy of the jury, his lawyer, his peers, and society.

"Tales of Raw Misery for Ages 12 and Up" is how a *New York Times* reporter, Tamar Lewin (2000), described *Monster* as well as *Speak* (Anderson, 1999), an Honor book for the 2000 Printz award that depicts a teenager who has been raped and the internal terror and outward rejection that renders her, for most of the novel, unable to speak about what has happened to her. Other journalists have written extensively about the grim novels on the current YA landscape. There is no question that many contemporary novels for young adults push boundaries far beyond where they previously existed in regard to topic, character, and setting.

With the publication of books such as *Monster* and *Speak*, YA literature is no longer "safe"—if, in fact, it ever was. With changing formats, perspectives, and boundaries that permit a more sophisticated, challenging body of literature, it is not surprising that some of these books become the "prime targets" mentioned in Chapter 4. Before thoroughly examining how this literature for young adults evolved from "safe" to "unsafe," just how unsafe it really is, and what this might mean for censorship in the 21st century, we will look at what is happening in literature for younger children—and how it, too, has changed.

Literature for the 21st Century Child

A glance at literature for pre-adolescent children reveals the same changes that have appeared in young adult literature—in the realm of a much wider expanse of formats, voices, and topics that may also be considered "unsafe." "Shocking subjects" include those subjects that are offensive to adults who view young children as innocent. The typical book for preteen children has in the past consisted of a simple plot (usually a mild adventure that involves some risk for the protagonist), a straightforward telling, and a happy ending with an embedded lesson. *The Little Engine That Could* by Watty Piper (1978) is a good example of this genre.

Departing radically from this tradition, Walter Dean Myers, author of *Monster*, also authored a nonlinear, multiple-perspective picture book biography on a once highly controversial figure. *Malcolm X: A Fire Burning Brightly* (2000) is labeled as reading level ages 4–8 by the publisher, HarperCollins. A reviewer for *The Horn Book Magazine* was quoted as commenting, "Not many writers could successfully pull off a picture-book biography of Malcolm X, but Walter Dean Myers does so with style and grace" (http://www.amazon.com/exec/obidos/ASIN/0060277076/qid=971969763/sr=1-24/002-9509043-7655245).

Looking at this book through the "radical change" lens, we see signs of the Digital Age appearing in its format. The first words (and others interspersed throughout) are direct quotes from Malcolm X. They appear in bold type, all caps, as follows:

WHOEVER HEARD OF A REVOLUTION WHERE THEY LOCK

ARMS AND SING "WE SHALL OVERCOME"? YOU DON'T DO

THAT IN A REVOLUTION. YOU DON'T DO ANY SINGING

BECAUSE YOU'RE TOO BUSY SWINGING!

YOU DON'T HAVE A PEACEFUL REVOLUTION. YOU DON'T

HAVE A TURN THE CHEEK REVOLUTION. THERE'S NO SUCH

THING AS A NONVIOLENT REVOLUTION! (Myers, 2000, p. 1)

In ordinary type, the text goes on: "The man talking was Malcolm X. The audience responded with applause and nervous laughter" (p. 1). Throughout the book other provocative quotes are presented in bold capital letters. Not all of them are as controversial as these first words appear, but they all provide a young reader with food for thought:

ANYONE WHO HAS READ A GREAT DEAL CAN IMAGINE

THE NEW WORLD THAT [READING] OPENED. (p. 12)

As in the digital world, words become pictures—with their bold, large type, these words call out "read me." A young reader could hardly miss them.

Both the pictures and the words in this book provide examples of changing perspectives. Malcolm X speaks for himself throughout, and the chronology at the end contains 24 direct quotes from *The Autobiography of Malcolm X* (X & Haley, 1965/1992). It is hardly typical to have this amount of primary material in a book for young readers. The sophisticated pictures by artist Leonard Jenkins bring multilayered art and multiple perspectives to the young reader, resulting in a feast for the eye and contemplation for the mind. For example, Malcolm X is pictured reading a book from a perspective that clearly shows that he is in jail (p. 15). The accompanying text demonstrates that he is where he is through his own actions. But on the next pages (pp. 20–21), though Malcolm X is still in jail, the bars are gone and the text helps the reader turn toward the future and the time when he will be free.

It is in the third area of radical change—that of changing boundaries—that this book breaks down the most barriers. Malcolm X represents a violent challenger to the nonviolent philosophy of Martin Luther King, Jr., about whom dozens of books for young children have been written, and the two men and their ideas are juxtaposed visually and verbally in Myers's book (pp. 20–21). Not only is this the story of a highly controversial, violent figure, but the book ends with his assassination—not exactly a fairy tale ending.

How different this biography is from the traditional biographies for children that focused only on acceptable heroes and positive behavior. *Malcolm X: A Fire Burning Brightly* respects the Digital-Age child's ability to confront more than one perspective on a topic, and because it is presented in an accessible format, the book gives a child the opportunity to ponder and compare. This is a lot to pack into 32 pages, but Myers knows how to address a young audience. He does not make Malcolm X into a George Washington—he invents no stories comparable to that of the cherry tree. But some adults may find this venture into the nursery with thought-provoking ideas far too unsafe for their children. Fortunately, many other adults will gladly accept the challenge to help young people think creatively and learn to deal with ambiguity and complexity. This book has not yet had time to win awards, but it has appeared on predecision discussion lists for the ALA Notable Books for Children honor.

Books on topics such as death, divorce, suicide, urban riots, and other subjects that were once deemed uninteresting or unintelligible to very young children now appear in print. Works that include wide-ranging perspectives and wildly innovative formats have been published in the past few years. Teachers and librarians, then, have a rich array of new formats, topics, characters, and settings to bring to their classrooms and libraries in the domain of literature for both younger and older children. But with these radical changes comes greater risk— risk of displeasing someone and facing a challenge. Plain old print text is not necessarily a "safer" format than digital type in the 21st century. In order to provide you, the "true heroes" named by Katherine

Paterson at the beginning of this chapter, with guidelines to face these challenges, it is important to understand more of the history of literature for young adults and children—to know that today's challenges and seemingly "unsafe" literature are not so different in the eyes of contemporary society than the books for youth that were challenged in the past.

What is it, aside from the prime targets, that brings out the censorious soul? The most frequently challenged books appear on lists of banned books again and again. New works are added as they are published and become targets, but the Digital Age censors are not so different from those who came before—and the literature to which they object contains elements that have always been considered radical. A historical context gives courage to contemporary teachers and librarians who believe that children have a right to read and that one can never really censor an idea, only an object. Knowing that both fear and courage have been necessary in the past—and that challenges have been successfully overcome—provides lessons that are perhaps the most useful guides for the present and future. After looking to the past, we will turn to the future and what we believe lies ahead in the arena of censorship of controversial books for youth.

Predecessors of Digital Age Change and Digital Age Censorship

Around the time of World War II, several U.S. authors broke barriers that had been placed around literature for youth and managed to publish a number of books that were predecessors to the vast number of radical, provocative books for youth today.

Radical Topics Shake Up the Status Quo

The early authors who courageously included revolutionary new topics in literature could not have realized the results of their efforts would lead to the great "political correctness" debates and to a new form of censorship with enormous complexities. Some young adult novels required serious reflection on children's or adolescents' personal, social, and cultural milieus in a time when concerns in these areas were not openly discussed. John Tunis's *All-American* (1939) explored racial, ethnic, and religious issues in a story about the career of a star high school athlete. In later novels, Tunis also examined anti-black and anti-Semitic feelings, and in one novel featured the deteriorating marriage of a high school athlete's parents—at that time still a taboo for literary exploration.

Poverty and rural culture were other topics present in society, but not in literature for young people. Then, in 1938, Marjorie Kinman Rawlings wrote *The Yearling*. The harshness of life endured by poor, rural, uneducated North Florida families was shown uncompromisingly in Rawlings's treatment of that remote area of the Depression-era Deep South. *Blue Willow* (1940) by Doris Gates was another of the first juvenile books to break the socioeconomic barrier, portraying a migrant child who longs for a permanent home—a place to house her "blue willow" plate.

These daring books were not so much the targets of active censorship as they were ignored—for they did not contain issues of importance to most U.S. citizens. After World War II, a period of stagnation set in and 1950s U.S. society was reflected in the lack of innovation in literature for children and adolescents. There were a few notable exceptions: One of these was E.B. White's *Charlotte's Web* (1952), which brought a level of sophistication to children's literature that most of its successors have found difficult to attain. Another in the young adult genre was J.D. Salinger's *Catcher in the Rye* (1951)—with its inner-city scenes, tough language, and memorable main character (Holden Caulfield), it is still considered a YA classic.

The next notable novel to bring the subversive into the mainstream is considered a watershed for YA literature. It is *The Outsiders* (1967) by S.E. Hinton, who was a 17-year-old high school student when she wrote the book. The novel includes treatment of alcohol consumption, brutality, hatred, despair, and contempt for the authority of various adults, as well as violent death. It is told from the point of view of Ponyboy, a 14-year-old lower-class member of a gang called "the Greasers." This gang is in constant struggle with a gang of upper-middle class boys called "the Socs," which is no less violent or cruel because of the members' relatively comfortable economic means. For over 30 years, Hinton's novel has ranked near the top of all reading interest inventories among young readers. It has been identified as one of the top three most important adolescent novels that all English teachers need to know; the others include *The Pigman* by Paul Zindel (1968) and *The Chocolate War* by Robert Cormier (1974), the latter a brilliant, symbolic exploration of alienation that is among the most taught—and most-censored—YA novels (Simmons & Deluzain, 1992, p. 112). The period of safe literature for children and adolescents had come to an end, and a new era was about to emerge full force with a dramatic toppling of taboos in literature for youth.

The Toppling of Taboos

In 1967, a syndicated New York sports columnist named Robert Lipsyte published his first attempt at fiction writing—a YA text titled *The Contender*. In it, Lipsyte created Alfred Brooks, one of the first teenage African American protagonists in the YA genre. Lipsyte violated a number of taboos observed by earlier YA novelists. The story was set in the poor urban area of Harlem, New York. Throughout the text, readers find instances of racial hatred, distrust for policy and other white authority figures, violence, cruelty, contempt for adults, both flaunting and breaking of the law, anti-Semitism, teenage sexual encounters, and drug and alcohol abuse. Yet Lipsyte handled these elements with such considerable restraint that, to this date, *The Contender* has not been named in any reports of censorship attempts. Although the novel has not remained as popular as *The Outsiders*, it has stayed among the top 15 books taught in English classrooms, according to a survey conducted by Theodore Hipple, an English educator at the University of Tennessee (1999).

Early in 1968, the popular YA novelist Paul Zindel published *The Pigman*, a book that gained the instant enthusiastic attention of the teenage reading audience. The probable reason for its great popularity lay in its ignoring of several taboos. The narration was presented in epistolary form, an early example of a format in which the young protagonists "speak for themselves." Flashbacks were employed as a stylistic feature in its chronology, an early example of nonlinear storytelling. The protagonists were involved in a teenage romance in which sexual involvement was evident, and which included unwanted pregnancy. Alcohol abuse was a popular teenage group activity and another prominent element of the plot. Probably the most flagrant violation of taboos, however, lay in the attitudes of the teenage coprotagonists, who both harbored contempt and profound dislike for their parents. When a lonely old man whom they befriend is murdered, they attempt first to repress their sense of responsibility for the act and then to rationalize it. Zindel's novel departs from the "good kid underneath" thesis of many YA texts of earlier times. There are no winners in *The Pigman*.

A great deal of these toppled taboos can be traced back to the multicultural movement that began in the 1960s. As pointed out in Chapter 5, Nancy Larrick's 1965 "All-White World of Children's Books" article caused publishers of books and curricular materials for youth to start thinking in more inclusive terms. The inclusion of ethnic minorities, gays and lesbians, nontraditional females, persons with disabilities, and other marginalized groups and their perspectives brought with it literature that was not as "safe" as that which told stories from a limited, mainstream point of view with a small range of acceptable protagonists.

Books for younger children did not become radical as quickly as those for young adults. But in 1963, a picture book author/illustrator equal in stature and groundbreaking work to Robert Cormier leaped onto the stage of children's literature. Maurice Sendak took a visual look into the psyche of a young child with his Caldecott Medal book *Where the Wild Things Are* (1963). The second book in what developed into a triology, *In the Night Kitchen* (Sendak, 1970), had a nude toddler boy protagonist. Even 30 years later, frontal nudity in U.S. books for young children is very rare, and when it appears, as in Robie Harris and Michael Emberley's incredibly well-researched and appealing *It's Quite Amazing: A Book About Eggs, Sperm, Birth, Babies, and Families* (1999), both author and illustrator know they are pushing boundaries. The same year that frontal nudity appeared in children's literature, Judy Blume's *Are You There God, It's Me, Margaret?* (1970) mentioned menstruation for the first time in a novel for elementary-aged children. Authors gradually and boldly started to include "dirty words," very scary stories, and dumb adults in books for children, all departures from the traditional literary paradigm. In 1990, Michael Willhoite broke through an enormous barrier by publishing the first widely distributed picture book with gay parents, *Daddy's Roommate*. Topics such as war, suicide, and rioting began to appear from time to time in picture books. Nonetheless, on the whole, books for younger children have never been and still are not as radical or controversial as those for older teens.

As the end of the 1970s approached, the themes and stylistic features of YA fiction began to display unmistakable signs of radical change. Concern for the taboos so characteristic of almost all earlier works largely vanished. After the watershed years of 1967–1968, a veritable avalanche of works appeared whose themes probed many of the social and psychological ills of the time. Holden Caulfield's blanket term for the adults with whom he associated was *phony*. In the YA novels that followed, that term of disparagement for adults became the watchword.

In today's YA novels, teachers can be assured of finding heavy doses of literary realism, along with a sometimes deeply pessimistic view of the world. The last 25 years paved the way for the drastically changing forms and formats, perspectives, and subjects of the late 1990s and early 2000s. By the mid-1990s, this environment encouraged the new type of change in literature for children and young adults that is exemplified in books such as Myers's *Monster* and *Malcolm X.* Teachers need to be aware of the presence of topics that many individuals, pressure groups, and communities find objectionable. But if the inclusion of these tough topics is so prevalent, why is one book challenged and not another? And why do some books (*The Outsiders, The Chocolate War, Catcher in the Rye*) continue to be challenged long after the first attempts have proved fruitless? The following tentative answers to these questions may help teachers and librarians understand the fundamental nature of a challenge, as well as how better to combat one.

Which Books Are Censored?

In Chapters 4 and 5 we examined the prime targets of and the emerging concerns about censorship. But with the toppling of taboos and the radical changes taking place in children's books in the 21st century, why are some books attacked repeatedly while others are largely ignored? Here is a suggestion: Serious censors must hit hard on books with visibility in order to make a significant impact; therefore, they choose targets that the public recognizes in order to capitalize on a potential "symbols of evil" phenomenon. Then they use the digital world to spread the message, promoting fear in order to gain control.

An examination of the most-censored book lists from both People for the American Way and the American Library Association shows that rather than seeking out new books (unless they are highly visible), censors target the same books year after year. Not all of the "radical" books mentioned earlier have been the frequent targets of censors, but many have. In Chapter 4, lists are provided of the most challenged books and authors over much of the 1980s and the mid-1990s (see pp. 72–73). In 2000, the American Library Association released their list of the most censored books of the 1990s (http://www.ala.org/bbooks/top100 bannedbooks.html). The authors and titles are largely the same, but their positions on the lists differ. Salinger's *Catcher in the Rye* is #10 on the ALA list. Hinton's *The Outsiders* and Zindel's *The Pigman,* are still among the top 100 challenged books of the 1990s (#38 and #39, respectively). Mark Twain's *The Adventures of Huckleberry Finn,* attacked by both the political right and left, remains the fifth most-challenged book more than 120 years after its publication. *The Chocolate War* is #4 on the list of most censored of the decade. Although their first books do not appear on the list, Maurice Sendak and Judy Blume have made the list with later publications, as have Robie Harris and Michael Emberley, and Walter Dean Myers. It is too soon to tell whether *Monster* and *Malcolm*

X: A Fire Burning Brightly will make their way to the censor's list—perhaps these books' popularity will first have to be measured.

A majority of books on the list of most-challenged works of the 1990s were published *before* that decade—some quite a few years before. One might conclude that in the children's genre it is not content alone that brings the censor to the door. Rather it seems that widely popular award-winning books with controversial content are the most likely to be those seized on by the censors and that many equally controversial (but perhaps of less literary merit or reader interest) books slip by without a glance. Ironically, once a book appears on the most-censored list, its sales immediately rise. The harder the censors try to block a book, the more curiosity the public has about it.

Harry Potter

J.K. Rowling's Harry Potter books provide a good forum for examining the future of censorship of books for youth. Because they are read aloud to children as young as preschool and have been "repackaged" (different covers on a paperback series in England) to appeal on the outside to more mature teens and adults, they qualify as both children's and young adult literature. *Harry Potter and the Sorcerer's Stone* (1998), the first of what will become a series of seven books, appeared in the United States in 1998, and was joined by the next two in the series later in 1998 and 1999. Just before the publication of the fourth book in the series in July 2000, Scholastic announced that there were more than 35 million copies in print. These books have received numerous awards and distinctions, among them inclusion on the 1999, 2000, and 2001 ALA Notable Books for Children and the 1999 and 2000 Best Books for Young Adults lists (*The Prisoner of Azkaban* [1999] was one of the 2000 Top Ten Best Books for Young Adults). Also for the year 1999, the three Harry Potter books received the most challenges of any book or series of books in the United States and were #60 on the most challenged books of the 1990s list.

The challenges to Rowling's books rest largely on their witchcraft and wizardry theme, which upsets many members of the Christian Right. The books have been challenged in at least 13 states, most notably by the State Board of Education in South Carolina, which considered banning them from the curriculum. The most visible actual ban occurred in Zeeland, Michigan, where superintendent of schools Gary Feentra was instrumental in removing the Potter books from library shelves and restricting circulation for elementary and middle school students. This action prompted the formation of an organization called Muggles For Harry Potter—now a national coalition of organizations, including the National Council for Teachers of English and the American Library Association—to defend the Harry Potter books. The organization apparently succeeded in Zeeland because on May 11, 2000, Superintendent Feentra announced that he was going to rescind most restrictions placed on the books, return them to the libraries, and allow students full access to them (http://www.mugglesforharrypotter. org/zeeland.htm). Four Zeeland citizens were honored at the Library of Congress during Banned Books Week 2000—two were adults who organized the grassroots effort for the Harry Potter books, a successful example of the very type of community-teacher-librarian-young person alliance advocated in Chapters 3 and 10. The other two honorees were students: Thirteen-year-old Julia Mayersohn wrote a strong letter to Family Friendly Libraries opposing the removal of the books, and demonstrated her leadership skills by organizing others to join the protest, while 11-year-old Billy Smith gave up his summer vacation to read the Harry Potter books to low-income children (http://www.mugglesforharrypotter.org/potter4.htm).

The Christian Right from which the challenges principally have come is divided on whether the Harry Potter books should be censored. An extensive article in *The Horn Book* lays out the position of one Christian commentator who does not believe the books should be banned, despite her own misgivings about witchcraft (Gish, 2000). With 35 million copies of the Harry Potter books in print, there has not been one publicly reported incident of a child becoming a witch on account of them.

Although the higher visibility of censorship challenges in the recent past seems pessimistic, the reality is that the anticensorship forces are just as strong or stronger than the censorship forces. Librarians and teachers are steeped in a long tradition of knowing why they choose books for youth—and of making well-defended choices. This must continue. Teachers and librarians have no cause to fear the introduction of radical elements into literature for youth—these elements have been there in the past and will be there in the future. What teachers and librarians must do is to arm themselves with knowledge, take heart in the successful battling of challenges, and confidently defend their professional judgment with contemporary facts. With this in mind, the authors who are courageous enough to write the books that break boundaries can become yet another ally of librarians and teachers. Mark West collected the censorship experiences of a number of well-known and well-respected authors in a book titled *Trust Your Children: Voices Against Censorship in Children's Literature* (1997). The courage of many of these authors should inspire others to use the literature that they were brave enough to create.

Library and Classroom Quest for Quality

The following is a highly selective overview of a long tradition in the world of books for children—the quest for quality. One of the most surprising and puzzling facts about the censorship of books for children and young adults is that until fairly recent times, most books read by children passed through the hands of several adult intermediaries—all working hard to select "the best." Professionals in schools reasoned that there was not enough money, space, or time to purchase everything, so very discriminating evaluative criteria were set. The result is that most challenged literature comes from an elite group selected with careful scrutiny and application of high standards. The problem is that these high standards in both the classroom and the library tradition do not advocate avoidance of controversial topics, but do advocate for inclusion of various points of view.

The evaluation of children's literature stretches back into the 19th century to Caroline M. Hewins's *Books for the Young: A Guide for Parents and Children* (1882), but 1918 is considered a more seminal year for the evaluation of children's literature. It was in this year that Anne Carroll Moore, who had been the visionary head of children's services at the New York Public Library and a professional leader for more than a decade, established her book review column in *The Bookman*. Margaret A. Edwards, a young adult librarian at Enoch Pratt Library in Baltimore, Maryland, also believed firmly in literature as inspiration for children and young adults. The following passage from Edwards provides a notion of how these early- to mid-20th century librarians viewed literature for youth.

> The book has been beloved over the world down through the ages as a symbol of wisdom and enrichment. People attribute to the printed word a kind of magic so potent that they throw what seem to them evil books into the fire to break their spells. For the reader, the book is escape when the world crowds in; it is courage and inspiration and vision; it is an extension and enrichment of one's limited experience. (Edwards, quoted in Hearne and Jenkins, 1999, p. 6)

Amelia Munson, another renowned young adult librarian, made clear that these 20th century library pioneers, with their high literary standards, were also strong advocates for intellectual freedom.

We are part of the great concourse of workers who are moved by a profound belief in three important factors: the power of the book to inject ideas...the power of the individual to dominate his materials and so to free himself to develop...the innate capacities of his nature; *and the power of democracy to seek its highest expression in the free circulation of ideas....* (Munson, quoted in Hearne and Jenkins, p. 14, emphasis added)

As early as 1909, the H.W. Wilson "canonical" selection tool, the *Children's Catalog,* was established and provided throughout the 20th century a carefully chosen recommended bibliography that was closely evaluated by experts in the field. In 1967 it was joined by a selection tool aimed specifically at school libraries, *The Elementary School Library Catalog,* published by Bowker. Comparable "best book" catalogs appeared for junior and senior high school libraries, as well. The American Library Association's Newbery Award was founded in 1922 to recognize the most distinguished children's book of the year, and the Caldecott medal for the most outstanding picture book followed in 1937. Both awards aimed at promoting excellence in literature for youth by encouraging highly inventive and risk-taking authors. *The Horn Book* started publication in 1924 and has provided serious criticism of children's literature in the eight decades since.

Meanwhile, another tradition for selecting the best in literature for young readers developed from the classroom perspective. During the early 1950s, increasing attention was paid to an emerging cadre of serious writers of books for an early adolescent reading audience. The eminent English educator of that era, Dora V. Smith, led a new wave of teacher educators, curriculum specialists, and authorities in library science to take a closer, more scholarly look at the young adult texts of that decade. In early 1961, Dorothy Petitt presented her exhaustive and meticulous doctoral dissertation on what makes a well-written YA novel. To complete her research, Petitt read and analyzed 20 scholarly treatises on long fiction, eventually synthesizing a set of judgment criteria. While completing this analysis/synthesis, Petitt developed a list of more than 500 YA novels currently in print. She sent that list to 18 critics to evaluate. Petitt asked her reviewers to give books they considered both popular and well written a rating of "1." She then took the 25 YA novels that received the most 1 ratings and analyzed them, using as a yardstick the criteria she had synthesized previously. She concluded that all 25 novels generally conformed to those scholarly criteria. (Petitt's criteria and original list can be found in Appendix A.)

Since Petitt's day, a large number of analyses of more recently produced YA novels has become available. In 1973, Al Muller completed a careful follow-up of Petitt's research, using her criteria as well as her sampling procedures. He analyzed the 25 novels that received the highest number of 1 ratings, and he found them once again to be well written. His most significant new finding had to do with the radical shift in choice of subject matter. Historical fiction and lighthearted treatments of human experience were almost nonexistent. The emphasis in the novels on Muller's list was contemporary reality, generally harsh in nature. (See Appendix B for Muller's list.)

While Petitt and Muller were studying the literary quality of young adult novels, others were promoting quality literature for youth in other ways. As early as the 1940s, August Baker of the New York Public Library and Charlemae Rollins of the Chicago Public Library had produced welcome annotated lists of recommended books about African American life and literature. In the 1970s, the Assembly on Literature for Adolescents, National (ALAN) was established and along with it, in 1978, the *ALAN Review*, a journal that contains literary criticism and cirtical reviews of Young Adult literature in each issue. The *Voice of Youth Advocates* was also established, another journal that reviews and promotes literature for young adults, using Petitt's approach of combining both quality and popularity. The journals that review and critique children's literature are numerous, and continue to enjoy brisk business to this day. All of these efforts toward establishing criteria for excellence in children's writing help to fortify the literature against censorship.

The work of Kenneth Donelson has also contributed to the dialogue on literary quality in YA fiction. A doctoral student of the widely respected adolescent literature authority G. Robert Carlsen, Donelson has been an outstanding contributor to the world of knowledge about literature for young people for the past 30 years. In 1980 he published *Literature for Today's Young Adults* with Arizona State University colleague and coauthor Aileen Pace Nilsen. This highly comprehensive overview of reading, literature, and young people (now in its fifth edition) has provided a valuable resource for teachers, librarians, supervisors, and teacher educators for the past 20 years. Its counterpart for children's literature is Charlotte Huck's *Literature for the Elementary School* (1996), now in its sixth edition. In the library field, Zena Sutherland's *Children and Books* (1996) (originally written by May Hill Arbuthnot) is now in its ninth edition. Each of the works has had a profound effect on influencing quality in the field of literature for youth.

A glance at the Web site maintained by Kay Vandergrift at Rutgers University (http://www.scils.rutgers.edu/special/kay) easily demonstrates just how many sources and resources, awards, and distinctions there are currently that assist in the selection of quality literature for youth. As Jenkins says, "In many ways, literary standards have changed very little from that day [early 20th century] to this. The field of writing for children has become larger and more varied due to technological and social changes, but reviewers still look for clear prose, interesting subjects, and engaging narratives" (Hearne & Jenkins, 1999, p. 9). Taking all of this into account, the conclusion is clear: Teachers and librarians must not allow the strident voices of a few censors to distract them from the more important, and historically evident, responsibility of assuring the best quality of literature for children and young adults.

Beneath the Surface of Censorship in the Digital Age

Although the censors' voices still can be heard loud and clear, some interesting new statistics on the number of challenges make it clear that beneath the strident surface, their numbers may be diminishing. The Office of Intellectual Freedom (OIF) of the American Library Association keeps statistics on the number of documented challenges to books reported to the OIF, as well as those found in newspaper reports or other public media. The surprise about these figures is that the number of challenges to books remained steady in the first half of the 1990s and then began to decline. Here are the numbers (estimated to be only about 25% of the actual number of challenges):

1992—641 challenges

1993—686 challenges

1994—758 challenges

1995—762 challenges

1996—661 challenges

1997—595 challenges

1998—478 challenges

1999—472 challenges

(http://www.ala.org/bbooks/challengesbyyear.pdf)

The drop is drastic. In the period of time that rates of crime, suicide, and pregnancy among young people have improved, the state of documented book censorship has dropped by 38%. All this has taken place in a decade during which children and adolescents have had the most widespread access to information in the history of the world.

These statistics, which seem to counter anecdotal evidence, require more analysis. Are the censors redirecting their attention to the Internet, and letting books "off the hook"? This question will be the focus of the next chapter.

Guidelines for Teachers and Librarians

- Keep abreast of the latest statistics on censorship attempts and make widely known facts about decreases and unsuccessful attempts.
- Join Muggles for Harry Potter and invite your students to join also. http://www.mugglesforharrypotter.org
- Be censored-book wise. Know that many of the same books will be censored over and over. Use a preemptive strike and inform parents of this, giving your reasons up front for not censoring quality literature.
- Prepare a short paragraph showing the century-long dedication of teachers and librarians to the selection of quality literature. Have it ready to hand to parents when necessary.
- Celebrate Banned Books Week every September. Enlist students and adults to read banned books.
- Distribute a survey of the 100 most censored books of the 20th century, asking adults and youth to check how many they have read. Chart the results for display in the library media center.
- Read *Hit List: Frequently Challenged Books for Young Adults* and its companion for children (available from ALA). Be confident about how you would defend each of these frequently challenged books. Use the resources and suggestions offered in these books.

RECOMMENDED WEB SITES

2000 Top Ten Best Books for Young Adults
http://www.ala.org/yalsa/booklists/bbya/2000top10best.html

Kay Vandergrift's Young Adult Literature Page
This Rutgers University professor has one of the most extensive sites on the Web related to literature for children and young adults. Many valuable links.
http://www.scils.rutgers.edu/special/kay/yalit.html

Muggles for Harry Potter Group
http://www.mugglesforharrypotter.org

CHAPTER 7

Internet Issues

The role that this technology is increasingly playing is the extension of rights of young people to speak out about themselves, to form affiliations with other teens, to find some way of understanding their plight in the modern world.

(Jenkins, 2000)

Columbine changed the world. Perhaps this statement is too strong, but it *is* accurate to say that when two teenagers came armed to Columbine High School in Littleton, Colorado, on April 20, 1999, and left a massacre in their wake, something stirred deep inside most caring human beings. This "something," however, was not the same for everyone.

In the aftermath of the Columbine shootings, Henry Jenkins, Director of the Comparative Media Studies Program at Massachusetts Institute of Technology, identified two of these reactions when he spoke on the topic of children's First Amendment rights to a room packed with concerned teachers and librarians at a program sponsored by the American Library Association's Intellectual Freedom Committee (2000). His remarks focused on two of the reactions that were raised about the Internet in school classrooms and media centers across the United States: one that values young people who speak for themselves and who seek connection through online communities, and one that fears children's and adolescents' access to information and its allegedly detrimental effect on young minds—as well as its potential for deadly results. The former view holds that in the wake of Columbine, the need has increased to reach out via digital and other means to form a community as a buttress against the isolation that the Columbine killers, Dylan Klebold and Eric Harris, clearly felt. The Internet is a means by which many have established a living memorial to those who died or were injured, also providing links to Web sites that will help teens in trouble (see "Remember Forever," http://redhare.com/columbine).

The latter view mentioned above leaps to find a causative factor for the terrible tragedy of Columbine. According to Jenkins, the digital media was the greatest demon in the eyes of most Americans. Censors of many sorts are ready to demand that the new media content be controlled. Without data to back up their judgments, and with little understanding of how most teenagers use new technologies, they are ready to filter every possible piece of information that might be harmful to minors. To quote Henry Jenkins, "a moral panic is when you stop asking questions and start jumping to conclusions" (2000).

Taking the middle view—that the Internet is neither savior nor demon—we now step back to examine the state of Internet access and use in our 21st century classrooms and media centers. We have already examined the changing content of texts and library books, their availability, and censors' partially successful attempts to control content and access for youth. Against this backdrop, we will juxtapose Internet issues and attempts to censor, observing similarities and differences and assessing the possibilities for success. As part of this assessment, we will consider new methods for delivering book content in the Digital Age, and how that also may increase or decrease potential censorship success.

Internet Access for Young People

Internet Connections in Schools and Classrooms

In 1994, President Clinton's National Information Infrastructure Initiative issued a challenge to the nation: to connect every school and classroom to the Internet by the year 2000. Each year since then, the National Center for Educational Statistics of the U.S. Department of Education has surveyed a scientifically selected random sample of schools in order to document progress and determine when or if this goal might be reached. The last such survey released before this book went to press took place in Fall 1999 and was reported in Spring 2000. The results show that the school objective nearly has been achieved, while the classroom objective has moved forward by leaps and bounds. Here are some of the statistics (available at http://nces.ed.gov/pub search/pubsinfo.asp?pubid=2000086):

- The percentage of public schools connected to the Internet has increased dramatically from 35% in 1994 to 95% in 1999.
- The percentage of public school classrooms (including library media centers, computer labs, and any other rooms used for instruction) connected to the Internet has increased even more dramatically from 3% in 1994 to 63% in 1999.

A study conducted in 1999 that surveyed nearly half the public schools in the United States projected that the "wired by 2000" objective would be met (Guernsey, 2000). The statistics for private schools were collected over a different time period, and are not as dramatic although the trend is the same.

- The percentage of private schools connected to the Internet has increased dramatically from 25% in 1995 to 67% in 1998.
- The percentage of private school classrooms connected to the Internet has increased, although not quite so dramatically, from 5% in 1995 to 25% in 1998.

(http://nces.ed.gov/pubsearch/pubsinfo.asp?pubid=2000044).

It must be noted that these statistics are aggregates, and many relevant differences are apparent according to a school's socioeconomic status, location (rural, suburban, or urban), parochial status, and possession of a dedicated line, although most of the public school differences were erased by the year 2000. The astonishing speed with which computers and Internet access have permeated schools is undeniable. The U.S. government has facilitated the rapid growth of this access through the Telecommunications Act of 1996, which produced the "e-rate" that makes Internet access possible for schools and public libraries at an affordable cost. The e-rate is a mandatory government/private sector partnership in which the Federal Communications Commission requires phone carriers to subsidize both the Internet hookups and the cost of bringing local phone service to customers in rural and other high-cost areas. By the spring of 2000, the third year of the e-rate program, more than 36,000 applications had been filed, 60% of those coming from the nation's neediest schools and libraries. Approximately $6 billion has been invested in this generally successful program (Carvin, 2000). The Supreme Court has refused to hear a case questioning the constitutionality of the e-rate private sector funding requirement, so it appears that this source of funding is secure for at least the short-term future ("Supreme Court Rejects," 2000). The e-rate has been hailed as the first government act that has a chance of succeeding in bringing equality of access—regardless of location, socioeconomic status, gender, or race—to the two things necessary to support our democratic ideal: communication and education.

The government has taken the stance that access to the Internet is healthy and good for all children and all schools. In introducing a U.S. Department of Education report, *Getting America's Students Ready for the 21st Century*, President Clinton stated,

> Our country was built on a simple value that we have an obligation to pass better lives and better opportunities on to the next generation. Education is the way we make that promise real. Today, at the dawn of a new century, in the

middle of an information and communications revolution, education depends upon computers. If we make an opportunity to every student, a fact in the world of modems and megabytes, we can go a long way toward making the American Dream a reality for every student. Not virtual reality—reality for every student. (http://www.ed.gov/Technology/Plan/NatTechPlan/priority.html)

As Clinton left office, his administration's goal of wiring every school was almost met. However, hand-in-hand with this rapid dissemination of technology has come the concern for protecting the innocence of children.

Internet Use in Schools and Classrooms

Many unanswered questions remain about how exactly the Internet is used in schools. Have computers with Internet access brought democracy to the classroom and reduced the digital divide? Do students have equal access regardless of age, gender, and race? Are the computers integrated with other school resources for curricular use? Are students information literate (see Chapter 3, p. 46)? For the answers to these questions, we have no comprehensive statistics such as those from NCES, but there are numerous "snapshots," or indicators that can give us some idea of the state of the art in various classrooms or disciplines. From these snapshots, we can find confirming evidence that the members of the Net Generation are as savvy about technology as they are reputed to be—as long as they have the chance for access.

Indicators of Internet use in classrooms appear everywhere. Many textbooks have been revised to provide links to Internet sites, sometimes provided on a CD-ROM to make the location of Web sites easy. The American Library Association has provided "700+ Great Web Sites for Children and Their Parents" (http://www.ala.org/parentspage/great sites/amazing.html) with evaluation criteria at the end, and has also published *Delivering Web Reference Services to Young People* (Minkel & Feldman, 1999), a basic guide for using the Web most effectively with students. The following snapshot is an account that appeared in the *New York Times* regarding one English teacher's use of his "wired classroom":

> Mr. Nellen wants his students to learn, above everything else, about writing and literature. His strategy happens to be through computers. One assignment, for example, is about Shakespeare's *Tempest*. Mr. Nellen posed discussion questions to his students in an e-mail message. Instead of discussing the questions orally, they are expected to send their answers in e-mail messages distributed to the entire class, so that everyone can read them and elaborate, again via e-mail, on what has been said. "This way you have time to think about it," said Jose Mendez as he typed. He also likes the technology for another reason. In this class of 35 students, he is able to communicate personally

with Mr. Nellen through one-on-one e-mail messages. In a traditional class, he said, teachers rarely talk to their students individually, except when they call them over to their desk. "Then," he added, "everyone thinks you are getting in trouble." Mr. Nellen is clearly not teaching English in a traditional way. He is no longer front and center, but moderating discussion, and not necessarily leading it. Around him, students ask each other questions instead of asking him for the answers. "What the technology is doing is forcing us to rethink how we do our jobs," he said. "You have to get rid of everything you ever learned about being a teacher." (Guernsey, 2000, http://archives.nytimes. com/archives)

Judith McGonigal, a teacher in the Haddonfield school district in southern New Jersey, states this same theme from another perspective. "[Technology] changes a lot of the power pieces in the classroom," she says. "The kids that have more experience become the co-teacher in the classroom. You are the co-learners with the kids" (Nussbaum, 1998, http://archives.nytimes.com/archives).

Advanced Technologies Academy (A-Tech), a new high school in Las Vegas, Nevada, is a school that has served as a test case for the integration of technology in the classroom. The Internet and computer are incorporated into almost every class. "Students in business communications classes use computers to present charts and use the Internet to research collaborative projects that are published on the Web. Students in chemistry classes create animated examples of atomic theories they have learned in class" (Guernsey, 2000, http://archives.nytimes.com/archives). This high school is located in an economically diverse area of Las Vegas, offering hope that perhaps technology may be the door to democractic education in the United States. A-Tech is one of three high schools in Clark County that boasts a 100% graduation rate, achieved as a result of every senior passing the state proficiency test (Guernsey, 2000).

While most educators agree that computers linked to the Internet are necessary and desirable for classroom use, not all hold this opinion. One of the most respected and vocal opponents of what she perceives as the misuse of classroom computers is Jane Healy, an educator with 36 years of experience. Healy is not concerned with the danger of Internet or computer content as much as she is concerned with the possible effects on the brain of learning through computers (Healy, 1999). In the fall of 2000, the Alliance for Childhood, a newly formed advocacy group for children, released a report titled *Fool's Gold: A Critical Look at Computers in Childhood* (http://www.allianceforchildhood. net/projects/computers/computers_reports_fools_gold_contents.htm). This report was signed by more than 75 prominent educators, child-development and health authorities, technology experts, researchers, and other advocates for children. The Alliance calls for a moratorium on the introduction of computers into early childhood and elementary school programs and for a comprehensive study by the U.S. Surgeon General on the effect of computers on the physical and emotional development of children. Both *Fool's Gold* and a book by Jane Healy titled *Failure to Connect: How Computers Affect Children's Minds and What We Can Do About It* (1999) have received a great deal of attention. Eliza Dresang recently encountered a technology teacher who uses the Internet daily, but who has decided that his children will not have access to a computer at home until they are past elementary school age. Should this type of backlash succeed on a large scale, it might prove to be yet another form of potential censorship, as it would become a block to information access. How accurate the concerns raised by these opponents of computer use for younger children are and what exactly their impact will be remains to be seen.

Teachers and Students and the Internet

Simply supplying the computers and gaining access to the Internet is not the end of technology integration. Massive amounts of money have been and will have to continue to be pledged to teacher education. Media specialists often take the lead in this teacher training as part of their special role on the instructional team. Students who have access to computers in their homes (just as students who have access to books in their homes), come to the classroom much more computer savvy than those whose only access is the school, library, or community center. "When it gets to the Internet I see more expertise," said Ginger Hovenic, executive director of the Harborside School in downtown San Diego, California, and a consultant to the Classroom in the Future Foundation, which trains teachers to use technology. "You can see the kids who have spent a lot of time exploring things. That's when I see the big gap begin to happen" (Nussbaum, 1998, http://archives.nytimes.com/archives). Closing this gap—teaching students to evaluate Web-based information with a healthy skepticism, conduct an orderly search in an entirely unruly medium, and go beyond the *use* of information to the *creation* of it in a multimedia environment—brings us to the importance of information literacy, and the development of strategies between classroom teacher and media specialist for teaching it.

The Academic Alliance and the Internet

Despite what may seem like large obstacles to wholesale success, an enormous enthusiasm is shared by the partners in the alliance referred to in Chapter 3—teachers, media specialists, students, and principals—that is buoyed by an understanding of the great wealth of information on the Web and the incredible learning experiences it can bring if used properly. However, this medium, unlike all others that formerly have been a part of school curriculum and use, does not reside in only one place at one time. If there is often more freedom of expression allowed in the school media center than in the classroom; if there is less angst on the part of the parents about media center materials than about those required for classroom study; if the history of litigation has, in general, held up the right of the student to free expression in the school library, then is it not sensible to view the Internet as a media center resource that is shared throughout the school? Is it not the best policy for the learning community to look to the media specialist for leadership in learning how to evaluate content, provide guidelines and policies for selecting resources, and teach the information skills necessary to use the Internet? With a sound instructional alliance, teachers will provide leadership about curricular needs, and students will lead with their skills and abilities at focusing on information and using it in a productive manner. Leadership in Internet use is one of several examples that indicate how the alliance described in Chapter 3 can provide a preventive buttress against censors' attacks.

Is the Internet a Print/Visual Medium or a Broadcast Medium?

The Internet is a multimedia medium. It contains printed visual images—both still and in motion—and spoken verbal content similar to radio. In the mid-1990s, when it became apparent that access to the Internet would soon be ubiquitous, the question arose whether it was more like print and visual media (books, magazines, newspapers, comics, films, videos) or broadcast media (radio and television). The answer to this question became extremely important both to those who would restrict the content of the Internet and/or access to that content, and those who would protect access and/or the content itself. In order to understand why this is a relevant question for those who must deal with attempts to censor Internet content, it is important to understand that there is legal precedence for interpreting "freedom of speech" in different ways for different media. It is also important to understand that some of this distinction is based on protecting youth from content that some adults think is inappropriate for young people to read, see, or hear.

Differing Interpretation of First Amendment Rights

At 2:00 p.m. on October 30, 1973, a New York radio station owned by the Pacifica Foundation broadcast a comedy routine by George Carlin titled "Filthy Words," which concerned "the seven dirty words you can never say on TV." The broadcast was part of a routine about society and language and a warning was given before this 12-minute broadcast that it might contain language "offensive to some." Carlin was satirizing the fact that the Federal Communications Commission (FCC) had indicated that these seven words would be considered offensive if used on television. He pointed out that there are many synonyms of these words that carry the same meaning and that some of these words have become common household words. A father heard this broadcast while driving in his car with his young son and wrote a complaint letter to the FCC. This complaint resulted in a July 3, 1978, Supreme Court decision in *FCC v. Pacifica Foundation* that upheld the FCC's right to threaten sanctions against the radio station because of its use of offensive, though not obscene, language. This contrasted with the print standard that protected all spech that was not obscene or "without redeeming social value" according to "contemporary community standards" (*Miller v. California*, 1973). Speaking for the majority of the Court, Justice Stevens said his argument was based largely on two principles:

> First, the broadcast media have established a unique pervasive presence in the lives of all Americans. Patently offensive, indecent material presented over the airwaves confronts the citizen, not only in public, but also in the privacy of the home, where the individual's right to be left alone plainly outweighs the First Amendment rights of an intruder.... Second, broadcasting is uniquely accessible to children, even those too young to read. Although [a] written message might have been incomprehensible to a first grader, Pacifica's broadcast could have enlarged a child's vocabulary in an instant. Other forms of offensive expression may be withheld from the young without restricting the expression at its source. Bookstores and motion picture theaters, for example, may be prohibited from making indecent material available to children. We held in *Ginsberg v. New York*, 390 U.S. 629, that the government's interest in the "well-being of its youth" and in supporting "parents' claim to authority in their own household" justified the regulation of otherwise protected expression. (*FCC v. Pacifica Foundation*, 1978)

The mention of *Ginsberg v. New York* in the judge's decision refers to a case that provided a different interpretation of obscenity than that in *Miller v. California*. The Ginsberg case "provides somewhat more leeway to specify the kind of sexual conduct depicted or described that would be patently offensive for minors" (Peck, 2000, p. 52). For adults, the work must appeal to prurient interest and taken as a whole lack serious literary, artistic, political or scientific value—but for minors the criteria for obscenity are not as rigorous. Can this standard be applied to the Internet regarding children without affecting access for adults? Often it is difficult to apply these standards. Nudity, for example, cannot be considered "harmful to minors" in all cases. Can this standard be applied to the Internet without abusing the First Amendment rights of youth by limiting their access to constitutionally protected speech—content that is not considered "harmful to minors"?

As we approach the issues that deal with limiting or censoring the enormous resources in cyberspace, the question arises, What other medium is the Internet like? Is it more like a printed book or video or is it more like radio or television? The answer is important, because thus far in the history of both legislation and court rulings a distinction has been made between the broadcast media and the print media. In general, the Supreme Court has established the principle that "differences in the characteristics of new media justify differences in the First Amendment standards applied to them" (*Red Lion Broadcasting Co. v. FCC*, 1969). Therefore, "each medium of expression...must be assessed for First Amendment purposes by standards suited to it, for each may present its own problems" (*Miami Herald Publishing Co. v. Tornillo*, 1974). As we have shown in *FCC v. Pacifica*, the differences of which these decisions speak have translated into tighter restrictions on the broadcast media.

How Has the First Amendment Been Interpreted for the Internet?

In the Telecommunications Act of 1996, a section called the Communications Decency Act (CDA) proposed restrictions on access to certain types of information on the Internet. The CDA proposed as a criminal act online transmission of anything that is either indecent or patently offensive to a person under 18. This brought the Internet in line with broadcast media: Material did not have to be obscene, only indecent or patently offensive to be considered unlawful. Immediately this law was contested by two groups that later joined forces. The American Library Association and the Freedom to Read Foundation—joined by online companies such as AOL, Prodigy, Microsoft, and numerous others—led the challenge for one set of plaintiffs (*Reno v. ACLU*, 1997).

Congress considered the Internet to be a broadcast medium, and the government took this position in defending it. The Supreme Court had another interpretation of this law. On June 26, 1997, the Court rendered its decision that the CDA was unconstitutional. The judges determined that the Internet was not like broadcast media in that users had to take a series of affirmative steps in order to access its content (*Reno v. ACLU*, 1997). They also found the difficulty and expense of enforcing the CDA prohibitive and the punishment for not doing so unjust. In relation to the First Amendment, the court equated the opportunity the Internet offers for individuals to be heard to that of the town crier of the 18th century:

> Through the use of chat rooms, any person with a phone line can become a town crier with a voice that resonates farther than it could from any soapbox. Through the use of Web pages, mail exploders, and newsgroups, the same individual can become a pamphleteer. (http://caselaw.findlaw.com/scripts/getcase.pl?court=us&navby=case&vol=000&invol=96-511)

The Supreme Court found that while trying to protect children, the CDA prohibited adults to access constitutionally protected information, and that there were ways that parents could shield their children from questionable material. Congress subsequently passed the Child Online Protection Act of 1998 (COPA, also known as CDA II), a narrower version of the original act that attempted to focus on a ban of commercial Internet content that was deemed harmful to minors. Immediately after passage of this legislation, the ACLU and others filed a lawsuit challenging the constitutionality of this law and seeking to have it overturned (*ACLU v. Reno II*, 2000). In 1999, a federal District Court issued a preliminary injunction against enforcement of the law, on the grounds that it is probably unconstitutional. On June 22, 2000, the Third Circuit Court of Appeals declared the law unconstitutional.

Starting in the mid 1990s, U.S. Senators and Representatives made several unsuccessful attempts to pass legislation requiring libraries that receive federal technology assistance to install filters on computers that are accessed by children. At the very end of 2000, the U.S. Congress finally enacted such a law, the Children's Internet Protection Act (CIPA), (http://www.cdt.org/legislation/106th/speech/001218cipa.pdf), which was passed as part of a massive budget bill.

The passage of this bill, unless it is declared unconstitutional by the courts, has the potential for widespread impact on school and public libraries. It applies to all libraries receiving funds from the following sources:

- Elementary and Secondary Education Act School Technology Funds
- Museum and Library Services Act Library Technology Funds
- E-rate service discounts for schools
- E-rate service discounts for libraries

The mandate will apply to most schools and public libraries. Schools and libraries are to file "Statements of Intent" with their applications for federal funding. If they do not comply, the funding will be withheld. The requirement is to install and use Internet filtering software to block obscenity, child pornography (both of which are illegal and not constitutionally protected) as well as material deemed harmful to minors. CIPA defines a minor as anyone 16 years of age or younger, a provision that will, of course, provide confusion at the secondary level.

Interestingly the "harmful to minors" definition in CIPA applies only to pictures, images, graphic image files or other visual depictions, not to text. The catch is that current technology filters either text alone or text and visuals but not visuals alone. The American Civil Liberties Union has declared its intention to file a suit to test the constitutionality of this new law; ALA will likely either join this action or initiate one on its own. Until the courts act, however, CIPA is the law of the land.

What the Future Holds for Legal Opinion and the Internet

What will the courts decide? Prior to the passage of this law, local library procedures and state laws (as well as the federal legislation already discussed) limiting access to the Internet have been put on hold or struck down by the courts. For example, in August 2000, a federal judge barred Virginia from enforcing a state law passed in April 1999 that criminalizes Internet content deemed harmful to minors. Similar laws were challenged successfully in New Mexico and New York. In a book for young readers on the Bill of Rights, Kathleen Krull (1999) cited the following statistic: "In 1998 some 1,400 proposed bills dealing with the Internet were argued about in-state legislatures—a surge from 1995, when there were only three proposed bills. Most of them have to do with how the Internet affects minors. So far supporters of free speech have won every case that has gotten to court" (p. 73). To date, challenges to libraries with Internet access for minors have been denied by the Court. One such court case—filed by a mother whose 12-year-old son was caught downloading pictures of nude women—against the Livermore, California, public library was dismissed by the Alameda County Superior Court, but has been appealed to the California First District Court of

Appeal. Incidentally, the citizens of Alameda County passed a bond referendum for the public library during the midst of this case.

The future of the Internet, with regard to both legislation and the place of the medium in home life and education, rests partially on the print versus broadcast media precedent. Decisions based on the print precedent have already laid the groundwork for less-restrictive legislation and practice in use of the Internet. We need to hold firmly in mind what attorney and author Robert S. Peck (2000) concludes from his analysis of case law:

> The U.S. Supreme Court has concluded that cyberspace receives the highest level of protection that the First Amendment affords. As a result, the same considerations that apply to printed words and images apply as well to the electronic word and the digital image. Any policy on Internet access that a...library adopts...must respect the rights of access of both older minors and younger minors who have a right to access protected speech and some speech that parents could find troubling but have serious value for youth and must respect the rights of parents who choose to permit their children to access sites that others might deem appropriate only for more mature individuals. Most importantly, such policies should be content and viewpoint neutral in all respects. (pp. 142–143)

The decisions to date suggest that the Court will view the Internet as it does books rather than as it does broadcast media, that it will hold it up as a medium deserving the highest of First Amendment protection, and that protection of children will have to be limited to enforceable, reasonable measures and will be left largely in the hands of parents.

In addition to CIPA, two U.S. national commissions set up by previous legislation worked throughout the year 2000. One set up by the Child Online Protect Act of 1998 held hearings in various parts of the country devoted to "Filtering," "Parents' Attitudes Toward the Internet," and other topics. In its report to the Congress in the fall of 2000, this commission recommended (ironically enough) against requiring the use of filters in libraries. The other piece of legislation, Protection of Children from Sexual Predators Act of 1998, dictated that a commission be set up by the National Research Council to examine tools and strategies for protecting youth from pornography and their applicability to other inappropriate Internet content (http://www4.nas.edu/cpsma/cstb/itas.nsf). This commission is still meeting as this book goes to press, but it will bring to Congress recommendations on the strengths and weaknesses of various youth protection strategies.

Congress also set up a bipartisan congressional Web-based Education Commission (http://www.webcommission.org), inviting a range of experts to submit online "e-testimony" on public policies needed to help fulfill the educational promise of the Internet. Specifically, the Commission sought concrete recommendations on a number of policy issues and questions related to access, professional development, distributive learning, assessment and accreditation, cost and financing, standards, intellectual property protection, online privacy, research and development, and marketplace forces. In December 2000 the commission submitted a report titled "The Power of the Internet for Learning" to Congress (http://interact.hpcnet.org/webcommission/text.htm). Included in the Executive Summary of this text are ideas that sound very similar to the 21st century learning discussed in Chapter 1 of this book. The report recognizes the importance of the Internet:

- to center learning around the student instead of the classroom
- to focus on the strengths and needs of individual learners and
- to make lifelong learning a practical reality.

(Web-based Education Commission, p. iii)

It goes on to state:

> We heard that the Internet enables education to occur in places where there is none, extends resources where there are few, expands the learning day, and opens the learning place. We experienced how it connects people, communities, and resources to support learning. We witnessed how it adds graphics, sound, video, and interaction to give teachers and students multiple paths for understanding. We learned that the Web is a medium today's kids expect to use for expression and communication—the world into which they were born.

(Web-based Education Commission, p. iii)

Unlike the Alliance for Childhood report, this report urges moving forward with all due speed to tap the fullest possible potential of the Internet for all kinds of learning. The report does state that "the power of the Internet to transform the educational experience is awe-inspiring, but it is also fraught with risk" (p. i). But it concludes that "working together, we can realize the full potential of this tool for learning. With the will and the means, we have the power to expand the learning horizons of students of all ages" (p. i). This commission called upon Congress for a national mobilization similar to the one that occurred after the launch of Sputnik.

Censorship in Cyberspace

This background of distribution, access, opportunity, and challenges brings us again to the issue of censorship in classrooms and media centers. As the reactions to the Columbine tragedy demonstrated, the U.S. public has a great fear of technology's unharnessed energy in schools and in the undisciplined hands of youth. If Klebold and Harris could use the Web to learn how to manufacture bombs and to spread hate speech, how many other young people are using the Web to evil ends? And how many of them are doing so in publicly supported places?

The prime targets for censors discussed in Chapter 4 include (1) profane, obscene, and otherwise objectionable language; (2) explicit depiction of sexual activity; (3) critical "anti-American" materials; (4) New Age selections; (5) satanism, witchcraft, the occult, and extraterrestrials; (6) the image of minorities; (7) violence, sadism, and rape. The CDA, CDA II, and the state laws discussed earlier have focused specifically on obscenity or material related to sexual matters. Local teachers and librarians, who generally will view the Internet as they do books and other written materials, must successfully and confidently deal with far more issues than obscenity. The Internet is a unique multimedia resource, and it incorporates potential censorship issues that arise in several other contexts.

The Trouble With Filters

The most controversial means of censorship in cyberspace is the use of filters on computers or networks to block certain content from the Internet user, and the passage of the CIPA does not magically remove the problems with these filters. Some opponents of blocking software refer to filters as censorship in a box. The American Library Association Council passed a resolution on filtering in 1998: "Resolved that the American Library Association affirms that the use of filtering software by libraries to block access to constitutionally protected speech violates the Library Bill of Rights" (http://www.ala.org/alaorg/oif/filt_res.html). Neither this resolution nor the Library Bill of Rights (1948, http://www.ala.org/work/freedom/lbr.html), a document that explains the First Amendment in the context of libraries, has any legally binding authority on libraries or librarians, but these documents are looked on by many librarians as the prime justifications for the defense of free speech in their workplaces. The filtering resolution has been controversial since it passed, but the American Library Association has stood firmly behind it. At the same time, the ALA has affirmed on numerous occasions the right of parents to determine what they wish their children to experience.

The principal argument for using filters in a school or classroom is to protect young people from inappropriate content. The majority of parents so far do not seem very concerned about the necessity of filtering. In a study done by the Annenberg Public Policy Center of the Univeristy of Pennsylvania titled *Media in the Home* (2000), researcher Emory Woodard found that only one third of parents with Internet access reported using blocking software (http://www.appcpenn.org/inhome.pdf). Parents express more concern about the television their children watch than about the content of the Internet.

The principal arguments made against the use of filters in libraries and classrooms are as follows:

- Filters are a means of censorship and as such violate First Amendment rights of students.

- It is better to teach students to use the Internet responsibly than to try to filter out mechanically certain kinds of materials.

- Most students can easily get around filters if they want to.

- Filters fail to block some sites or types of sites they purport to block. Therefore, a school system could be held legally responsible if parents have been assured that unsavory material will be blocked.

- Filter manufacturers often have social and political agendas.

The first two of these principles will be taken as self-evident. The third is backed up by such organizations as Peacefire, an anticensorship Web-based organization run by teens, which provides information on its Web site about how to disable all of the major filtering software packages (http://www.peacefire.org). For this reason, Peacefire is a Web site blocked by some of the filtering software packages it reviews. Peacefire, in fact, sells T-shirts emblazoned with the phrase "Censored by Censorware," which list blocked sites and the products used to block them.

The fourth and fifth principles are legitimate concerns. Peacefire representatives submitted three reports to the COPA Commission on filtering companies, purported by their own statements to be state-of-the-art technology. One report demonstrates inappropriate blocking by a filtering program called ClickSafe, and the other report provides evidence of how sites that the software claims to block are not blocked. (Both reports are linked from the Peacefire Web site, http://www.peacefire.org.) According to Peacefire, ClickSafe makes the following claims:

- ClickSafe uses state-of-the-art, content-based filtering software that combines cutting-edge graphic, word, and phrase-recognition technology to achieve extraordinarily high rates of accuracy in filtering pornographic content.

- ClickSafe can precisely distinguish between appropriate and inappropriate sites (i.e., it has both remarkably low underblocking and overblocking rates).

Peacefire further noted that the sites blocked by ClickSafe's pornography category (on July 18, 2000) included the following:

Frequently Asked Questions about the COPA Commission (http://www.copacommission.org/commission/faq.shtml);

Biographies of three COPA Commission members (http://www.copacommission.org/commission/hughes.shtml); (http://www.copacommission.org/commission/balkam.shtml); (http://www.copacommission.org/commission/bastian.shtml); and

Technologies and methods within the scope of the COPA Commission—a list of the different software and age verification techniques that the commission was appointed to consider (http://www.copacommission.org/commission/technologies.shtml).

("Sites Blocked," 2000, http://peacefire.org/censorware/ClickSafe/ screenshots-copacommission.html)

In addition, the homepages of several companies and organizations that have members on the COPA Commission were also blocked by ClickSafe under the category of pornography, including:

About the Internet Content Rating Association

(http://www.icra.org/about.html);

The Center for Democracy and Technology's home page—one of Washington's most prominent civil liberties groups opposing Internet censorship

(http://www.cdt.org); and

The National Law Center for Children and Families—a list of activities and lobbying efforts that the organization has conducted at the federal level

(http://www.nationallawcenter.org/federal.htm).

("Sites Blocked," 2000, http://peacefire.org/censorware/ClickSafe/ screenshots-copacommission.html)

Sites for the ACLU and the Electronic Frontier Foundation were also blocked as was that of one conservative organization, the American Family Association.

Another Peacefire report on Basic Artificial Intelligence Routine (BAIR), a program that claims to recognize and block pornographic images through advanced artificial intelligence, found 0% accuracy when testing this product (Haselton, 2000, http://peacefire.org/censorware/BAIR/first-report.6-6-2000.html). The report on Peacefire's Web site explains how the study was conducted and provides information for anyone who wants to test the accuracy of this filtering product for themselves. SurfWatch, another filtering program that Peacefire studied for accuracy in blocking explicit materials, was found to have "an error rate of 42/51 = 82%, or roughly four non-pornographic domains blocked for every one pornographic domain blocked" (Haselton, 2000, http://peacefire.org/censorware/SurfWatch/first-1000-comdomains.html).

Similar results are revealed by The Internet Filter Assessment Project (TIFAP), a study conducted in 1997 by librarian Karen Schneider, who writes a column titled "The Internet Librarian" in the *American Libraries* journal. The study neither recommends nor rejects filters, but rather attempts to do what the title says—assess them. According to TIFAP, many sites that are blocked by filters prevent students from doing needed research: "keyword blocking obscured everything from nursery rhymes ("pussycat, pussycat" was blocked repeatedly, even, in one case, when the tester used the search terms "nursery rhymes") to government physics archives (the URL began with XXX)" (http://www.bluehighways.com/tifap/learn.htm). Numerous students have also independently documented excessive blocking of Web sites that provide information for gay or lesbian students. The evidence on filters available in early 2001 tells us that teachers or librarians who believe that filters are protecting them or their students are naive. Those who support open access to constitutionally protected speech believe that teachers or librarians who have faith in filters are shirking, at least in part, their duty to protect the First Amendment rights of the students they teach.

Perhaps more sophisticated products that are more successful at blocking constitutionally protected speech are just around the corner. At this time they have not yet been invented. Or, following the example of a company called KidsNet, perhaps a method to evaluate Web sites on a massive scale will be implemented. KidsNet, which will be officially launched in the spring of 2001 at http://www.kidsnetinc.com, uses a rating system that rates sites against levels of sex, violence, etc.

The system allows a user to set the controls to see only the rating level he or she choses (or someone else sets). Rather than asking creators of sites to self-rate (as hardly any do), KidsNet plans to have the 100,000 most-visited Web sites evaluated by trained raters. Although this system definitely leans more toward selection than blocking, it has features that allow whole categories to be blocked, so users are in effect able to choose to block, for example, art works containing nudity.

Practical Responses to Filtering

So, what are teachers and librarians to do about this filtering legislation, a new law as this book goes into print? Some suggestions are as follows:

- Keep yourself and others informed about the state of the laws and court cases. (This can be accomplished by joining an on-line news service such as those of the Center for Democracy and Technology, or the People for the American Way. See their respective Web sites listed at the end of Chapter 9 for how to join.) Also, reading *American Libraries* online each week is a good way to keep up to date (http://www.ala.org/alonline). Particularly keep abreast of challenges to this legislation.

- Strengthen the coalitions recommended throughout this book; involve young people. Let them explore the consequences of this filtering law, help them understand the current lack of sophisticated programs. Communicate with the community.

- Get involved in the decision about whether to forego funds or comply. If complicity is the local decision, do not hesitate to advertise the consequences as they occur, seek better alternatives, and explore new products such as KidsNet.

- Be proactive in analyzing and articulating what is going on.

- Promote the image of the child of the 21st century and what Internet access means for him or her (see Chapter 1).

- Regard this situation as temporary, and be open to the possibility of changing paradigms in the digital world. The flow of information in the digital world is ultimately unstoppable, and the answer lies in individual responsibility rather than technology.

Censors Using Cyberspace

A byproduct of the connectivity of the Internet is the ability of censors to broadcast their messages far and wide in a manner of seconds.

Dr. Laura Schlessinger, an online and broadcast commentator on contemporary society in an alliance with David Burt of the Filtering Facts organization, launched a particularly vindictive and relentless campaign against the American Library Association in 1999. ALA's reputation for defense of Intellectual Freedom became a target for mud-slinging and fear-inducing tactics. The disturbance started over a Web resource linked from Teen Hoopla (http://www.ala.org/teenhoopla)—a Web site with resources for teens maintained and disseminated by the Young Adults Library Services Association of ALA. The controversial linked site was Go Ask Alice! (http://www.goaskalice.columbia.edu), created and maintained by the Columbia University Health Education Programs. Some of the questions asked by teens require answers involving explicit sex. The site does not attempt to moralize but only to provide information.

Schlessinger not only used her Web site to accuse the ALA of attempting to destroy the morals of youth, but she also waged a campaign to get librarians to disassociate themselves from ALA. (See http://www.drlaura.com/action/index.html?mode=view&tile=1&id=63 for some of Dr. Laura's commentary on the ALA.) In the September 1, 2000, issue of *Family Circle Magazine*, an article titled "Is Your Library X-Rated?" appeared. In it, author Schlessinger condemns the ALA and praises Family Friendly Libraries, as well as Charles Reed of the Christian Coalition of Ohio. She concludes that with her initiative, libraries will be saved from the fate of movie theaters that have become X-rated.

It is this type of campaign that forces those who are committed to free access to information to grit their teeth and remember that it is not only the sought-after speech that needs to be protected by the First Amendment, but also the unreasonable and distasteful. A belief in democracy dictates a belief that such campaigns will die a natural death, killed by those who do not buy into the rhetoric.

Overreactions to Student Cyberspeech

The open access that gives Laura Schlessinger her forum also provides young people with a place to express their thoughts. The Web allows every student who so desires to become an editorial columnist. Following is a quick synopsis of three of the most visible cases of Web site censorship that represent the fear felt by principals and other school officials, and their readiness to censor without rational consideration of the effects of their acts.

Paul Kim, Bellevue, Washington. In the spring of 1995, Paul had acceptances from Harvard, Stanford, and Columbia, a National Merit

Scholarship, and a bright future ahead. Then, joining the "crowd" on the World Wide Web, Paul created "The Unofficial Newport High School Home Page." As a parody, Paul posted jabs at classmates and also links to sexually explicit Web sites. The principal at first said there would be no punishment, but then complaints came from the outside. Kim took down his Web site, but the principal decided to withdraw her recommendations from the seven colleges to which he had applied and the National Merit Foundation—without informing him. Kim took his case to court and won, but lost his acceptance to Harvard and his scholarship (which the school had to make up).

Brandon Beussink, Marble Hill, Missouri. In 1998 Brandon Beussink used his home computer to create a Web site that poked fun at his school's official Web site, using vulgar language. He, like Kim, took it down when approached by the administration, but nonetheless was suspended and not allowed to graduate on time. The court sided with Beussink. In this decision, Judge Rodney Sipple wrote that, "Beussink was not disciplined on February 17, 1998, because he was disrespectful or disruptive in the classroom. Beussink was disciplined because he expressed an opinion on the Internet that upset Principal Poorman.... Indeed, it is provocative and challenging speech, like Beussink's, which is most in need of the protection of the First Amendment" (Carvin, 2000, p. 29).

Nick Emmett, Kentlake, Washington. Nick Emmett was a varsity sports team member and had a 3.95 grade point average. He, too, created an "unofficial home page" from his home. He expanded on an idea from one of his classes in which students had been asked to write obituaries; he asked fellow classmates to vote on who would "die next" and write an obituary. The school found this objectionable and suspended him. The court ruled in Emmett's favor, and the school district eventually settled out of court.

In each of these cases, the school administrator acted too hastily and, perhaps out of fear, violated the students' right to free expression. Each of these are examples of the kind of moral panic that can occur when questioning ends.

Acceptable Use Policies: A Tentative Solution

In Chapter 9, the recommendation to create a school district instructional materials selection policy is joined here by a recommendation to have a school board-approved acceptable use policy for Internet use. The AUP may, in fact, no longer be voluntary because the CIPA requires that schools and public libraries have what are called Internet Safety Policies (http://www.cdt.org/legislation/106th/speech/001218cipa.pdf, p. 3). The CIPA dictates what must legally be in this policy, but schools and libraries have the option of writing more about acceptable use than is required. Nancy Willard has collected a fine document on the Web titled "A Legal and Educational Analysis of K-12 Internet Acceptable Use Policies" (http://www.erehwon.com/k12aup/legal_analysis.html) that offers suggestions of elements that should be included in a district's policy.

An attitude supportive of intellectual freedom is as appropriate in the creation of an Internet acceptable use document as it is in one for nonnetworked materials: In defining "acceptable" it is important to bring calm questioning rather than moral panic to the table. In all of the Web censorship cases discussed earlier, the principals went far beyond what the situation required in their punishments and reactions. A good acceptable use policy will have the minimal constraints necessary to preserve equity of access and educational responsibility in the school environment.

From the time this chapter was originally written until the time this book was about to be published, much of the text in this chapter had changed. Two commissions had completed their work. A new law had passed. This demonstrates how timely the librarian and the teacher in the cyberspace world must be in keeping abreast of what is happening and providing information to others. Many of the details may have changed, but the overall theme has remained the same: The policy of open access to information and defense of intellectual freedom will not evaporate in the cyberage. It takes clear thinking and commitment to see one's way through the fog of filters and fear, but a calm and reasonable approach, and commitment to the teacher-media specialist-student alliance will provide the strength that is needed when freedoms are at stake.

Guidelines for Teachers and Librarians

- Develop an Internet bulletin board where current events dealing with Internet laws and litigation are posted.

- Be sure every instructional team member understands the Internet legal precedents that have been set already.

- Integrate use of Internet resources into every lesson taught.

- Encourage students to become information literate. Help them to become information literate.

- Ask students to create an Internet acceptable use policy for their media center and classroom.

- Ask students to identify a time when they have had some kind of information they needed withheld from them. Ask how it felt and what happened.

RECOMMENDED WEB SITES

American Library Association
700+ Great Web Sites
http://www.ala.org/parentspage/greatsites/amazing.html

American Library Association—Teen Hoopla
http://www.ala.org/teenhoopla

Q&A about Go Ask Alice
http://www.ala.org/yalsa/askaliceq&a.html

Center for Democracy & Technology
This site provides update on legislation and court actions relating to Internet free speech. Monitors and presents positions.
http://www.cdt.org/speech

Dr. Laura
http://www.drlaura.com/main

Electronic Frontier Foundation
This is an intellectual freedom issues site. See also: Know Your Enemies
http://www.eff.org
This page has extensive annotated list with contact information of groups with agendas to limit access to information (Christian Coalition, Phyllis Schlafly).
http://www.eff.org/pub/Groups/BCFE/bcfenatl.html

Enough is Enough
This is home to a group against children's free access to Internet.
http://www.enough.org

Family Friendly Libraries
FFL is a national grass-roots network of concerned citizens, librarians, and library trustees that believe in
- more common sense access policies to protect children from exposure to age-inappropriate materials without parental consent, and
- a return to policies placing libraries under maximum local control with more acknowledgment of taxpayer authority and community standards.

http://www.fflibraries.org

Findlaw U.S. Constitution: First Amendment
This resource gives a list of links to legal summaries of cases on all aspects of First Amendment case law.

http://caselaw.findlaw.com/data/Constitution/amendment01

First Amendment Cyber-Tribune
This is a great site for legal info and news of challenges; has links to other sites.

http://w3.trib.com/FACT

Free Access to Information and Freedom of Expression (part of International Federation of Library Associations and Institutions)
In their own words, "FAIFE monitors the state of intellectual freedom within the library community worldwide, supports IFLA policy development and cooperation with other international human rights organisations, and responds to violations of free access to information and freedom of expression."

http://www.faife.dk

Free Expression Network
"The Free Expression Network (FEN) is an alliance of organizations dedicated to protecting the First Amendment right of free expression and the values it represents, and to opposing governmental efforts to suppress constitutionally protected speech."

http://www.FreeExpression.org

The Freedom Forum
This site contains mostly news stories.

http://www.freedomforum.org

Global Internet Liberty Campaign
This site provides links to news articles and documents.

http://www.gilc.org

Institute for First Amendment Studies
This site presents news stories from other sources, some original opinion articles.

http://apocalypse.berkshire.net/~ifas

Internet Free Expression Alliance
This site provides news on Internet filtering/rating and links.

http://www.ifea.net

Library Watch Online Magazine
"Library Watch Online Magazine covers issues related to Public Libraries using public tax dollars to distribute materials to children that are pornographic, obscene,

and/or otherwise illegal."
http://netwinds.com/library

National Campaign for Free Expression
This campaign focuses on artistic expression, and the page has a section of news article summaries on youth and free expression.
http://www.artswire.org/~ncfe

Peacefire: Open Access for the Net Generation
http://www.peacefire.org

Remember Forever: Columbine High School April 20, 1999
http://redhare.com/columbine

CHAPTER 8

An In-Depth Look at Censorship Litigation

The people of the United States have unquestionably become a more litigious breed in recent decades. In the current era, "I'll sue you" seems to have taken the place of "Go to hell" as a response to some effronteries. The emergence of the political correctness and affirmative action movements has served to increase the use of the lawsuit as a means of dealing with charges of various kinds.

To truly understand censorship, it is important to fully comprehend its legal ramifications. A study of court battles that have been fought on this issue can provide valuable insight into the mentality and methods of censors and would-be censors, while also offering guidance to the defenders of free speech. Several court cases relating to the issue of censorship have been mentioned in the preceding chapters. This chapter offers a more in-depth review of certain key legal battles involving formal censorship challenges; the impact of certain court decisions emanating from those challenges; and a profile of several groups of U.S. citizens who have encouraged, supported, and frequently financed censorship attacks. The increased power and responsibility of school administrators that has resulted from one of those Supreme Court cases deserves special attention, because in the final analysis, curricular directions in a democratic society are based, at least in part, on a political rationale. The significant increase in formal challenges to those curricula in the last 25 years reflects the will of those with specific political agendas.

Because most of the formal litigation of school censorship challenges devolves into matters of freedom of expression, the First Amendment is usually the rule against which those suits are pressed. When that freedom becomes the issue, the federal courts are often the ones in which these suits are filed. Federal courts also deal with state laws concerning public school curricular mandates, many of which have been challenged as unconstitutional. The most notorious censorship cases in recent years are cases that have moved from Federal District Courts to regional Circuit Courts of Appeal and then to the U.S. Supreme Court. A closer look at three of these—*Tinker v. Des Moines*

Independent Community School District (1969), *Island Trees v. Pico* (1982), and *Hazelwood School District v. Kuhlmeier* (1988)—will demonstrate some of the major issues surrounding censorship court battles, including the changing face of the Supreme Court itself.

Censorship Challenges and the Supreme Court

Tinker v. Des Moines Independent Community School District

A significant case testing students' right to First Amendment freedom occurred in 1966 at East High School in Des Moines, Iowa. A number of students wore black armbands to school to protest against the war in Vietnam. When ordered by their principal to remove the armbands, they refused to do so and were disciplined—suspension and loss of membership in certain honor societies. A group of their parents, among them a family named Tinker, sued the school and school district under the First Amendment. The case wound its way through the courts and, in 1969, the Supreme Court decided in favor of Tinker over the Des Moines Independent Community School District in a vote of 7-2. Writing for the majority, Associate Justice Abe Fortas stated, in essence, that a person does not surrender his First Amendment Rights at the schoolhouse door (*Tinker*, 1969). But that was another era and another Supreme Court—one composed of Justices Black, Douglas, Fortas, Marshall, White, Stevens, Stewart, Brennan, and Chief Justice Earl Warren. Eight years of Supreme Court Justice appointments by Presidents Nixon and Ford, followed by 12 years of those by Presidents Reagan and Bush, would radically change the Warren Court's philosophical bent.

Board of Education, Island Trees Union Free School District v. Pico

The Island Trees case, finally settled in the Supreme Court in 1982, represents a classic example of school versus community in relation to book banning. It also reflects the changing face of the Supreme Court. In 1976, a group of school board members physically removed a number of books from the high school library in Levittown, Long Island, New York. These board members, responding to a group of complaining community members, made claims that the books were "anti-American, anti-Semitic, anti-Christian, and just plain filthy" (*Island Trees v. Pico*, 1982, http://www.fac.org/columns/970919b-s.asp). These books included,

Slaughterhouse Five, by Kurt Vonnegut, Jr.

The Fixer, by Bernard Malamud

The Naked Ape, by Desmond Morris

Down These Mean Streets, by Piri Thomas

Best Short Stories by Negro Writers, edited by Langston Hughes

Go Ask Alice, Anonymous

A Hero Ain't Nothin' But a Sandwich, by Alice Childress

Soul on Ice, by Eldridge Cleaver

A Reader for Writers, edited by Jerome Archer

Laughing Boy, by Oliver LaFarge

Black Boy, by Richard Wright

A group of parents, represented by the Pico family, sued the school following the removal. It is worth noting that the Island Trees district is an affluent, upper middle class, largely Caucasian bedroom community—the large majority of whose residents work at white collar jobs in New York City. In the summer of 1982, the Supreme Court voted 5-4 against the school board and for Pico, et. al. The five justices in the majority contended that it is not constitutionally permissible for school boards to remove books from school libraries simply because they dislike the ideas contained in those books. That majority consisted of Justices White, Blackmon, Brennan, Marshall, and Stevens. Opposing were Justices Powell, Rehnquist, O'Connor, and Burger—all Nixon, Ford or Reagan appointees. Of further note was the statement contained in the majority opinion, written by Justice William Brennan: "This case is about a library, not a school's curriculum...we freely concede that the school board has the right and duty to supervise the general content of a school's course of study (Simmons, 1990, p. 116–117)." A prophetic statement indeed, as later events would corroborate.

On the matter of school-community relations, the *Island Trees v. Pico* case offers an excellent illustration of the complex, often volatile balance between these two groups, regarding what should be taught and how. James Anthony Whitson (1998) has studied the curriculum governance aspect of *Pico* in detail. He explains the motivation for the case in this manner:

> In *Board of Education v. Pico* (1982), three school board members attended a political rally where they obtained a list of "objectionable" books. After determining that 11 books on the list were included in the district's school libraries and/or the curriculum, the board sent an "unofficial direction" to the superintendent and the principals directing them to remove the books from their

schools and send them to the school board office. The superintendent objected to this course of action, recommending that the established procedure for reviewing challenged books should be used instead. The board responded by repeating its demand that all copies of the books be removed and sent to them.

At a public meeting shortly after this, the superintendent reiterated his position in a prepared statement, in which he argued that it was "wrong for the Board or any other single group to act to remove books without prolonged prior consideration of the views of both the parents whose children read these books, and the teachers who use these books to instruct," that it was "wrong to judge any book on the basis of brief excerpts [taken] out of context," that it was "wrong to take action based on a list prepared by someone outside the...community," and that it was "wrong to by-pass the established procedure for reviewing the challenged books." A "Book Review committee" made up of four parents and four school staff members was eventually appointed and finally recommended removing two of the books. The board substantially rejected the committee's report and decided that nine of the books should be removed from the libraries and from use in the curriculum.

Of course, the superintendent is legally answerable to the school board, so after giving them his own recommendations, the superintendent in *Board of Education v. Pico* did carry out the school board's orders. This case illustrates the typical situation of the superintendent who, like the principal, finds herself caught in the middle between politically elected school board members and the teaching faculty. By comparison, the building-level principals are closer to the faculty and are likely to be more intimately engaged in the actual process of educating students. (p. 4)

The narrow margin by which the Supreme Court Justices voted in the *Pico* case in accordance with an anticensorship stance (5-4) stands in sharp contrast to that of *Tinker* (7–2), reflecting a shift in attitudes toward civil and human rights between 1969 and 1982. The four dissenting members clearly reflect the attitude of their time, which viewed certain matters of intellectual freedom in a manner different from many of their predecessors.

Hazelwood, Missouri School Board v. Kuhlmeier

A little over a year after the *Island Trees v. Pico* decision was rendered, another, more significant case began its inexorable journey to the Supreme Court. In May 1983, the editorial staff of the newspaper published by Hazelwood East High School in St. Louis, Missouri, decided to run two controversial stories—one on teen pregnancy, the other on the effects of divorce on adolescents. When the principal of Hazelwood East had both stories deleted, the students (all members of a course titled Journalism II) sued him under the First Amendment, and the case began its journey through the federal court system.

Hazelwood, an affluent suburb of St. Louis, is not measurably different from the Island Trees school district mentioned earlier.

The principal's decision to remove the stories was upheld in a U.S. District Court late in 1986, but that decision was reversed by the 8th U.S. Circuit Court of Appeals in the summer of 1987. Then in January 1988, the U.S. Supreme Court voted 5-3 in favor of the principal's decision to censor the stories. Justice Byron White, writing for the majority, stated that, in effect, a school need not tolerate student speech that is inconsistent with its educational mission and therefore school officials may impose reasonable restrictions on the speech of students, teachers, and other members of the school community (*Hazelwood*, 1988). Editorial opinion was somewhat divided in this nationally celebrated case, although it was probably more sympathetic to the students. The most significant ramification of the *Hazelwood* decision lies in the power that it placed in the hands of building principals to decide what can and cannot be included in their school's curricula. Because broad curricular knowledge is not always a significant strength of such administrators, the long-range effects of this Supreme Court decision are incalculable.

Some Ramifications of the *Hazelwood* Case

One measurable effect of the *Hazelwood* decision was its use as a precedent to decide a critical censorship case in which classic works of literature were removed from a high school English course. In April 1986, a clergyman supported by a number of angry parents in Lake City, Florida, enjoined the school board to remove a book from an elective twelfth-grade humanities course being taught at Columbia County High School. The text, *The Humanities: Cultural Roots and Continuities* (Witt, 1980), contained two selections that the clergyman and his followers deemed particularly offensive: Aristophanes's play *Lysistrata* and "The Miller's Tale" from Chaucer's *The Canterbury Tales*. With little hesitation, the school board gave the building principal absolute authority to remove the text and any other curricular materials that he felt might be objectionable. (The banished text was the only humanities book on the state-approved list in 1986.) A Lake City parent, who was at that time a doctoral student in English at Florida State University, sued the school and the school board under the First Amendment. Once again, the case drew the attention of the national media.

In late January 1988, U.S. District Court Justice Susan Black upheld the right of the school board to banish the text. In her decision, Justice Black cited as precedent the January 1988 (2 weeks earlier) *Hazelwood v. Kuhlmeier* journalism case, laying emphasis on the powers bestowed by that decision on the building principal. Reacting to this decision, the plaintiff voiced the feelings of many people when she said, "It's one thing to censor 17-year-old writers in a school paper, but it's another thing to censor Chaucer and Aristophanes" (Johnson, 1994, p. 112). Nevertheless, the decision of the District Court was upheld at the 11th U.S. Circuit Court of Appeals in January 1989. In his written opinion, Justice R. Lanier Anderson wrote, "Of course, we do not endorse the [school] board's decision.... We seriously question how young persons just below the age of majority can be harmed by these masterpieces of Western literature. However, having concluded that there is no constitutional violation, our role is not to second guess the wisdom of the board's action" (Johnson, 1994, p. 133). The court went on to point out the opinion that in issues of curriculum, schools have been accorded greater control over expression than they may enjoy in other spheres of activity. The plaintiff decided to carry the case to the Supreme Court despite both of the setbacks she experienced and the unwillingness of the American Civil Liberties Union to continue their support of her petition. As this chapter is being written, more than 10 years have elapsed, and the Court has as yet not been willing to hear the case.

James Anthony Whitson, previously quoted regarding the *Island Trees v. Pico* case, also examined the interrelationships among censorship adjudication, school implementation of curricula, and community activism in relation to the *Hazelwood* decision. According to Whitson (1998), this case has had a broad impact on students' right to read, listen, view, write, and speak, as well as teachers' right to teach in a manner they deem effective, and principals' roles as curricular leaders in their schools:

> In *Hazelwood* (1988), the Supreme Court decided that a high school principal had not violated the First Amendment rights of students when he censored a student newspaper by removing the pages that included articles that he considered inappropriate. Although the case itself involved only this one conflict over the contents of a student newspaper, the sweeping language of the Court's majority opinion made it clear that this decision would have profound and far-ranging implications for censorship-related issues involving not only student newspapers, but school plays, library holdings, and even assigned readings and classroom instruction in the school courses themselves. As one high school principal stated flatly, in justifying his own censorship action: "As you're aware, a Supreme Court ruling allows principals to censor" (*Newsletter on Intellectual Freedom*, 1991).
>
> In large part, the eventual legacy of *Hazelwood* may depend on whether educators do, in fact, take on the responsibility of exercising their authority in such a way as to enhance the intellectual freedom and capabilities of their students. When we focus on this question, we can see that those who fear,

instead, the onset of an "Orwellian nightmare" in the wake of *Hazelwood*, do so precisely on the basis of a fear that the discretionary authority that the Supreme Court has recognized for school officials might not always be used by educators for real educational purposes. (p. 3)

The power over curriculum bestowed on principals by *Hazelwood* will continue to reverberate throughout the school systems of the United States into the foreseeable future. The attitudes, intellectual awareness, and curricular backgrounds of these administrators has been touched on in Chapter 4 and will be further considered in Chapter 9. If the past performance of the professional organizations currently representing school principals is any harbinger, the prognosis of curricular leadership on their part is not overly optimistic.

Challenging the Curriculum

The Significance of the Hatch Amendment

In August 1978 Senator Orrin Hatch (R-Utah) introduced an amendment to the General Education Provisions Act that provided a wedge for those who disagreed with the curricular decisions made by many education professionals. Originally passed by Congress in 1979, the amendment is formally titled The Protection of Pupil Rights Amendment, and was further amended under the "Goals 2000: Educate America Act" on March 31, 1994. It is more commonly called "the Hatch Amendment." The complete text of this amendment follows:

Sec. 439.(a) All instructional material, including teacher's manuals, films, tapes, or other supplementary material which will be used in connection with any survey, analysis, or evaluation as part of any applicable program shall be available for inspection by the parents or guardians of the children. (b) No student shall be required, as part of any applicable program, to submit to a survey, analysis, or evaluation that reveals information concerning:

- political affiliations;
- mental and psychological problems potentially embarrassing to the student or his family;
- sex behavior and attitudes;
- illegal, anti-social, self-incriminating and demeaning behavior;
- critical appraisals of other individuals with whom respondents have close family relationships;
- legally recognized privileged and analogous relations, such as those of lawyers, physicians, and ministers; or

- income (other than that required by law to determine eligibility for participation in a program or for receiving financial assistance under such program), without the prior consent of the student (if the student is an adult or emancipated minor), or in the case of unemancipated minor, without the prior written consent of the parent. (Protection of Pupil Rights Amendment, 1994, http://www.freerepublic.com/forum/a3702579e0817.htm)

Briefly, the amendment establishes two principles: parental access and parental consent. First, schools must make available to parents all instructional materials used in connection with federally funded research or experimental programs or projects in which their children are involved. Second, schools operating such programs or projects must obtain written parental permission before requiring a student to submit to certain kinds of psychiatric or psychological testing or treatment when the primary purpose is to reveal information concerning any of those seven areas listed under Sec. 439(b).

When the Hatch Amendment was passed in 1979, it evoked little discussion among educators. The principle of prior parental consent for psychological testing in experimental projects had already been established in congressional legislation 4 years earlier; indeed, the principle of parental access to instructional materials had long been observed even without such a mandate. Where adopting materials was a matter of local option, many schools had opened access to such materials prior to their adoption. Federal regulations concerning implementation of the Hatch Amendment that were announced in early 1980 by the Department of Education consisted largely of a restatement of the provisions of the law and some further definitions of terms. Among educators there seemed little new policy about which to be concerned.

But if the Hatch Amendment elicited little discussion among educators, it encouraged considerable discussion among pressure groups who saw great potential in the amendment for restricting the school curriculum and controlling teaching methods. The frequent and often enthusiastic alliance of the Reagan and Bush administrations with conservative and fundamentalist causes provided momentum to these pressure groups and encouraged them to press forward with their efforts.

Led by the Reverend Pat Robertson, founder and director of the (now defunct) National Legal Foundation, an emerging group of ultraconservative organizations sought increasingly to use the Hatch Amendment as a lever to control school curricula. The nature and constituencies of these groups will be described later in this chapter, but their primary objective was to assert parents' rights in decisions concerning materials of all kinds in their children's (and, by extension, *all* children's) education as well as the manner in which curricular goals were conveyed in the classroom. The 1980 landslide election of Republican President Ronald Reagan, accompanied by the downfall of such senatorial leaders as Gaylord Nelson (D-Wisconsin), John Culver (D-Iowa), Warren Magnuson (D-Washington), Frank Church (D-Idaho), Birch Bayh (D-Indiana), and George McGovern (D-South Dakota) provided further impetus to these activists.

Legal Battles Over Curriculum Content

A number of challenges to curricular decisions—some made by school systems, others by legislative mandates—have arisen over the past two decades. Laws passed in Louisiana and Arkansas in the early 1980s determined that creationism would be granted equal time with evolution in required high school science classes. Both were overturned at the U.S. Circuit Court of Appeals. In Tennessee, a large group of parents petitioned certain school systems to prohibit their children from being provided early reading instruction through certain "secular humanist" materials. They, too, were shot down by the courts. In Alabama in 1984, a district court judge ruled that some 44 instructional (print) materials were inappropriate for use in the schools (all were on the state-adopted list) because of their secular humanist leanings. That decision got the judge some space in *Time* and *Newsweek* magazines, a couple of features in the international press, and interviews on CNN. His ruling, however, was quickly reversed at the Circuit Appeals Court.

Another court case, one that pitted a citizens' group called CHOICE (Citizens Having Options In Their Children's Education) against the Bay County (Florida) School Board, illustrates the profound effect that ultraconservatives can have on curricular decision making:

Late in the spring of 1986, a fundamentalist parent entered Mowat Junior High School in Panama City, Florida, to complain about her daughter's having to read *I Am the Cheese*, a novel by Robert Cormier (1977). Although over 90% of the parents polled by the school had given their consent to the all-class use of the book, the parent refused the teacher's offer of an alternative selection for her daughter. She demanded, instead, that all copies of the book be removed from the school. The English department, chosen that year by the National Council of Teachers of English (NCTE) as a "center for excellence," refused that demand. The parent went to the (elected) county superintendent and reiterated her demand. An active member of a local Assembly of God church, the superintendent ordered that book, plus two other "young adult" novels (*About David* by Susan Pfeffer and *Never Cry Wolf* by Farley Mowat) to be removed immediately. The county school board backed his decision. The teachers resisted, groups supporting both sides of the issue organized, and the school board dealt with the petitions late that summer.

The confrontation swelled and exploded early in 1987. A group of teachers and parents had filed suit in the U.S. District Court. Rigid guidelines for book selection and retention were imposed unilaterally by the superintendent. In April, he threw out 64 books in current use in the high school English courses, noting that there was "some profanity" in each one. All of Shakespeare's plays were removed; so were such classic works as *Oedipus Rex*, *Wuthering Heights*, *Animal Farm*, *Call of the Wild*, and *The Red Badge of Courage*. The community was thrown into an uproar. Two weeks later, the school board overruled the superintendent and restored all of the books. The board retained its original guidelines, however, and in the fall refused the Mowat teachers' request to restore *I Am the Cheese*. By the end of the calendar year, the beleaguered but prayerful superintendent announced that he would not run for re-election in 1988. (Simmons, 1990, p. 119)

John Simmons, one of the authors of this book, was coordinating a graduate English Education degree program at the Florida State University–Panama City Campus at the time, and was the major advisor to the Mowat teachers. During the course of this case, Simmons was verbally attacked by one of the incensed citizens during a Rotary Club luncheon as being the true malefactor who had brought his university's "godless" curriculum to Bay County. Also, he was deposed by one of the CHOICE attorneys in a suit that was settled for the CHOICE plaintiffs some years later. On a more significant level, the leader of the Mowat English teachers, Gloria Pipkin of Panama City, was in 1989 given a Courage Foundation award for bravery in adhering to her principles on a controversial issue. Her fellow awardees that year were U.S. Surgeon General C. Everett Koop, Securities and Exchange Chair Paul Volcker, and New York City District Attorney Rudolph Giuliani. That same year, Pipkin resigned her teaching position under pressure from certain elements of the local community.

Organizations Attempting to Influence Curriculum

Earlier in this chapter, mention was made of the rise of a number of organizations whose avowed goals include the exertion of strong influence over public school curricula in the United States. Although some of these organizations have been in existence for a long time, most of them have been established during the period ranging from 1970 to date and have grown rapidly, both in membership and financial strength. These groups represent both the left and right wing ends of the political spectrum; the "both ends" also refers to the fact that many of these views—on U.S. society in general and on appropriate school materials in particular—seem to be extremist to most of that vast, largely uncommitted population, often referred to as "Middle America."

The Moral Majority.   Once a great presence under the leadership of the Reverend Jerry Falwell, the organization is now defunct. It flourished during the 8 years of the Reagan administration, and has dissipated since.

The Citizens United for Responsible Education.   Another Christian fundamentalist group that was once extremely active, CURE is now moribund. Once the group's leader, the Reverend Jimmy Swaggart, became embroiled in personal problems, CURE faded away.

The Christian Coalition.   A relatively new and increasingly powerful consortium, the Christian Coalition originally was under the leadership of the Reverend Pat Robertson. This group is closely allied with Robertson's National Legal Foundation and his Christian Broadcasting Network's 700 Club. Many disaffected followers of Falwell, Swaggart, and Jim Bakker have joined the Robertson coalition. They target anything that smacks of "New Age" and "Godless" philosophy in relation to materials and teaching strategies. This is probably the most influential group at present. Ralph Reed was successful in following Robertson as head of this group, but he left in 1997 to become a consultant for conservative agencies. He turned the reins over to the current director, Donald Hodel.

The Eagle Forum.   An Illinois-based political action group with strong orthodox Christian leanings led by Phyllis Schlafly, this group has been intensely opposed to such activities as journal writing in English classes (invasion of privacy), and the use of the Impressions Reading Series (accusations of devil worship, occult happenings, sorcery, etc.). This antifeminist, antiabortion, antisex education, and ultra-right wing group came into prominence as the women's group that most vigorously opposed the Equal Rights Amendment. The Eagle Forum also opposes live rock concerts, successfully lobbying for the San Antonio anti-rock concert legislation; and the group helped inflame legislatures in Florida, Missouri, and Tennessee against pop music lyrics. Tipper Gore of the Parents' Music Resource Center has run an antirock "workshop" for them, which created a cadre of antilyrics lobbyists including Shirley Marvin of Missouri Project Rock and Carol Griffin, Florida's "Key Eagle." This group also wants to see creation theory included in textbooks.

Focus on the Family.   This is a strong national organization under the direction of Dr. James Dobson. With the increasingly extensive and acrimonious debate over abortion rights, the group has grown dramatically. Its monthly magazine has become a major vehicle for the promotion of the Christian lifestyle and regularly features pieces on ultraconservative perspectives on the way to the Good Life. These include criticisms of immoral literary selections, multicultural curricular offerings, gay/lesbian discussions in the classroom, and frank considerations of certain health issues. Focus on the Family supports the American Family Association's media boycotts, the antiabortion tactics of Randall Terry, Phyllis Schlafly's antifeminist Eagle Forum, and other evangelical activities. Leader James Dobson is not a minister, but he is a family values counselor who has preached against parental permissiveness since the 1960s. In addition to being antiabortion, Focus on the Family is pro-school prayer, antievolution, and wary of too much information about the Holocaust being presented in schools. Its board of directors includes Susan Baker, wife of former U.S. Secretary of State James Baker and cofounder of the Parents' Music Resource Center.

Concerned Women of America. A highly popular national organization headed by Beverly LaHaye, Concerned Women of America has led the attack on pro-choice legislation and has been a strong advocate for school prayer and the use of public schools for religiously oriented meetings and events. In 1986, LaHaye and her followers attracted national attention by providing legal, moral, and financial support for 11 fundamentalist parents in Hawkins County, Tennessee, who objected to their children being taught basic reading skills through a Holt, Rinehart & Winston basal series. They claimed that the selections used in this series contained "occultism, secular humanism, pacifism, feminism, and disobedience to parents" (Hulsizer, 1989, p. 20). Although their suit was ultimately turned down by the U.S. Circuit Court, the case gave LaHaye's group inspiration to become major opponents of the Impressions series. Litigation against this series is pending.

Educational Research Analysts' Corporation. This organization has a long and unusual record. Initiated in a small community near Dallas, Texas, it was the brainchild of Mel and Norma Gabler, who decided to invest their time and resources combing through potential state-adopted textbooks for instances of "un-American and un-Christian" elements. From the mid-1970s to the present day, the Gablers have had a significant influence on textbook choice in the nation's second largest state. In the past few years, that influence has diminished somewhat, but Mel and Norma Gabler are still active.

The National Association of Christian Educators (NACE). Headed by Robert L. Simonds, this popular and financially potent organization has been around for a long time. In recent years, however, it has expanded its influence by forming the Citizens for Excellence in Education (CEE). This subgroup has established chapters in hundreds of communities across the United States. The main goal of the CEE is to examine curricula and "to save America's public school children from atheism, homosexuality, the occult, drugs, children having children, abortion, brainwashing and crippling psychology" (http://www.web com.com/webcee/strategy.html). This group has been particularly active in reviewing elementary curricula for evidence of imaging, meditation, witchcraft, and devil worship.

Simonds, in authoring the NACE constitution, included the following three goals as primary in importance: (1) to bring public education back under the control of Christians; (2) to take control of all counterproductive, secular humanist (now "New Age") curricula from local schools; and (3) to take control of all school boards. He's made some progress. In his President's Report of February 1994, he stated, "We are in the process of putting born-again Christians in every school board in America.... A school Board with five members needs only three Christians to take complete control of a school district. You can literally own that system and control all personnel, curriculum, materials, textbooks, and policies" (Marzano, 1994, p. 40).

The American Family Association, with the Reverend Donald Wildmon. The Rev. Wildmon's antipornography crusade through the AFA is a vehicle for censorship that often advocates boycotting the sponsors of "anti-Christian" television shows and the use of motel chains it believes show pornographic (i.e., R-rated) movies. Wildmon orchestrated the campaign that successfully severed Pepsi's sponsorship ties to singer/actress Madonna because of her supposedly blasphemous video for "Like a Prayer," and was at the center of the campaign against Martin Scorsese's film, *The Last Temptation of Christ.* Wildmon's statements about the management of Universal Studios during the latter campaign, along with his publication of a survey of how many Jews work in Hollywood, earned him condemnation as an anti-Semite from, among others, the Roman Catholic Archbishop of St. Louis, the head of the Mennonite church, and the head of one Lutheran synod. Working through such offshoots and affiliates as the National Federation for Decency (NFD) and CleaR-TV (Christian Leaders for Responsible Television), Wildmon boasts of preventing CBS from basing a cartoon series on the Garbage Pail Kids, and of spending $50,000 campaigning for 1988's ultra-repressive Child Protection and Obscenity Enforcement Act.

Because Wildmon is regarded skeptically, many activists tend to shy away from direct identification with him. When one of his publications reprinted a chapter from Tipper Gore's rock-bashing book, *Raising PG Kids in an X-Rated World*, then-Senator Al Gore was forced to issue a statement denying any association with Wildmon and condemning his anti-Semitism. Yet the press rarely mentions this aspect of Wildmon's agenda, and as a result, the threat of a Wildmon boycott often intimidates advertisers. In November 1990, Burger King announced that it was withdrawing its commercials from several television shows to which Wildmon's CleaR-TV objected. The same week, CleaR-TV called off a boycott of Burger King.

National Organization for Women (NOW). This organization consistently adopts pro-censorship positions on subjects ranging from Bret Easton Ellis's novel *American Psycho* to Bruce Springsteen's use of the word "girl" in his song lyrics. NOW is always careful to couch its advocacy of censorship in careful terms, but this left-wing organization uses the same tactics as many right-wing advocates. Sometimes it seems as if NOW wants to be let off the hook because it represents a vulnerable constituency.

NOW has been known, vis-à-vis censorship activism, for its crusades against texts, plays, and films that depict women in stereotypic roles and/or compromised positions. The organization's attack on both Vladimir Nabokov's novel *Lolita* (1961), and the later dramatization of the same title, gained national attention. More recently, NOW's continuing criticism of the work and attitudes of Madonna have been frequent and acerbic.

The National Association for the Advancement of Colored People (NAACP). The presence of the NAACP on this list may come as a surprise to those who have generally viewed this organization as a supporter of equality for all liberal causes. But the great concern of its leaders for texts that place African Americans in pejorative, demeaning roles has sometimes led to the NAACP's opposition to the use of those texts in U.S. classrooms. This opposition has grown in intensity since the early successes of the Civil Rights movement. As early as 1964, the Illinois Chapter of NAACP was temporarily successful in forcing the removal of *The Adventures of Huckleberry Finn* from all public school classrooms in that state. Since that time, and encouraged by the growth of the black middle class, NAACP state and local chapters have campaigned for the novel's removal—meeting with sporadic success over the past 30 years. In the 1990s, that success had grown to the point at which the Twain novel—long a required text in U.S. high schools, junior colleges, and universities had risen to a place in the top five of People for the American Way's 1993 "most censored" list. Other well-known works, written by such celebrated authors as William Faulkner, John Steinbeck, John Updike, Walker Percy, and Lillian Hellman, to name a few, have also been questioned for use in classrooms. Interestingly, the writing of celebrated African American authors such as Toni Morrison, Alice Walker, James Baldwin, Toni Cade Bambarra, August Wilson, and others who depict the plight of African Americans seem to have avoided such attacks. Clearly, the impetus of the political correctness movement has added fuel to the NAACP's book-banning fires.

The Family Research Council. This relatively new organization led by Gary Bauer grew rapidly in numbers during the 1990s. It shares many of the goals and precepts of companion groups such as the Christian Coalition, Focus on the Family, and the American Family Association, and it has attacked certain liberal targets ferociously. The Council was outspoken in its support of former Vice President Dan Quayle's denouncement of the television show *Murphy Brown* and his attendant espousal of family values in 1992. The group's presence in the presidential election during the fall of that year logically followed, strongly supporting the orthodox positions on family expressed in the Republican National Platform. Its leadership also provided funds, phone banks, and door-to-door support for Republican candidate Michael Farris in his campaign for the lieutenant governorship of Virginia in 1994, as well as giving firm backing to Oliver North in his senatorial bid that same year. This organization was one of the most vocal attackers of President Clinton during the months of the Monica Lewinsky ordeal. It is axiomatic that Bauer and his colleagues are firm opponents of literature that, in their opinion, reflects secular humanist or "New Age" perspectives on life in the United States.

John Birch Society (JBS). One of the most venerable organizations in the censorship business, the JBS has stood since the Cold War beside such time-honored groups as The American Legion, the Daughters of the Revolution, and the Daughters of the Confederacy to oppose anything that might challenge "the American Way of Life"—as they define that "way." JBS founder Robert Welch amassed a fortune creating and administering a candy conglomerate during the years of World War II, and he became a committed anti-Communist crusader at the outset of the Cold War. Welch founded the ultra-conservative *American Opinion* journal in 1956 and followed it with the John Birch Society in 1958. His accusations against supposed Communist agents, "fellow travelers," and sympathizers became increasingly venomous and continued to be so until his death in 1985. His organization continues to exist, but with the death of its founder and the razing of the

Berlin Wall in 1989, it has pulled back considerably on the scope and intensity of its activities.

During its salad days, the JBS was deeply concerned with any materials found in schools and libraries that contained any hint of left-wing ideology. Inspired by Hollywood blacklisting and the success of Senator Joseph McCarthy, the group devoted great amounts of time and energy to exposing "Communistic" materials in U.S. schools. Although the prime target of such investigation was social studies (especially history), literature choices also received extensive review. So it was that the works of John Hersey, Sherwood Anderson, Robert E. Sherwood, Sinclair Lewis, Kurt Vonnegut, and John Steinbeck became the object of complaints and challenges due to their "unpatriotic" nature. For some reason, the racial epithets in *The Adventures of Huckleberry Finn* were never criticized by the John Birch Society.

To further illustrate the attitudes and feelings of some of the highly visible supporters of such groups as those listed here, we present the following statements from various censorship advocates:

> *There is nothing in the U.S. Constitution that sanctifies the separation of church and state.* (Pat Robertson, televangelist/founder of the Christian Coalition, 1984)

> *The Supreme Court's school prayer decisions were bad law, bad history and bad culture. It was just wrong.... And if the court doesn't want to reverse itself, then we have an absolute obligation to pass a constitutional amendment to instruct the court of its error.* (Newt Gingrich, former Speaker of the U.S. House of Representatives, 1994)

> *I want to be invisible. I do guerrilla warfare. I paint my face and travel at night. You don't know it's over until you're in a body bag. You don't know until election night.* (Ralph Reed, Christian Coalition [quoted in Alley, 1991])

> *Modern public education is the most dangerous single force in a child's life: religiously, sexually, economically, patriotically and physically.* (Reverend Tim LaHaye, cofounder, Moral Majority and Concerned Women of America [quoted in Marsh, 1991])

> *I hope I live to see the day when, as in the early days of our country, we won't have any public schools. The churches will have taken them over again and Christians will be running them.* (Reverend Jerry Falwell, founder, Moral Majority [quoted in Hulsizer, 1989])

Attitudes such as these have contributed enormously to the continuing attempts to legislate censorship in the United States. The persistent growth of the Christian Right contributes to a climate of fear and suspicion—an "us against them" mentality in which those supporting censorship defend themselves as "God-fearing" and "concerned" citizens who worry about the morality of their children's schools and who are justified in defending themselves against the attacks of liberal "pagans." Two parents' rights excerpts from a 1991 issue of *Citizen*, published by Focus on the Family, demonstrate this attitude:

> Throughout the nation, parents who try to play an active role in their children's education are increasingly ridiculed and demeaned. Using terms like "censorship" and "attacks on freedom," liberal groups have painted parents who exercise their democratic rights as fascists bent on suppressing free expression.
>
> "It used to be that censorship was considered an act by government to keep certain information from the public," said John Whitehead, president of the Rutherford Institute, a Christian legal foundation. "Now, if citizens attempt to influence the government—in this case the schools—that is called censorship. But it goes on every day. Every special interest group in Washington is trying to wield influence."
>
> Whitehead said that by seizing the censorship debate, liberal groups are promoting their own agendas while keeping others out.
>
> "There was a time when censorship was used to protect the public good. Today certain groups are using it as a way to beat back decent people who want to see some sort of moral standards in the classroom." (Ebert, 1991, pp. 1–6)

And consider this statement by Greg R. Jesson in the same publication:

> [I]n recent years, "censor" has been applied by liberals to anyone who disagrees with them. If you don't want your tax dollars to subsidize profane art, you are a "censor." If a publisher doesn't want to publish a violent novel, he is a "censor." If a local cable system refuses to carry MTV, it is a "censor."
>
> As the word "censorship" has come to be applied to almost anything, it has come to mean nothing.... If a parent expresses concern over a child's third-grade reader, for example, the parent is a "censor," according to People for the American Way, the National Education Association and other like-minded groups.... How do parents refute the charge that they are "censors"?
>
> Point out this unexpected consequence: "If my attempting to restrict what you teach my children constitutes censorship, then you attempting to restrict what I can disagree with does, too. If my disagreeing with you is censorship, then you disagreeing with me is also. You can't have it both ways; if one is censorship, then they both are." (Jesson, 1991, pp. 2–3)

Convoluted "Catch-22" thinking such as this only serves to confuse the issue of what censorship really is and how the restriction of free thinking and ideas can ultimately undermine the goals of U.S. democratic society. Disagreeing with a person or group's attempts to censor materials, and referring to these persons as "censors," does not amount to censorship unless those individuals or groups' freedom of speech is denied or restricted.

Meanwhile, legal challenges by left-wing censors continue to undermine school curricula as well. From the other side of the spectrum, Mark Walsh, writing in the November 5, 1995, issue of the *San Francisco Examiner* made the following comments about a controversial censorship case in Arizona:

> The parent, Kathy Monteiro, alleged that the assignment of *Huckleberry Finn* and the William Faulkner short story "A Rose for Emily," which also uses the racial epithet ["nigger"], in her daughter's freshman English class amounted to racial harassment.
>
> Her lawsuit also alleged that her daughter and other African-American students at McClintock High School in Tempe, Ariz., were subjected to racial taunts from other students, which increased after the assignment of the Twain and Faulkner works. School district officials did not respond to the complaints of racial harassment, the suit contended.
>
> Ms. Monteiro sued the Tempe Union High School District under the 14th Amendment's equal-protection clause and Title VI of the Civil Rights Act of 1964, which prohibits racial discrimination in programs receiving federal funding.
>
> A federal district court threw the lawsuit out. The 9th Circuit court upheld the lower court's ruling on challenges to controversial literary works, but it reinstated the portion of the suit alleging that district officials failed to respond to racial harassment of Ms. Monteiro's daughter by other students. (Walsh, 1995 [quoted in *Education Weekly*, 1997])

Also quoted in the article was a San Francisco-based appellate panel, which stated, "Permitting lawsuits against school districts on the basis of the content of literary works...could have a significant chilling effect on a school district's willingness to assign books with themes, characters, snippets of dialogue, or words that might offend the sensibilities of any number of persons or groups."

Strident censorship disputes that find their way to the courtroom have increased dramatically in recent years, due in part to the number of local, state, and national organizations that have chosen to enter the censorship fray. Both left- and right-wing organizations have helped support this rise in litigation, backing individuals as they take challenges to educational materials in their schools to court. Challenges to specific texts or publications, however, are now also being augmented with challenges to overall curriculum, especially by members of the Christian Right who have increased their efforts to use legislation to impose their values and religious views on the United States educational system. The legislative climate in the United States has gone through dramatic swings in the last two decades of the 20th century. The elected and appointed officials of the next administration will face difficult choices about our democratic ideals and the lengths to which they will allow certain factions of U.S. society to dictate the morality of the country as a whole.

RECOMMENDED WEB SITES

700 Club
http://www.cbn.org/the700club

The American Family Association
http://www.afa.net

The Christian Coalition
http://www.cc.org
http://www.cbn.org/about/bios/pat.robertson.asp

Citizens for Excellence in Education
http://www.nace-cee.org

The Citizens United for Responsible Education
http://www.eskimo.com/~cure

Concerned Women of America
http://www.cwfa.org

Family Research Council
http://www.frc.org

Focus on the Family
http://fotf.org
http://www.family.org

National Association for the Advancement of Colored People
http://www.naacp.org

National Legal Foundation
http://www.nlf.net

National Organization for Women
http://www.now.org

Protection of Pupil Rights (Hatch Amendment)
http://www.freerepublic.com/forum/a3702579e0817.htm

CHAPTER 9

Reasonable Responses to Censorship

It is better to light one candle than curse the darkness.

—Motto of the Christopher Society

Picture this scenario: A newly graduated, certified language arts teacher accepts a position in a middle or high school in a moderately sized community, which, she later learns, is led politically and spiritually by rather conservative council and church members. She is assigned to the basic classes, where students are largely unmotivated, and she also has last pick of available teaching materials. In an attempt to get the students involved, she photocopies a short story that clearly violates one or more of the taboos discussed in Chapters 4 and 5. Then the landscape darkens.

An angry parent storms into her classroom, or maybe the principal's office, demanding that the text be removed immediately and that the teacher show cause of why she distributed this "filthy" selection. A well-connected member of the community, he threatens action against the teacher in question. As is often the case, the principal waffles. When he realizes that he cannot assuage the outraged parent, he moves in certain predictable directions: He orders the text removed at once and calls the teacher, and possibly her department head, into his office for admonishment, declaring that such choices will not be tolerated in the future. At the end of the school year, he writes a negative evaluation of this first-year teacher and indicates to her that a continuing contract (tenure) is not likely for her at this school. Soon after learning of her fate, she seeks another opening in another community, pleading with her principal not to give her a questionable letter of recommendation.

Could this tragic sequence of events have been avoided? Maybe, maybe not. As indicated in Chapter 1, an imposing number of censorship complaints and challenges are totally unexpected, idiosyncratic, narrowly reasoned, and charged with emotion. An Associated Press piece by Judie Glave, published in the November 26, 1998, issue of the *Tallahassee Democrat*, demonstrates how inflammatory the opposition to books can become, and how easily teachers can find themselves in the midst of controversy:

162

Teacher Is Threatened for Using Ethnic Book

A white teacher who had to be taken out of her New York City classroom after community members complained she used a racially insensitive book says her life was threatened and she may not return.

"They had to sneak me out of the school," Ruth Sherman, a third grade teacher at Public School 75 in Brooklyn, said Wednesday. "They were screaming racial slurs and profanities at me." She said one woman lunged at her and threatened her saying, "You'd just better watch it."

Asked if that was a threat, the woman replied "It's not a threat. It's a promise," according to Sherman. She said she did not recognize her as a parent of anyone in the school.

The children's book that caused the furor in the largely black and Hispanic community is the critically acclaimed *Nappy Hair*. Written by black author Carolivia Herron, the book—which celebrates racial differences—is recommended for classroom use by Columbia University's Teacher's College.

Sherman said 50 community residents confronted her at a school meeting Monday. Only one was a parent of a student in her class. She said that parents had photocopied pages of the book, taken out of context and distributed them through the neighborhood, with a note about her.

The author defended Sherman.

"She could have taught *Mary Had a Little Lamb*, or some other books that had nothing to do with the African-American culture," Herron said in a telephone interview from Chico, Calif., where she is an assistant professor of English at California State University.

"Instead, she tried to relate to the culture of the children she was teaching."

The teachers union said District Superintendent Felix Vasquez told Sherman to report to district headquarters instead of her classroom pending further investigation.

Later Tuesday, school officials decided the book was appropriate classroom material and Sherman could return to the classroom Monday, though they still said the book should have been cleared with the principal.

Sherman says she's not sure how she'll respond to the invitation to return to class.

"I am afraid to go back to that area, not only the school but the area because my life was threatened," Sherman said. At the same time, she said she has received many calls of support from colleagues and gotten flowers from parents who want her back.

"She's a wonderful teacher," said Lydia Flores, mother of 8-year-old Jennifer. "You don't find teachers like that."

Dennis Herring, president of District 32's school board, said the entire incident was the result of miscommunication. He said the photocopies did not properly relay what the book was really about. Taken out of context, he said, "it looks like pictures to degrade African Americans."

Told in a gospel-like, call-and-response style, the book is about a little girl with the "nappiest, fuzziest, the most screwed up, squeezed up, knotted up" hair. It received rave reviews, including one from the *New York Times*. (Glave, 1998, p. A3) (Reprinted with permission of The Associated Press)

Any teacher is vulnerable—the neophyte described in the opening of this chapter, an experienced teacher who moves to a school in an unfamiliar community, or even a teacher who is well established in his or her school or town. Classroom teachers need to stay alert to the political, social, and cultural atmosphere that affects all phases of public school life. New city and county commissioners are elected, new clergy assume leadership of various churches, and, most pertinently, new school board members are chosen by the people. In 1994, three candidates, all heavily supported by the local Christian Coalition chapter, were elected to the five-member school board of a rural Central Florida county. One of the new board's first acts was to mandate that all relevant curricula be modified to indicate the superiority of white Caucasians to other racial/ethnic groups. This decision received widespread publicity in Florida and elsewhere. Two years later, one of these school board members had resigned and another was defeated at the polls, but the damage had been done. Imagine the situation of a senior high school social studies department head during that 2-year interlude!

"Aeterna Vigilia": Awareness for Educators

The old Latin axiom, *aeterna vigilia est pretium libertatis* (eternal vigilance is the price of liberty), is especially relevant to today's public school teachers. The best advice to give teachers, administrators, and librarians is to be proactive—as well as alert. Proactivity is anticipating complaints and challenges from virtually any direction. Teachers should know their materials extremely well and stand ready to defend their inclusion in the curriculum.

Because any text can be challenged, it is necessary for teachers to analyze their choices for possible multiple interpretations. Proponents of the Reader Response movement in literary study have claimed that a writer ceases to be involved in determining the meaning of a text once he or she has completed it—the meaning of the finished text is made by the reader. Even if a text seems to contain a clear and valuable meaning to a teacher, the majority of his or her students, and most parents and citizens, it only takes one challenger with a vastly different perception to stir up a hornets' nest of controversy. Teachers should, therefore, examine all texts—especially those to be studied by the entire class—for possible alternate meanings. Those that could conceivably generate debate on some touchy issue need to be shared with fellow faculty members and, most importantly, the building principal. Communication with district curriculum supervisors is also a good idea.

This caution does not represent a belief that all significant-but-controversial issues found in texts should be avoided by teachers. First, there are no "safe" texts, and trying to find universally accepted materials is a waste of time and energy. Second, there is the undeniable goal of education, particularly in the upper grades, that school should be an institution that assists in preparing young people for an informed, insightful, and appropriately realistic introduction into the adult world. The choices of the right materials to meet that goal will be debated forever, but this does not imply that teachers should include *Naked Lunch* or *Tropic of Cancer* in their programs of study—common sense should always be exercized in text selection.

It is in preparing substantial, persuasive rationales for valuable materials that teachers' academic backgrounds come into play. Teachers should keep handy bibliographies of scholarship related to the texts they are teaching. It is also helpful to read journals that offer new, meaningful insights into worthwhile selections both new and old (they're still writing about *Hamlet*, after all). Keeping a dossier of scholarly and professional literature (*English Journal, Social Education, Journal of Adolescent & Adult Literacy*, etc.)—or at least knowing where to locate these resources on the Internet or in the media center—will help teachers by providing a stockpile of professional "backup" for their curricular literary choices.

Of particular concern is the distinctive dilemma of middle school and junior high school teachers and librarians as they try to defend selections categorized as young adult (YA) literature. For example, when teachers are questioned about the use of *Romeo and Juliet* (the text, not the film) in their courses of study, they have a very large fund of academic reference sources to which they can allude. That is not the case for teachers who use YA texts, most of which are about contemporary life and few of which are supported by abundant scholarly literature. Teachers who make YA selections for their classes would do well to familiarize themselves with the *ALAN Review*, a publication of the National Council of Teachers of English (NCTE), and the *Journal of Adolescent & Adult Literacy*, a publication of the International Reading Association (IRA). A number of other texts, which will be described later in this chapter, are also helpful in establishing sound rationales for text choices.

Materials available for teachers to use as defense against complaints regarding commercial films, videotaped dramas or documentaries, and CD-ROMs are a bit more problematic. The current rating system for Hollywood films is not very helpful—but teachers should keep in mind that the showing of R-rated films in the classroom is a dicey choice at best. Thus, while the study of the text of *Romeo and Juliet* is broadly defensible, the showing of the recent film is another matter. Media personnel in the school, public library, and district curricular office are the best and most immediate consultants for teachers in need of assistance on this issue. It is unwise for a teacher to assign a text, show a film, or play a taped song whose contents of which have not been closely scrutinized beforehand.

Teachers also need to have a background in district policy regarding subject matter appropriate for class study. If a district does not have such a policy expressed in clear, unequivocal language, one should be formulated. In case after case of censorship controversy, the underlying problem has been the lack of policy at the district level. Almost invariably, such districts go through an ordeal of emotional, extended arguments with community members who represent both sides of the censorship challenge—neither of which typically is willing to back off or even compromise. If ever the old adage "An ounce of prevention is worth a pound of cure" applies, it is in this type of situation. If no official school board policy is in place, it is professionally sound for a group of teachers and media specialists to approach the governing body with a request that one be created. These school personnel should be eager to serve on a committee to hammer out such a policy. After all, educators are taxpayers, too.

At the state level, teachers and other interested school personnel should investigate whatever set of criteria exists for selection of instructional materials. As noted earlier, that search is much easier in those 27 states that have a statewide adoption policy. Awareness of the statements and actions of officially appointed textbook evaluation committees should be part of the "aeterna vigilia" posture of all educators who wish to be genuinely proactive. It also would be helpful for teachers to petition the Commissioner of Education in their state to publicize the NCTE's *Students' Right to Read* (Donelson, 1972) commitment as part of their presentation to the committee in question. Contacting local legislative members regarding the stance taken by most professionals on this issue is also a potentially valuable activity. Over the years, it has not been uncommon for the citizenry to regard teacher activism as suspect or even inappropriate. Significantly, there are also many teachers who harbor such skepticism. But in the matter of blunting irrational censorship vendettas, teachers need to accept the proposition that they are in the best position to influence statewide decisions.

Teachers should also be attentive to the rhetoric emanating from candidates during their campaigns for public office. When candidates stress issues such as "parents' rights," "questionable teaching materials and approaches," or "Christian morality" as fundamental in their appeal to the voters, educators need to start a portfolio on such aspirants. Their actions, upon election, are frequently more extreme than they were during their campaign days. Letters to such elected officials early in their term of office, reminding them of what they did or did not promise their public school teacher constituency, are a smart idea.

Anticensorship Tactics for Teachers

There are quite a few concrete, immediate, and school-related tactics that may anticipate or deflect the kinds of censorship episodes described earlier in this chapter. (Note: A particular set of suggestions, labeled "Outreach," has been saved for Chapter 10.) The following guidelines should be kept uppermost in teachers' minds as they select texts for study in their classrooms:

Clear all selections that might even hint of controversy with appropriate superiors—high school department heads, middle school team leaders, assistant principals for curriculum, even the principal him/herself. The unhappy new-in-town teacher described in the scenario that began this chapter could have avoided, or at least significantly reduced, her problems by taking such steps. Because censorship challenges can come from virtually any direction, it is advisable to take such insurance action with all materials proposed for classroom use.

Ask the head of the media center/library in your school to peruse all materials lists—both print and nonprint—before you distribute them in your classes. It is the media specialist who knows about availability, potential dangers in wide-reading selections, and past incidents of complaints about certain texts or films. The media center/library specialist may have filed annotations concerning questionable materials. The strong intellectual freedom stance of the ALA is usually reflected in the positions taken by these professionals, and they often have good advice about how to ward off problems.

Solicit and, when possible, save students' responses to any material that you even vaguely suspect contains elements of controversy. The "save" suggestion obviously applies only to written responses. The establishment and maintenance of portfolios is high on the list of writing instruction authorities at this time. Saving what your students write can be enormously valuable when some irate parent charges into your room demanding to know why his or her child was exposed to such "filth."

Showing this parent your students' written responses—that never allude to the allegedly filthy elements—could well have a calming effect.

Prepare lists of alternate choices for texts you feel may be objectionable for one reason or another. Be sure that texts from such lists are available in your classroom, your department's workroom, or in the media center/library. These alternate choices should be consistent with the objectives of the instructional unit in which they are to be included. Teachers may not have the time to read each title on an alternative choices list, but becoming familiar with them is an important antidote to parental objections to what their children have been assigned to read. The NCTE text, *Reading Ladders for Human Relations* (Tway, 1981), will provide a useful resource in this. (Note: In making up alternate choices lists, request copies of texts you know are not available from your librarian. Such texts should be placed on the next year's list of library acquisitions. Librarians often complain of not receiving enough input from teachers as they prepare their acquisition requests.)

Prepare a letter to be sent home describing the subject matter and style of the potentially objectionable material. Include a space in the letter that allows the parents to indicate their approval or disapproval of this text as an assignment that is suitable for their child. Urge parents to return the reply either with their child or by mail. Encourage them to contact you with any further substantive questions about the text or the manner in which it will be presented. It is not unreasonable to assume that some highly productive dialogue could be initiated by such letters and requests for feedback. The value of alternate choices and parental permission requests has been reported by many teachers—it seems to be a consistently effective means of warding off parental complaints.

Use the censorship unit as a proactive strategy. One of this book's authors learned of a particularly good strategy a few years ago from Mrs. D, who was, at the time, supervising a Florida State University student teacher in English. Mrs. D is a lifelong resident of the small, rural, Central Florida community in which she teaches 10th- and 11th-grade language arts. She is also the director of the choir at the First Baptist Church where her husband is a deacon. It is safe to say that she is a well-respected member of her community.

Early each school year Mrs. D assigns her 10th-grade classes a potentially censorable novel. Some of her recent choices have included Steinbeck's *Of Mice and Men*, Huxley's *Brave New World*, Salinger's *Catcher in the Rye*, and Vonnegut's *Slaughterhouse Five*. In distributing the text, Mrs. D assigns her students to one of two debate teams—one team will argue for and one against the censorship of the book in question. At the same time, she sends a note home to her students' parents that announces the debate and offers them the option of precluding their child from it. She also invites parents' input in, and attendance at, the debate. Mrs. D gives her students three class periods of research time to prepare their arguments. She then referees the debate, awarding points for pertinence of contributions and clarity of statements rendered. She names a winner at the conclusion of the debate, and then assigns the students an essay in which they defend either point of view based on what they have concluded through participation.

Through the use of this strategy, Mrs. D defuses most, if not all, potential parent challenges. She acquaints her students with reasons why books are attacked, as well as how they are defended. Finally, she leads them in the study of an acclaimed work of fiction using the censorship debate as a preteaching tool. She claims this procedure has never failed her.

Show visible support for fellow teachers whose choices of materials or approaches have been challenged. Teachers should support colleagues who are under fire from individuals or groups who accuse them of making unacceptable choices of study material. That support should be expressed in writing to district school superintendents, school board members, local text selection oversight committees, and the community at large through letters to the editor of the local or regional newspaper. Remembering the any-text-at-any-time warning issued earlier in this chapter, fellow teachers would be well advised to rally around their beleaguered fellow professionals. They may return the favor at a future time.

The importance of community and professional support during a censorship controversy is illustrated in the highly popular monograph *Stifled Laughter* (Johnson, 1994), in which a woman recounts the turmoil she experienced when fighting the removal of a text in her local high school's 12th-grade elective humanities class. In the late 1980s, Claudia Johnson was a community college English teacher at Lake City Community College in Lake City, Florida. She learned one day of the interventionist actions of the principal of Columbia County High School who, at the insistence of a local fundamentalist minister, had removed from the class the state adopted text *The Humanities: Classical Roots and Cultural Traditions*. The Columbia County School Board had upheld the removal by a vote of 5–0. (For a full description of this case, see Chapter 8, pp. 147–148.)

Ms. Johnson was outraged and brought suit against the principal and the school board in Federal District Court under the First Amendment. This action did not come at a propitious time for Ms. Johnson, who was, aside from her teaching duties, a homemaker, a mother of two teenage children, and a doctoral student at Florida State University. In staying with her litigation, Ms. Johnson experienced unpleasantness in the form of hate mail, threats, obscene phone calls, and vilification of her children. The most discouraging aspect of the entire episode, however, was the feeling of loneliness she experienced. Fellow teachers at the community college avoided her. So did her neighbors. Members of her church, including her minister, looked the other way. At gasoline stations, in malls, and in the supermarkets, some people made cruel and obscene remarks. An occasional female, an erstwhile friend, would sidle up to her in the frozen food section and whisper a word of terse, nervous encouragement. But that was about it for community "support." *Stifled Laughter* is now-Dr. Johnson's account of the whole fiasco—with considerable emphasis placed on what it was like psychologically to confront censorship all alone.

Become aware of the professional and political organizations that offer support and tangible assistance to teachers who are enveloped in the tentacles of a censorship challenge. This is among the most important support mechanisms that can be offered. Claudia Johnson's feeling of alienation from such support is as good a reason as any for thoughtful, pragmatic teachers, at all levels, to familiarize themselves with data of agencies that stand ready, willing, and able to assist teachers under fire.

Helpful Organizational Resources

American Library Association (ALA, 50 East Huron Street, Chicago, Illinois 60611)

Of all the organizations that offer assistance on censorship issues, the ALA is the most comprehensive and may well be the most effective. This is a dedicated, research-based, and intellectually solid organization. The following three services illustrate the kind of help that the ALA provides:

1. Banned Books Week—Each autumn, the group sponsors this celebration in conjunction with the American Booksellers Association, the National American Publishers, and the American Society of Journalists and Authors. In libraries and bookstores all over the United States, the ALA presents a program of authors, aca-

demics, political leaders, newspaper editors, and publishing firm executives who address the right to read and the right to learn issues—along with symposia, student panels, displays, and free literature. Some truly renowned U.S. citizens have been presenters during this popular, well-publicized week of activities. The introduction to the ALA's 1988 resource book, *Celebrating the Freedom to Read*, speaks eloquently to both the goals of the event and the mission of those organizations that proudly sponsor it. (See Appendix C for the complete text of this introduction.)

2. The ALA also publishes a bimonthly *Newsletter on Intellectual Freedom*, created by its Office of Intellectual Freedom, which includes a series of reports on current censorship cases, plus position papers, bibliographies, and more. Its "scoreboard" feature describes cases involving classrooms, school and public libraries, commercial booksellers, music of various kinds, and litigation summaries.

3. The Library Bill of Rights—In 1948, the ALA created a set of guidelines that explicilty explains the basic right to intellectual freedom that people in all parts of the world should be able to enjoy. This list should be displayed in every library and school—public or private—all over the world. The text of this bill appears in Appendix D.

The Association for Supervision and Curriculum Development (ASCD, 1250 North Pitt Street, Alexandria, Virginia 22314-1453)

The mission of this organization spans a wide range of concerns for professional educators in the United States and beyond. It has produced a number of themed issues of its major periodical, *Educational Leadership*, that deal with concerns specific to educational censorship. ASCD also provides a newsletter titled *Update*, which included a question-and-answer dialogue about the right to read in its January 1995 issue. A statement of ASCD's position on censorship was included in a 1983 issue of *Educational Leadership*. It is stated as follows:

The Association for Supervision and Curriculum Development affirms that:

• Parents and other citizens have the right and the responsibility to express their views about the merits and appropriateness of public school curriculum and materials.

• School systems should have well-defined procedures by which concerns can be communicated to school officials and responded to promptly, thoughtfully, and courteously.

- Adoption of such procedures is based on the presumption that some complaints may be valid; that decisions about choice or use of materials are properly subject to reconsideration.

- The best hope for a sound decision when materials are questioned is through use of a predetermined process that ensures thorough consideration of the issues by an objective group. Actions by individuals—whether citizens or educators—that circumvent such deliberations are a threat to individual liberty and democratic process.

- Materials should always be evaluated in reference to educational criteria formulated in advance of any particular controversy.

- As stated by the United States Supreme Court in *Island Trees vs. Pico*, materials must never be removed or restricted for the purpose of suppressing ideas.—*Approved by ASCD Executive Council, October 1982*

(*Educational Leadership*, 1983)

International Reading Association (IRA, 800 Barksdale Road, Box 8139, Newark, Delaware, 19714)

This large, prestigious organization has increased its consideration of right-to-read matters over the past 20 years. Today, issues of its major journals—*The Reading Teacher, Journal of Adolescent & Adult Literacy*, and *Reading Research Quarterly*—as well as its newspaper *Reading Today*, regularly feature pieces on the topic of censorship. IRA's longstanding Committee on Intellectual Freedom established a Joint Task Force on Intellectual Freedom with NCTE in 1991. In 1992, the Task Force produced a pamphlet on the topic, espousing a pro–right-to-read position and offering advice to teachers, especially those at the lower grade levels, who are faced with criticism of their curricular text choices by parents and other citizens. In 1994, the Association published an anthology of articles on school censorship titled *Censorship: A Threat to Reading, Learning, Thinking* (Simmons, 1994), which contains essays on censorship in grades K–12 in an array of content areas. The text also provides suggestions for dealing with the problem. Several key resolutions passed by the Association appear in Appendix G of this text.

National Council of Teachers of English (NCTE, 1111 West Kenyon Road, Urbana, Illinois 61801)

Already cited on several occasions in previous chapters, this organization has stood for the rights to read, learn, and teach for all of its nearly 90-year history. The following is a brief summary of NCTE services and activities:

1. *The Students' Right to Read* pamphlet, reproduced for over 50 years, an excerpt of which is included in Appendix E.
2. The Standing Committee Against Censorship, a long-term, active subgroup of the organization.
3. The Joint Task Force on Intellectual Freedom (with the International Reading Association).
4. The publication of anticensorship texts, including the anthologies *Dealing with Censorship* (Davis, 1979) and *The Students' Right to Know* (Burress & Jenkinson, 1983).
5. The passage of a number of anticensorship resolutions, including a basic one regarding attacks on teachers, abridgments/adaptations, freedom of the student press, and others.

Several of these resolutions can be found in Appendix F. There is one, however, that merits some discussion in this summary, largely because of its impact on one U.S. school district and the political fallout it has created in others. *The Students' Right to Their Own Language* was debated and passed first by the NCTE subgroup, the Conference on College Composition and Communication (CCCC), in 1972 and by the entire Council in 1974. It reads,

> We affirm the students' right to their own patterns and varieties of language—the dialects of their nurture or whatever dialects in which they find their own identity and style. Language scholars long ago denied that the myth of a standard U.S. dialect has any validity. The claim that any one dialect is unacceptable amounts to an attempt of one social group to exert its dominance over another. Such a claim leads to false advice for speakers and writers, and immoral advice for humans. A nation proud of its diverse heritage and its cultural and racial variety will preserve its heritage of dialects. We affirm strongly that teachers must have the experiences and training that will enable them to respect diversity and uphold the right of students to their own language.

> (National Council of Teachers of English, 1972)

When publicized in November 1974, this resolution evoked considerable criticism from a number of the country's leading newspapers and popular periodicals. It also received accolades from well-known civil rights organizations. It evoked a rather stony silence from the prestigious Modern Language Association and was condemned by a number of conservative organizations. When several publishers produced texts that reflected this philosophy, there was a mixed response, with the majority of school districts responding negatively. Of all the stands taken by the NCTE on curricular issues with social ramifications, none has created more controversy than this one.

National Coalition Against Censorship (NCAC, 275 7th Avenue, New York, New York 10001)

This is a small but active alliance of national, noncommercial organizations that includes religious, professional, artistic, educational, labor, and civil rights groups, with established chapters in a number of states. NCAC publishes a monthly newsletter, *Censorship News*, which deals with a broad range of First Amendment issues. While school censorship is a frequent topic in NCAC literature, the organization's scope is quite broad. Its position statement includes these key ideas:

- Censorship of books and films in schools and public libraries restricts the right to read, to see, to learn, to teach, and to think. It encourages ignorance.

- Government secrecy inhibits access to information necessary for democratic decision-making and exposure of abuses and illegalities.

- Too many groups, going far beyond expression to persuade others about their own concerns and values, try to impose their way of thinking on entire communities. Film, television, and cable are some of the affected media.

- The television industry, locked into attracting the largest possible audience at every possible moment, gives short shrift to issues of access, diversity, and fairness.

- Attempts to restrict "obscenity" and "pornography" have led to widespread confusion, intimidation and wasted resources. They have limited art, literature and scientific inquiry. (National Coalition Against Censorship, 1985)

This group is useful because, through its newsletter, it keeps its readers abreast of current censorship episodes of note and discusses how they are being confronted. The members of its alliance include several whose help can be solicited by teachers who have been challenged, such as the American Civil Liberties Union, ASCD, IRA, NCTE, Student Press Law Center, and others. Thus, the NCAC newsletter is a useful reference source, one that should be included in every school media center/library.

People for the American Way (PFAW, 2000 M Street, NW, Washington, D.C. 20036)

PFAW is another broad-based, highly active group whose former annual publication, *Attacks on the Freedom to Learn*, once provided a state-by-state review of school censorship cases and their status at the time the reports were received. The publication attained great national visibility and its key findings were quoted in hundreds of U.S. newspapers. Its "Top Ten" included the 10 most challenged authors, literary texts, and overall publications for a single and multiyear period. Unfortunately, the PFAW governing body decided to end this annual print publication with its 1996–1997 issue, but it continues in online form and is available for subscription at http://www.pfaw.org/activist. In Fall 1997, PFAW published a journal titled *A Right Wing and a Prayer*, a text that included coverage of activities of the religious right in several areas of concern. The state-by-state summaries and "Most Wanted" lists, however, have been eliminated. The value of this publication to schools has been therefore diminished, but because of the commitment of the organization to anticensorship issues, special publications bearing the PFAW imprimatur should never be ignored.

National School Board Association (NSBA, 1680 Duke Street, Alexandria, Virginia 22314)

Although this organization has the potential to provide great assistance, the NSBA faces somewhat of a dilemma: Its member groups do not necessarily support any goal that the parent group may promote or adopt. As discussed in Chapter 2, all school boards are elected by the citizens of their districts and thus exist in total autonomy. As a result, the NSBA executive board can do no more than make suggestions to its constituent groups. Local control of public schools, a major tenet of public policy across the United States, keeps authority out of the hands of the national group.

In 1989, however, the NSBA leadership authorized the publication of *Censorship: Managing the Controversy*, a periodical-sized document that was distributed to all local district boards. The rather demure tone of the publication was set by President James R. Oglesby and Executive Director Thomas A. Shannon in its foreword:

> Controversy is something educators must live with. In fact, the effective management of controversy may be one of the most basic responsibilities of elected officials in a democracy. As school board members, you are called upon constantly to address the questions underlying the challenge of censorship. These questions concern the very mission of public schools:
>
> • What should students learn?
>
> • How should they be taught?
>
> • What learning materials should be used?
>
> • How should curriculum decisions be made?

Rather than defending one position or another in this monograph, NSBA has gathered a wide variety of VIEWPOINTS from the vast spectrum of contemporary opinion that make censorship challenges facing public schools today. Without endorsing any particular viewpoint, sometimes it is helpful to look at them less subjectively than usual and reassess the process by which your school district handles censorship challenges.

When the waters are calm, take the opportunity to reconsider policies and procedures for handling material that is challenged. Schools that implement effective policies have a better chance of resolving conflicts with fewer restrictions on the instructional and library materials available to students. (Oglesby & Shannon, 1989)

The five sections that make up the rest of the previous document provide a series of suggestions that are thoughtful, practical, and gently persuasive. Furthermore, its appendixes include a number of position statements from such organizations as ALA, NCTE, and NSSC. These are balanced by statements from such censorship-prone groups as Educational Research Analysts and the Eagle Forum.

Thin Ice on the Front Lines

Unfortunately, this chapter ends on an enigmatic note. The person any teacher under attack most needs to provide help and support is the building principal. But this fact represents a serious dilemma: Those front-line administrators frequently do not support—or even listen to—their teachers, who naturally seek their help when they are verbally attacked by a parent or concerned citizen about classroom materials or procedures. To an alarming degree, school principals peremptorily side with the outsider instead of their faculty members. Many will merely tell the teacher to remove the questioned text, stop showing the film, desist from playing the tape, or rescind the invitation to the "questionable" guest speaker. The outcome of the *Hazelwood* decision, discussed in Chapter 8, gives principals significant leverage in making those choices. This is particularly true when the school or teacher in question has experienced a previous censorship challenge. Some principals make these decisions immediately, and in doing so, ignore the established district policy on responding to such challenges. Once that ultimatum has been made, what are teachers to do? If they knuckle under without a murmur, that's a win for the censors, who will strike again because victory came so easily. If teachers go over the principal's head to request district action from the superintendent or school board, they may become ensnared in a bureaucratic briar patch.

Moreover, in taking this step, their effrontery will almost certainly be rewarded by an irked principal's negative annual evaluation.

There is no doubt that the principals of all public schools are in a stressful position. They are the mediators between the educational goals and strategies of their teachers and the public, whose taxes underwrite the whole operation. In any conflict between town and gown, principals cannot escape their roles as decision makers and arbiters. Principals must be more than public relations experts, however; in the final analysis, they must be philosophically aware, sensitive professionals. The whole educational landscape is almost always in a state of flux, and educational leaders must stay up-to-date—much as a teacher attends staff development sessions or a medical doctor reads the current issues of the *Journal of the American Medical Association.* Arguably, one of the main sources for such ongoing education are the professional organizations, such as the American Association of School Administrators (AASA), the National Association of Secondary School Principals (NASSP), and the companion elementary group (NAESP), together with their publications and state affiliates.

In Fall 1989, one of the authors of this book, John Simmons, was appointed Chair of the Standing Committee Against Censorship of NCTE. Soon after this appointment, Simmons contacted the editor of the *NASSP Bulletin,* requesting a themed issue on the secondary school principal's role in censorship cases. The ensuing agreement called for the submission of essay manuscripts—all written by nationally recognized authorities—all nine of which met the February 1 deadline. No word was forthcoming from the NASSP office until late July, and then only after several letters and calls were placed. The reply stipulated that only five of the nine essays were acceptable, that the rhetoric in three of the surviving ones would have to be "toned down," and that additional essays had to be submitted representing the other side of the issue. When those conditions were rejected, the NASSP backed out of the whole arrangement. In Winter 1993 a modified version of the original collection was published as a themed issue, "Censorship and the School Principal," in the *ALAN Review.*

The metamessage here is clear: The principals' organization was not at all eager to express a position of leadership in the right-to-read, right-to-teach dialogue. Teachers looking for support in censorship challenges are advised to make immediate contact with their principal but those teachers may not receive the kind of backing from that key individual that they so desperately need. In the uncertain world of censorship challenges and attacks, teachers and librarians are walking on ice that is very thin indeed. Without enlightened, unequivocal, and courageous support from the personnel and organizations representing leadership in our public schools, too many teachers may find themselves struggling out there all alone.

Guidelines for Teachers and Librarians

- Set up a classroom or library activity for students in which they investigate an important text, some of the scholarly support related to it, and some of the published complaints/challenges to it. Then stage a "pro vs. con" debate during class time.

- Invite a "concerned" panel of parents to present their thoughts on curricular issues (only) at a meeting of the Parent/Teacher organization. An administrator who is well informed on the school's program of studies should moderate. All teachers and support staff members should attend.

- Ask the school librarian to collect all issues of professional periodicals that deal with censorship and place them in a prominent location on school library shelves. Also request that the same library staff use any available budgetary resources to acquire publications by organizations that focus on intellectual freedom.

- Form a "watchdog" committee of faculty and staff to peruse available newspapers and news magazines for articles, essays, position statements, etc., on school censorship. Regularly post these items on a designated bulletin board.

- Ask those who draw up your school's student council agenda to include the censorship topic at least once a year. Ask that the pertinent dialogue be video- or audiotaped. Save the tapes for review by administrators, teachers, parents, and concerned citizens.

RECOMMENDED WEB SITES

American Association of School Administrators
http://www.aasa.org

American Library Association—Banned Books Week
http://www.ala.org/bbooks/resource.html

See also:
Coping with Challenges in School Libraries
http://www.ala.org/alaorg/oif/coping_inf.html#schoollibs

Dealing with Concerns about Materials
http://www.ala.org/alaorg/oif/dec_lib.html

Freedom to Read
http://www.ala.org/alaorg/oif/freeread.html

Guidelines for Policy Development and Implementation
http://www.ala.org/alaorg/oif/pol_reg.html

Newsletter on Intellectual Freedom
http://www.ala.org/alaorg/oif/nif_inf.html

Interpretations of the Library Bill of Rights
http://www.ala.org/work/freedom/interprt.html

Association for Supervision and Curriculum Development
http://www.ascd.org

See also:
Educational Leadership
http://www.ascd.org/frameedlead.html

Education Update
http://www.ascd.org/frameedupdate.html

Curriculum Update
http://www.ascd.org/framecupdate.html

Center for Demoncracy and Technology
http://www.cdt.org

International Reading Association
http://www.reading.org

See also:
The Reading Teacher
http://www.reading.org/publications/journals/RT/index.html

Journal of Adolescent & Adult Literacy
http://www.reading.org/publications/journals/JAAL/index.html

Reading Research Quarterly
http://www.reading.org/publications/journals/RRQ/index.html

Reading Today
http://www.reading.org/publications/newspaper/rty.htm

Censorship: A Threat to Reading, Learning, Thinking
http://newbookstore.reading.org/cgi-bin/OnlineBookstore.storefront/1417134553/Product/View/123&2D553

National Association of Elementary School Principals
http://www.naesp.org

National Association of Secondary School Principals
http://www.nassp.org/index1.html

National Coalition Against Censorship
http://www.ncac.org

See also:
Censorship News
http://www.ncac.org/cen_news/cnhome.html

National Council of Teachers of English
http://www.ncte.org

See also:
The Students' Right to Read
http://www.ncte.org/censorship/right2read.shtml

The Students' Right to Their Own Language
http://www.ncte.org/ccc/12/sub/state1.html

National School Board Association
http://www.nsba.org

People for the American Way
http://www.pfaw.org

See also:

Attacks on the Freedom to Learn Online
http://www.pfaw.org/issues/education/aflo/index.shtml

A Right Wing and a Prayer
http://www.pfaw.org/issues/education/rwp97.summary.shtml

CHAPTER 10

Outreach Approach—
Hope for the Future

For too long, many school employees have assumed the roles of reactors in censorship challenges. The classic censorship episode begins when parents or concerned citizens hear of a text, song lyric, film or videotape, teaching strategy, or controversial speaker about to be introduced to students. Immediately their often-angry initiatives throw schools into the defensive role. The trends in litigation described in Chapter 8 place the burden of proving the educational value of a given material or strategy on the teacher rather than on the individuals who lodge complaints. The all-too-frequent censorship scenario—a parent raises an objection, the teacher/media specialist responds, the school administrator waffles, a negotiated decision is reached, and the teacher/media specialist's capacity to provide meaningful learning opportunities is diminished—could be modified, or eliminated altogether, through the use of proactive moves that anticipate the problem and resolve it before it becomes a contentious issue.

The word *proactive* has been tossed around by educational spokespersons for a long time and in a multitude of contexts. As it relates to censorship, proactivity can have real significance. School employees must understand their potential roles in conveying to concerned community members the vital message implicit in the *Students' Right to Read*. Classroom teachers, school and district administrators, librarians, guidance personnel, and members of the district supervisory staff all need to be alert to opportunities for initiating dialogue with those outside the school, as well as nonprofessional decision makers within it.

John Simmons has been a teacher educator in English and reading at the same university for almost 40 years. Having experienced one career-threatening censorship challenge in his early years as a high school English teacher, Simmons has been acutely aware of the problem and the potential it has for causing serious personal and institutional damage. In 1976, as a university educator, he decided on a plan of action that he has followed each semester since, and which will serve as an introductory example of the proactive "Outreach Approach" to potential censors.

Implementing the Outreach Approach

The Citizens' Panel

The topic of censorship is part of Simmons's undergraduate peda-gogical course in teaching literature, a required course designed for students who aspire to be English teachers. The author seeks out a neutral site (public library conference room, bank meeting facility, etc.) to hold an evening session during which a panel of citizens addresses the undergraduates on the topic of Appropriate/Inappropriate Materials for Classroom Use. That panel has consisted of the following representative citizens:

1. A member of the clergy, usually from a traditionally conservative Protestant church (although not always);
2. An elected member of the county school board;
3. An experienced, articulate middle or high school English teacher, locally employed;
4. A building principal from a local middle or high school (from a different school than the teacher); and
5. A citizen of the county who has, in the past, expressed objections to materials or teaching strategies introduced into upper grade classrooms.

Though Leon County, Florida, Simmons's home district, has two large universities; one large community junior college; and is the seat of city, county, and state government, it retains many of the characteristics of a small, Deep South community. Thus, there is always an ample pool of concerned citizens from which to choose the person in the #5 slot described above.

Student attendance at this 7 to 9 p.m. session is required. Other English/English Education students, both undergraduate and graduate, are invited to attend. Panelists, as well as students in the teaching-of-literature course are provided with the NCTE pamphlet, *The Students' Right to Read* (1972), well in advance of the meeting. Each panelist makes a brief (10-minute) statement of his or her perspective on the topic. The audience, with Simmons as moderator, is invited to direct questions to specific panel members. (The students are warned in advance about the absolute requirement of courteous behavior and admonished to ask questions, not make speeches.) The moderator stands always at the ready to deal with any counterproductive behavior. The session usually runs over its allotted 2-hour time frame. There are nonalcoholic beverage refreshments in the rear of the meeting room, encouraging further discussion among the members of the panel and students after the formal program is over.

For nearly a quarter-century the censorship panel presentation has consistently been deemed a success. In promoting concerned, frank dialogue, it unites town and gown in an off-campus setting. Moreover, it introduces teachers-to-be to opinions and attitudes in the "real" world where they will teach once they graduate. This Outreach Approach also provides a perspective on literary choice that students seldom hear from their literature professors in arts and science venues. Finally, the event sensitizes the panelists to the kinds of frequently naïve perceptions of what is "okay" to introduce to teenage students in the English classroom.

The citizens' panel is one way to establish a prearranged, focused dialogue among prospective teachers, librarians, school officials, and the citizens who live in the community. Most communities, however, do not have a large university that boasts a well-established program in English Education or Information Studies/Library Science. In those thousands of cities and towns where such assistance is not readily available, it is the school personnel themselves—primarily English, social studies, science, health, even home economics teachers and librarians—who must take the initiative for creating outreach activities.

The Faculty Consensus

In order to approach citizens' groups with invitations to dialogue, teachers and administrators must first be sure that their own house is in order. Faculty meetings with long, pontificating statements on topics that seem trivial, obvious, or marginally germane to the real task of teaching less-than-academically-inspired students might be improved by the introduction of a refreshingly relevant topic such as "Controversial issues: What and what not to teach in classrooms." Fellow teachers, administrators, librarians, and other school personnel are all citizens, and many are also parents who have established personal positions on the subject of what materials and topics are permissible in the classroom. Better to have individual teachers raise such concerns in faculty meetings than later on when they learn that a fellow teacher has just assigned a "dirty book." Ideally, these kinds of issues should be introduced in meetings before the school year even begins. In addition, district supervisors who are informed on these issues should review established district policy—documents of which can be photocopied, distributed in advance, and discussed. A related issue could be the topic of self-censorship (see description in Chapter 2). After these steps are taken, a school policy, consistent with that of the teacher/parent group but embellished with other staff input, should be put in writing and ratified. Once teachers are reasonably sure they share a common understanding with fellow staffers, they can face the outside world with professional confidence. An unsuspecting teacher should not be the object of Pogo's claim, "We have met the enemy and he is us."

The consortium of International Reading Association (IRA), the American Library Association (ALA), and the Association for Supervision and Curriculum Development (ASCD) produced this list of helpful suggestions for school personnel as they ready themselves for outreach gestures:

- Establish, in writing, a materials selection policy. It should specify the local criteria and procedures for selecting curricular and library materials, and all school personnel should strictly adhere to the policy.

- Establish, in writing, a clearly defined method for dealing with complaints. An important part of this policy statement should be formal review procedures for challenged material. A form should be used to identify the complainant's specific concerns; a broad-based committee that includes parents and other citizens as well as school personnel should be established to review challenged materials; and no restrictions should be placed on the use of the materials until the review process has been completed.

- Establish continuing communication with the school community. It should be kept informed about educational objectives, curricula, and classroom and library programs. The community should especially be informed about policies and procedures for selecting instructional and library materials.

(*Newsletter on Intellectual Freedom*, 1996, p. 11).

The Author's Forum

Including an established author, especially one who has been through the censorship fires over his or her texts, as a speaker could add definition to outreach gatherings. During the past decade, one of the most effective and willing author/speakers was the renowned young adult novelist Robert Cormier. His novel *I Am the Cheese* (1977) was the center of a notorious 1986 book-banning episode in Panama City, Florida, described earlier in Chapter 8 (see pp. 151–152). In 1990, Cormier was invited by the Bay County Friends of the Library chapter to speak to anyone—including hostile citizens' groups—about the censorship issue from his perspective. John Simmons and his Florida State University (Panama City Campus) literature class were in attendance as Cormier made his presentation, which showed him to be a sincere, articulate, and tactfully uncompromised professional. This author of a controversial book proved himself to be also a sympathetic, open-minded, spiritual human being, as well as a devoted husband, father, and citizen—not evil incarnate. This author of "sinister" works, such as *The Chocolate War, I Am the Cheese,* and *Fade* was also revealed to be the author of a short story collection, *8 Plus 1,* which contains stories that would move many family values apostles to appreciative tears. An initially hostile audience was charmed, and the man who wrote the text in question was perceived in an entirely different light.

In his essay, "A Book Is Not a House: The Human Side of Censorship," Cormier offers a statement of understanding and conviction that may be of some use in the outreach or faculty/staff gatherings described earlier. In recalling a particularly painful censorship incident, he writes,

> Those parents on Cape Cod continue to haunt me.
>
> I am a parent as well as a writer and I sympathize with them. They acted in what they felt was the best interest of their daughter. They tried to protect her from the world. They had a right to do this, a responsibility to do it, in fact. Who can quarrel with parents who try to shelter their children from what they perceive as bad influences, whether it's a book or friends or strangers on the street?
>
> My wife and I did the same as we ushered our three daughters and son through the frenzied days of childhood and the lacerating time of adolescence, setting up our family rules, our own curfews, our own rules of behavior.
>
> But there's a place where we sharply differed from that Cape Cod family.
>
> Those parents did more than send their daughter away from the classroom and into the library. They also became part of a movement to censor *The Chocolate War.* They didn't want anyone else's daughter to read the book, either.
>
> This is censorship in its most basic, purest form.
>
> And this is why censorship is so difficult to fight.
>
> It's the act of sincere, sometimes desperate people who are frightened by the world they live in and in which they are bringing up their children. They are trying to do the impossible, to shield their children from this world, to control what they see and do, what they learn. At a moment when their children are reaching out beyond the boundaries of home and family, they are raising barriers to that reaching out. Instead of preparing them to meet that world, they want them to avert their eyes and remain in impossible exclusion. Beyond that, they insist that this same kind of sheltering be extended to the people next door or down the street or in the next town.
>
> Various organizations—religious and social—are quick to support these parents, and that's when headlines scream across the front pages, voices are raised in anger, picketing begins, and the threat of violence, or even violence itself, erupts.

The supporters of books also have their organizations. Teachers and librarians can turn to organizations within the American Library Association, the National Coalition Against Censorship, the Freedom to Read Foundation, and authors and publishers themselves for help in their battles against the removal of books from libraries and classrooms.

Every writer I know whose books are challenged enters that battle, flies across the country, makes the speeches, debates opponents, offers encouragement to educators who find themselves the targets of the book-banners.

I believe, however, that the greatest thing writers can do is simply to keep writing. Writing honestly with all the craft that can be summoned. Writing to illuminate as well as entertain. Writing to challenge the intellect and engage the heart. To make the reader, in Robert Daley's words, laugh and cry and suffer and triumph and understand. (1992, pp. 73–74)

(From "A Book is Not a House: The Human Side of Censorship" by Robert Cormier in *Author's Insights: Turning Teenagers Into Readers & Writers* edited by Donald R. Gallo. Copyright ©1992 by Robert Cormier. Published by Boynton/Cook, a subsidiary of Reed Elsevier Inc., Portsmouth, NH. Reprinted by permission of the publisher.)

The experience with Cormier well illustrates that it is worth taking the time to find authors who may be willing to come to your community and make the case for critical reading of quality literature to an audience of interested community residents. (Many publishers will underwrite the travel expenses of their star authors.)

The Role of the Library/Media Specialist

The role that media center/library specialists play in the censorship issue has been treated extensively in this text. They can also play a significant role in the outreach effort. Public libraries should be contacted and their help solicited. Librarians are almost without exception well informed about the Right to Read struggle. The anecdotes they can recount are reason enough to establish a connection with them. Their support group, Friends of the Library (usually a cross-section of community residents) can assist with publicity and the arrangement of meetings outside the school on the censorship topic. The library facility itself makes an excellent site for such a gathering. In terms of promoting intellectual freedom, public libraries can prove to be a valuable ally, and school personnel should take the initiative in establishing a communication link.

Reaching Out to Religious Organizations

The local ministerial association is another group to consider in the outreach effort. Although this has traditionally been an organization of the Protestant faith, a growing spirit of ecumenicism has broadened this group to include religious leaders who may be of Catholic, Jewish, Unitarian, Muslim, Hindu, and other faiths. Thus, in establishing contact with religious organizations, school representatives will probably be dealing with a range of spiritual leaders.

Significantly, some churches have already taken it upon themselves to promote the Right to Read. Unitarian/Universalist churches regularly hold colloquia on intellectual freedom. For centuries, the Roman Catholic Church published *The Index*, a lengthy list of forbidden books. Then, in 1966, the Vatican passed a resolution titled *Nihil Obstat*, a Latin phrase meaning that any print material could be read by practicing Catholics. In light of the Nihil Obstat proclamation, it is ironic that Cormier's *The Chocolate War*, a novel about corruption in a Catholic high school, is acceptable for study in Catholic schools but is roundly condemned by Christian fundamentalist groups.

In Chapter 8, the review of groups that often challenge "objectionable" materials, strategies, and choices includes a number that bear the Christian fundamentalist imprimatur. While these groups certainly have established themselves as a political force to be reckoned with in the post Civil Rights era, their actual power has been somewhat exaggerated by both opposing liberal groups and the national media. The 1998 off-year election would seem to corroborate that contention. In the week before polling day, the Christian Coalition spent a large sum of money on a Voter's Guide mailing to millions of eligible voters. Not surprising, the preferred candidates, affiliated with the same political party, were all highly conservative. The outcome of that election clearly reflected voters' preferences for candidates who were moderate or pragmatic. As reported in the November 5, 1998, issue of the *Tallahassee Democrat*,

> Barry Lynn of Americans United for Separation of Church and State said a backlash against the [Christian Fundamentalist] movement has begun. "It was a humiliating defeat. They've really hit the wall. They have embarrassingly little to show for the millions they poured in."
>
> Mike Lux of People for the American Way said "they put in more resources than with any other election."
>
> The movement's most publicized organization, Christian Coalition, said it spent $1.3 million distributing 35 million voter guides to churches, plus a million postcards and 500,000 phone calls to get supporters to the polls.
>
> Another group with money and moxie, Campaign for Working Families, said it pumped nearly $3 million into 225 races at the federal and state level.... The broadest indicator of the movement's grass-roots impact was the fate of the 115 candidates for the U.S. House endorsed by CWF.... In the post-ballot recriminations, Christian Coalition executive director Randy Tate said the

Republicans failed to offer a "clear conservative agenda" to match Democratic proposals, as they had done in 1994.

(Ostling, 1998, p. A8)

These statistics should encourage public school staff members to approach their local ministerial groups, the members of which are usually moderate, open-minded, and cooperative. They are men and women who have found that they have more to agree on within their ranks than to contest. Many of them would welcome a dialogue with local educators on the issue of what materials are appropriate in schools for assisting students through the shoals of adolescence and into a viable life in the adult community. Furthermore, like the public librarians, they can provide a meeting facility with adequate seating and microphones, away from the school building.

As Robert Cormier noted in "A Book Is Not a House," there will be members of the ministerial organizations who will raise pointed objections to certain curricular choices. *They must be heard in full* and only in the most extreme instances interrupted or heatedly challenged. Ideally, all persons who attend topical meetings are there to listen as much as to speak. As they engage in dialogue and assemble their supporting literature for distribution, school personnel should be patient and respectful of all who participate. In addition to printed materials, videotapes such as People for the American Way's *Redondo Beach: A Stand Against Censorship* (1995)—an account of the Redondo Beach, California School Board's handling of the Impressions series challenge—can be illuminative. Because this is a time when school emissaries should use courteous tones in their carefully crafted negotiation, any hint of contempt for those who oppose the Right to Read position is unacceptable. In his 1969 inaugural address Richard Nixon said, "We cannot talk to each other while we are shouting at each other." The tone of such meetings, then, is at least as important as the content.

Involving Civic Organizations

School personnel can also approach a cluster of local civic organizations concerning the Right to Read movement. First on the list is the Chamber of Commerce (the statewide Chamber might be included here, at least via correspondence). This group regularly expresses its commitment to enhancing life in the community: What more important facet of community life is there then the well-being of its children? Using literacy—cultural, functional, and computer—as a lever, school representatives can stress the community-wide need for promoting wide and critical reading. The citizens of today and tomorrow need to be able to discern bias, hidden persuasion, and doublespeak in the documents with which they will be immersed as consumers, voters, taxpayers, and, indeed, as civic group participants. The demand of the Citizens for Excellence in Education for schools to restrict the scope of their curricula to "factual knowledge," bereft of critical reading goals, should be stressed to the Chambers of Commerce, as well as to such fraternal organizations as the Lions' Club, the Kiwanis, the Rotary, and other organizations—both those with national affiliations and those that are primarily local. If the community climate is right, the Knights of Columbus, the Masons, and the YMCA/YMHA, YWCA/YWHA can be consulted; they all present educational programs to their members. All these efforts will also facilitate outreach to parents who, after all, are likely to be members of one group or another.

Closely associated with the civic organizations described here, at least in many citizens' minds, are patriotic organizations such as The American Legion, Veterans of Foreign Wars, and Daughters of the American Revolution. Because the members of these groups may cherish positions that are more traditional or conservative, they may be more resistant to dialogue about censorship issues. In any case, they should be approached, and their passionate patriotism may well provide an avenue. Many of their members conceivably may have used the GI Bill of Rights to gain higher education in colleges and universities, at which they probably read materials that the current would-be book banners condemn. Has that reading weakened the moral fiber of those veterans? Has it hindered them as voters, neighbors, consumers, or civic activists? Do they want the freedoms (such as the Right to Read or Teach) that *they fought for* weakened? The answer is probably "no" to all of the above. Furthermore, educators might want to point out that critical thinking, reading, and viewing are fundamental skills that ensure that the members of this democratic society remain informed, alert, and patriotic. What better place to enhance those capacities than in the public schools? Teachers may find an unlikely source of support for anti-censorship positions in the members of these groups who are rarely, if ever, invited to enter the dialogue.

Informing Professional and Parent-Teacher Organizations

Closer to (professional) home, some teacher or parent-teacher groups need to be sensitized to the nature of the censorship problem, its growth in recent decades, and the wide-ranging threat it poses to intellectual freedom in U.S. public schools. In most school districts, there are classroom teachers' associations in place that exist under many different names. These are the agencies for collective bargaining between public school teachers and their employers. The power and influence of such agencies varies across the United States; in some large cities, these groups have much to say about the acquisition and distribution of funds and the enhancement of the working conditions of their constituents. It is the latter aspect of the bargaining process to which challenges to text and nonprint media relate. A few appropriate censorship safeguards written into teachers' bargaining agreements or contracts could have the dual effect of calling would-be book banners to account and upgrading teacher morale. Guidelines adopted by the district school board should be in the hands of the lead bargaining agent, and they should be discussed in dialogue between teacher representatives, the school board, and principals' organizations. As in other instances within this chapter, the bargaining agents probably will not come to the teachers; once again, the teachers must take the initiative.

Parent-teacher organizations represent another important target of teacher initiative on the censorship challenge issue. Traditionally, parent-teacher groups have been an important agency in clarifying various school situations and supporting worthy causes proposed by schools. In an era of increased censorship activity, they could prove to be a valuable ally. The PTA/PTO regular meeting agendas should include the censorship issue as an item, especially in the early fall, because the overt, stated support of these organizations is vital in proactive endeavors. These meetings can be a venue for honest, thoughtful, extended dialogue when they are led by teachers who have been well prepared in both content and style of delivery. The question-and-answer phase of the meeting can be used to correct parent misconceptions, often created by unfounded rumors, and to clarify teacher positions on a range of issues—from the philosophy of intellectual freedom to the criteria for choosing "questionable" materials or teaching strategies. The minutes of the meeting should clearly reflect all the above.

Another traditional PTA/PTO sponsored event, Parents' Night, is a good forum for teachers to answer parents' questions and clarify the reasons for their choices of educational materials and methods. Statements of rationale and purpose in the teachers' learning activities can be composed, copied, and distributed to all visitors during that evening. Productive dialogue about the *why* of certain units, texts, authors, and assignments is better raised in this context, rather than in an angry telephone call to the teacher or principal later. One result of this outreach strategy is the creation of a nucleus of PTA/PTO parents who will be informed and ready for indignant, reactionary friends who call to enlist them in a challenge or protest.

Given the two previous suggestions, it would be somewhat redundant to describe teacher initiatives taken to district school boards as another proactive strategy. However, the potential significance of such requests for a place on the agenda should not be overlooked or underestimated. In his 35-plus years as a community resident, parent, taxpayer, and educator, coauthor John Simmons has, on occasion, appeared before the district board—either by request or at his own initiative. The agenda of these meetings is often slanted toward fiscal rather than curricular issues. Although fiscal concerns are pressing, curricular issues are also important and should be reviewed. School board meeting dialogue on the Right to Read and Teach is important; but once again, it is the teachers who must proactively create the reasons for requesting these agenda additions.

Suggestions for Preparing Outreach Statements

The content of a teacher presentation to any group should be developed carefully and reasonably. Thus, the final matter of concern in this review of outreach possibilities is a clarification of suggested items for inclusion in prepared statements on censorship and the Right to Read and Teach:

1. Keep a list of previously recorded instances of complaints or challenges. Remember that according to *Attacks on the Freedom to Learn* only 15–20% of such episodes are ever repeated (People for the American Way, 1996). For those that are, record the significant data, focusing particularly on the material or strategy targeted, and the individual or organization responsible. It is helpful to know all this when preparing for dialogues with any of the groups described earlier.

2. Keep supplies of generic material at the ready, such as the Library Bill of Rights, the *Students' Right to Read* pamphlet, and the *Students Right to Their Own Language* NCTE resolution. Watch for opportunities to distribute and review or critique such documents.

3. Keep a copy (when available) of the past minutes of the organizations being approached. These minutes can be revealing as to the sentiments of various vocal group members. While it is not wise to brandish these documents as weapons, the more you know, the better.

4. Keep a list of likely speakers, such as Richard Peck, who have status, who oppose censorship, and who are willing to address

the group in question on the author's perspective on censorship and the Right to Read and Teach.

5. In presenting the teachers' perspective, stress the educational value of materials that may evoke challenges. Emphasize that the purpose of certain materials is not to criticize or satirize family values, traditional community mores, or patriotism. Make sure that no one in the education community tolerates or defends a teacher whose ostensible goal is to titillate his or her students—stress that teachers are reasonable, honorable, and trustworthy adults.

6. Emphasize the long-range goals of critical reading and thinking: These skills provide crucial preparation for college success, professional competence, alert consumerism, and enlightened citizenship. In a democratic society governed by free enterprise principles, the mere assimilation of factual knowledge is very seldom adequate for meeting crucial challenges in adult life. In this fast-paced Information Age, businesses seek employees who can think quickly and creatively, holding their own in electronic interaction and boardroom strategy sessions.

7. When reviewing literacy choices, remember that competent, well-trained teachers and librarians strive for the goal of balance. This literary balance is illustrated in the following truths:

   a. Some texts are about good people, some are about bad ones.

   b. Some texts are about pugnacious people, some are about tranquil ones.

   c. Some texts are about happiness, some are about sadness.

   d. Some texts are about success, some are about failure.

   e. Some texts are about familiar lifestyles, some are about unfamiliar ones.

   f. Some texts are about good neighborhoods, some are about bad ones.

   g. Some texts are about law-abiding citizens, some are about criminals.

   h. Some texts are about healthy people, some are about the infirm.

   i. Some texts are about younger people, some are about older ones.

   j. Some texts are about great people, some are about common ones.

k. Some texts are about people from the North, some are from the South, some from the East, some from the West, and some from foreign lands.

l. Some texts are about city people, some are about suburbanites, and some are about rural people.

m. Some characters speak Standard English, some don't—such as those by John Steinbeck, Charles Dickens, Langston Hughes, Jack London, Tennessee Williams, George Bernard Shaw, and many other writers. (Stress here that the goal of all teachers is to introduce and maintain instruction in correct English. It is only when studying literary selections of a certain nature that a variety of language styles are to be found; the reading of such texts in no way represents the acceptance or promotion of these styles with students.)

When all is said and done, stand your ground; it's what self-confident, professionally competent educators do.

In summary, the Outreach Approach should be used to establish school-community relationships in matters of material and strategy choices. With the increasing diversity of the U.S. population and the alarming nature of reported censorship episodes over the past quarter-century, this approach may well be the proactive weapon of choice.

Guidelines for Teachers and Librarians

- Petition the local school board to review selected lists of outside reading and nonprint media items distributed by various district faculty members. If there are titles that raise questions in the minds of any board members, invite those individuals to discuss their concerns with the faculty members who use them.

- Join with public librarians and their Friends of the Library to mark Banned Books Week with substantive public events such as a panel of citizens, presentations by guest authors, a forum with members of the legal profession speaking on the Right to Read issue, and presentations by invited spokespersons from state and national professional groups.

- Keep a close check on staff/school board contract negotiations under the rubric of "working conditions," especially those items that affect academic freedom. Prevail upon those faculty/staff representatives to review and critique those items at meetings of the school faculty and staff.

- Invite an editorial representative from a major English dictionary publisher (G. C. Merriam Webster, Random House, Thorndike-Barnhart, etc.) to address a session of the PTO. Ask that individual to include in his or her remarks (1) the function of the dictionary and (2) criteria for adding and defining words (especially when such additions could be considered "dirty").

RECOMMENDED WEB SITES:

American Legion
http://www.legion-aux.org

Campaign for Working Families
http://www.campaignforfamilies.org

Freedom to Read Foundation
http://www.ftrf.org

Knights of Columbus
http://www.kofc.org

Masons
http://freemasonry.org
http://web.mit.edu/dryfoo/www/Masons

National Coalition Against Censorship
http://www.ncac.org

National Council of Teachers of English
http://www.ncte.org

   See also:
   The Students' Right to Read
   http://www.ncte.org/censorship/right2read.shtml

The Students' Right to Their Own Language
http://www.ncte.org/ccc/12/sub/state1.html

People for the American Way
http://www.pfaw.org

Veterans of Foreign Wars
http://www.vfw.org/home.shtml

YMCA
http://www.ymca.int
http://www.ymca.net

YWCA
http://www.ywca.org

Epilogue

John O'Hara leads into the final chapter of his novel, *Appointment in Samarra* (1934), in this manner:

Our story never ends.

You pull the pin out of a hand grenade, and in a few seconds, it explodes and men in a small area get killed and wounded. That makes bodies to be buried, hurt men to be treated. It makes widows and fatherless children and bereaved parents. It means pension machinery, and it makes for pacifism in some and for lasting hatred in others. Again, a man out of the danger area sees the carnage the grenade creates, and he shoots himself in the foot. Another man had been standing there just two minutes before the thing went off, and thereafter he believes in God or in a rabbit's foot. Another man sees human brains for the first time and locks up the picture until one night years later, when he finally comes out with a description of what he saw, and the horror of his description turns his wife away from him.... (p. 192)

Similarly, John Simmons was in the midst of completing his work on this book when he received a telephone call from a local middle school English teacher. This person—a 25-year veteran of the middle school classroom, an undergraduate and graduate advisee of the author, and a supervisor of one of his student teachers—had just received a call from two enraged parents. Mrs. Angry Parent demanded that all copies of Katherine Paterson's Newbery Award-winning novel, *Jacob Have I Loved* (1980), be removed from her daughter's seventh-grade class. She cited the "extreme religious overtones" found in the title and a scene in which a teenager reports a dream about killing her sister. Soon after this demand, the teacher in question received another call, this time from Mr. Angry Parent, threatening to "call in the ACLU" on "this serious case."

Before calling Simmons, the teacher reported this problem to her principal, *who supported her 100%*. She then consulted the senior librarian, who did a search on her computer and found a number of award citations the novel had received, including the Newbery Award. The librarian also provided a list of texts on the statewide adoptions list, three of which were anthologies that included the Paterson novel. Finally, she reported that, to date, no complaint had been registered by any parent or other citizen about this text.

Next, the teacher contacted the school district media coordinator, who confirmed the report that no complaint had been registered about the text at any other school. He reminded the teacher of the adopted district policy on a citizen's request to review material. (This policy was closely patterned after the model in NCTE's *The Students' Right to Read* pamphlet.) He also promised to appear at any case conference that might ensue.

In her call to Simmons, the teacher first requested his support of the student teacher, an excellent classroom performer who was considerably shaken by the whole episode. A mother of two teenage children, this individual was dumbfounded by the nature and intensity of the attack. Once Simmons had promised to support his advisee, the cooperating teacher shared more particulars, all of which should have resonance with readers of the previous chapters:

1. In 2 years, the parents, both college educated, had never complained about a teacher's choice of materials.

2. The area in which the school is situated is an upper middle class, predominantly white suburb (just like Island Trees and Hazelwood).

3. The mother would not accept an alternate text for her child, but instead vociferously demanded that the text be removed from the classroom, the library/media center, and the school. Her husband supported this demand, threatening legal action if it was not met.

4. Earlier in the term, the teacher had sent home a letter to all parents, announcing the future assignment of the Paterson novel and the context in which it would be taught. The letter asked if parents had any objections to that choice. It went on to request that the parents provide money for their children to purchase a paperback edition of the text, available in a local bookstore. The parent in question signed and returned this permission letter, agreeing to allow her child to purchase the book. Fortunately, the teacher had filed that letter and retained it.

5. The incident took place in late fall of this school year. Thus, the teacher and her student teacher had assigned for all-class reading at least five selections—including poems, short stories, and one-act plays—that contained spiritual and/or religious, even Christian elements. No complaint had come from these particular parents—nor from any parents of students in that seventh-grade class.

6. The mother demanded an immediate, on-site conference (it was the day before Thanksgiving break) to "settle the matter once and for all," i.e., to remove the text. When asked if she had fol-

lowed district policy to date, or if she was even aware of such a policy, she stated that she had not, and was not, but that "that didn't matter." She wanted resolution then and there. The school and the district representative denied that request. Predictably, the episode is far from over.

Does all of the above sound familiar? Most pertinent is the fact that the unpredictability—and the intensity—of censorship challenges remain a fact of life in U.S. education. Such challenges continue to rear their contentious heads long after anyone finishes reading the final sentence in this or any other book on the topic. This is all the more reason to keep in mind that the best defense for censorship challenges is not offense; it is proactivity.

Petitt's Criteria for Judging Fiction for Adolescents

I.   Definition: Is this a novel?

    A. Is it extensive enough to qualify (at least 50,000 words)?

    B. Does its length reveal Change?

    C. Is it structued without having its vital qualities destroyed?

    D. Is it fiction, and invented story, or is it history or some other form of prose?

    E. Does it, as fiction, have the individuality characteristic of the novel which immediately sets this novel off as different from any other novel?

    F. Are values communicated by indirection?

II. Unity: Is the novel unified?

    A. Do all technical aspects work together to present the whole?

    B. Is the totality of the novel achieved through the presence of alternatives or oppositions?

III. Theme: Does the theme emerge as the controlling element to which all other aspects can be seen finally to contribute?

    A. Is the theme a facet of the general theme of all fiction—the individual in society?

    B. At the same time is the individual facet of the theme unique because of the way it has been developed?

    C. Is the theme skillfully developed?

       1. Do the characters signify some universal truth beyond the meaning of their own existence?

       2. Does the theme have a mystic kinship which universalizes its particularity?

    D. Is the theme developed rhythmically?

       1. Are repetitions and variations in time, action, in minor themes and in symbols without monotony?

2. Does the rhythm of repetitions and variations cause an explosion of meaning beyond the particular people, events or objects?

IV. Plot: Is the plot a purposely directed pattern of events?

   A. Does the story, a series of events, dominate?

   B. Is there a plot which links inner and outer experience by telling why events come about?

   C. Does the plot have mythic similarities to other plots?

   D. At the same time is it unique?

   E. Do events of the plot reveal the characters?

   F. At the same time are events partly shaped by the characters?

   G. Is the structure of the plot self-contained?
     1. Does foreshadowing operate to make the plot coherent?
     2. If used, is coincidence used to develop a theme?

   H. Has the author solved the central technical problem of all novelists—the choice of point of view?
     1. Is it clear from what point of view, on whose authority, the story is told?
       a. Is the point of view at all times clearly defined?
       b. Is it convincing, apart from the authority of the author's assertions of validity?
     2. Has the author fully exploited the advantages of his choice and contrived to turn the disadvantages into virtues?
       a. If he has chosen to speak in the first person, has the author achieved unity, immediacy, and significance while compensating for the limited authority?
         (1) Is the single mind telling the story a believable one?
         (2) Does it have a believable depth of sight sufficient to be capable if probing beneath the surface?
         (3) Do the events told in the first person acquire a dramatic immediacy?
         (4) Are the limitations of single compensated for?
           (a) Are events outside of the scope of the first person narrator's observations adequately handled?
           (b) His bias recognized?
           (c) Is his bias used to revel him as well as the events?
       b. If he has chosen to speak in the third person is this revealing of his theme?

      (1) If he has chosen to be omniscient, has he been able to show the minute human scene as well as the scope of human life?

      (2) If he has chosen to limit omniscience to action, is his theme a limited one in which action contains feeling?

      (3) If he has chosen the method of the effaced narrator, has he exercised sufficient subtlety in moving from the limited physical sight of the narrator to his own omniscient moral sight?

    c. Does the round character change in the course of the novel?

      (1) Is the change significant?

      (2) Is the degree of change in keeping with the scope of the novel?

    d. Does the flat character serve as a medium to reveal the complex change of round characters?

V. Dialogue: Does the dialogue simultaneously further plot and express character?

  A. Is the voice of each character individual?

  B. Does the interaction of speech between characters reveal their relationships to each other?

  C. Does the dialogue advance the story?

  D. Is the dialogue reserved for culmination scenes?

  E. Is the dialogue artistically valid?

    1. Does it imitate without transcribing?

    2. If it attempts to make the inarticulate articulate, does it do so always as a means of clarifying character? (never as a vehicle to express abstract ideas for their own sake?)

VI. Setting: Is particularity given to character and event through descriptions of setting?

  A. Is the setting subordinate to the human element?

  B. Does the setting have dramatic use to reveal character?

  C. Does the setting have dramatic use to synthesize place and events?

VII. Style: Do the elements of style all reveal theme?

  A. Is the sentence structure relevant to the theme?

  B. Do the metaphors reveal the individuality of the novel and thus of its theme?

C. Are symbols relevant projections of the material?
  1. Do they exist believably on a literal level?
  2. Do they serve as a means to disclose the meaning of the literal level of existence?
D. Is the tone, the attitude of the author toward the material of the novel, established by a consistent use of language?
  1. Does overdone language or editorializing produce a sentimental or condescending tone?
  2. Does the tone allow character and event to make their own case?

Petitt's Books for Adolescents Ranked as Those "Best Written"

Judges: 18 of the Outstanding Critics of Books for Adolescents

Author   Book

Ranked in order of number of votes:

	Author	Book
1.	Forbes, Esther	*Johnny Tremaine*
2.	Rawlings, Marjorie	*The Yearling*
3.	Daly, Maureen	*Seventeenth Summer*
4.	O'Hara, Mary	*My Friend Flicka*
5.	Street, James	*Goodbye, My Lady*
6.	Knight, Eric	*Lassie Come Home*
7.	Walker, Mildred	*Winter Wheat*
8.	Annixter, Paul	*Swiftwater*
9.	Brink, Carol	*Caddie Woodlawn*
10.	Fuller, Iola	*Loon Feather*
11.	Benary-Isbert, Margot	*The Ark*
12.	Stolz, Mary	*Ready or Not*
13.	Gray, Elizabeth J.	*Adam of the Road*
14.	Ullman, James R.	*Banner in the Sky*
15.	Richter, Conrad	*Light in the Forest*
16.	Gipson, Fred	*Old Yeller*
17.	James, Will	*Smokey the Cowhorse*
18.	Yates, Elizabeth	*Patterns on the Wall*
19.	Bro, Marguerite	*Sarah*
20.	Catton, Bruce	*Banners at Shenandoah*
21.	Chute, Marchette	*Innocent Wayfaring*
22.	Clark, Ann Nolan	*Santiago*
23.	Kelly, Eric P.	*Trumpeter of Krakow*
24.	Krumgold, Joseph	*And Now Miguel*
25.	O'Hara, Mary	*Thunderhead*

(From Petitt, D. (1961). *A Study of the Qualities of Literary Excellence Which Characterizes Selected Fiction for Younger Adolescents.*)

Muller's List of Quality Young Adult Fiction

Armstrong, William	*Sounder*	1969
Bonham, Frank	*Durango Street*	1965
	The Nitty Gritty	1968
Craig, Margret	*It Could Happen to Anyone*	1961
Dizenzo, Patricia	*Phoebe*	1970
Everly, Jeanette	*A Girl Like Me*	1966
	Drop-out	1963
Freedman, B. & N.	*Mrs. Mike*	1947
Head, Ann	*Mr. & Mrs. Bo Jo Jones*	1967
Hinton, S.E.	*The Outsiders*	1967
	That Was Then, This Is Now	1971
Hentoff, Nat	*I'm Really Dragged But Nothing Gets Me Down*	1968
	Jazz Country	1965
Hunter, Kristin	*Soul Brothers and Sister Lou*	1968
Kingman, Lee	*The Peter Pan Bag*	1970
Laing, Frederick	*Ask Me If I Love You Now*	1968
Maxwell, Edith	*Just Dial a Number*	1971
Neufeld, John	*Lisa, Bright and Dark*	1969
Neville, Emily	*It's Like This, Cat*	1963
Sherburne, Zoa	*Too Bad About the Haines Girl*	1967
Spear, Elizabeth	*The Witch of Blackbird Pond*	1958
Stirling, Nora	*You Would If You Loved Me*	1969
Swarthout, Glendon	*Bless The Beasts and Children*	1970
Wojciechowska, Maia	*Tuned Out*	1968
Zindel, Paul	*I Never Loved Your Mind*	1970
	My Darling, My Hamburger	1969
	The Pigman	1968

(From Muller, A. (1973). *The Currently Popular Adolescent Novel as Transitional Literature.*)

Introduction to the American Library Association's *Celebrating the Freedom to Read* (1988)

> To deny free speech to engineer social change in the name of accomplishing a greater good for one sector of our society erodes the freedoms of all and, as such, threatens tyranny and injustice for those subjected to the rule of such laws.

This excerpt from the court's decision in ABA et al. V. Hudnut III acknowledges that today's recurring threats to the First Amendment are the result of well-meaning citizens attempting to "engineer social change." Censorship attempts often are motivated by the desire to remove evil as exemplified in racist, sexist, or sexually explicit materials. Bernard E. Rath, American Booksellers Association executive director, calls upon "bookstores and libraries as oases and storehouses of information for all Americans thirsting for knowledge and solutions" to protest these attempts to restrict information. To focus on the concept that reading opens minds, eliminates fear and breeds tolerance, the theme for the 1988 Banned Books Week is "Open Books for Open Minds."

Banned Books Week 1988—Celebrating the Freedom to Read takes place September 24–October 1, 1988. Now in its seventh year, the event is jointly sponsored by the American Booksellers Association, the American Library Association, the American Society of Journalists and Authors, the Association of American Publishers and the National Association of College Stores. It is also endorsed by The Library of Congress' Center for the Book. These groups have joined together to emphasize that imposing information restraints on a free people is far more dangerous than any ideas that may be expressed in that information.

The week-long observance is designed to be a positive educational program of exhibits, lectures, discussions, plays and films demonstrating the harms of censorship. This publication can help bookstores, schools and libraries to organize their programs in affirmation of the First Amendment. It includes a historical annotated list of books that have been banned or have been the object of controversy from 387

BC to the present; an annotated list of books challenged or banned this year; a collection of quotations on the First Amendment; camera-ready art for ads and bookmarks; posters; display ideas and sample news releases.

The freedom of speech and freedom of press, rights guaranteed by the First Amendment of the Constitution, are continually challenged by groups and individuals attempting to restrict what others can read or see. As examples in this publication make clear, most complaints about books are concerned with sex, obscenity, and "objectionable language." Challenges, however, are not limited to any one political perspective or special interest group. Parents have objected to books dealing with rebellion, sexual references, drug use or crime, feminists to unfair gender stereotypes, and atheists to biblical references. In the 19th century, *The Adventures of Huckleberry Finn* was challenged for poking fun at conventional morality and for bad grammar. Today, the novel is attacked by civil rights groups for its alleged demeaning portrayal of blacks. Other frequently challenged works such as *Of Mice and Men*; *Our Bodies, Ourselves*; *To Kill a Mockingbird*; *Are You There God? It's Me, Margaret*; and *Catcher in the Rye* are similarly misunderstood and attacked.

The freedom to choose and the freedom to express one's opinion even if that opinion might be considered unorthodox or unpopular is the message of Banned Books Week. These freedoms, guaranteed by the U.S. Constitution, have lasted over 200 years. The Constitution speaks—today more than ever—that it is only when all speech is protected for all citizens that everyone's rights are guaranteed.

The Library Bill of Rights

The American Library Association affirms that all libraries are forums for information and ideas, and that the following basic policies should guide their services.

1. Books and other library resources should be provided for the interest, information, and enlightenment of all people of the community the library serves. Materials should not be excluded because of the origin, background, or views of those contributing to their creation.

2. Libraries should provide materials and information presenting all points of view on current and historical issues. Materials should not be proscribed or removed because of partisan or doctrinal disapproval.

3. Libraries should challenge censorship in the fulfillment of their responsibility to provide information and enlightenment.

4. Libraries should cooperate with all persons and groups concerned with resisting abridgment or free expression and free access to ideas.

5. A person's right to use a library should not be denied or abridged because of origin, age, background, or views.

6. Libraries that make exhibit and meeting rooms available to the public they serve should make such facilities available on an equitable basis, regardless of the beliefs or affiliations of individuals or groups requesting their use.

(http://www.ala.org/work/freedom/lbr.html)

Excerpt from *The Students' Right to Read*

What should be done upon receipt of a complaint?

If the complainant telephones, listen courteously and refer him or her to the teacher involved. That teacher should be the first person to discuss the book with the person objecting to its use.

If the complainant is not satisfied, invite him or her to file the complaint in writing, but make no commitments, admissions of guilt, or threats.

If the complainant writes, contact the teacher involved and let that teacher call the complainant.

Sometimes the problem seems less serious and more easily resolved through personal contact over the phone. If the complainant is not satisfied, invite him or her to file the complaint in writing on a form prepared for this purpose. (See sample.)

Citizen's Request for Reconsideration of a Work
Author _____
Paperback_____ Hardcover _____
Title _____
Publisher (if known) _____
Request initiated by _____
Telephone _____
Address _____
City _____
Zip Code _____

Complainant represents
____ Himself/Herself
____ (Name organization) _____
____ (Identify other group) _____

1. Have you been able to discuss this work with the teacher or librarian who ordered it or who used it?
   ____ Yes ____ No

2. What do you understand to be the general purpose for using this work?

    a. Provide support for a unit in the curriculum?

       ___ Yes ___ No

    b. Provide a learning experience for the reader in one kind of literature?

       ___ Yes ___ No

    c. Other _____

       _____

    d. Did the general purpose for the use of the work, as described by the teacher or librarian, seem a suitable one to you?

       ___ Yes ___ No

       If not, please explain.

       _____

       _____

3. What do you think is the general purpose of the author in this book?

    _____

    _____

4. In what ways do you think a work of this nature is not suitable for the use the teacher or librarian wishes to carry out?

    _____

    _____

5. Have you been able to learn what is the students' response to this work?

    ___ Yes ___ No

6. What response did the students make?

    _____

    _____

7. Have you been able to learn from your school library what book reviewers or other students of literature have written about this work?

    ___ Yes ___ No

8. Would you like the teacher or librarian to give you a written summary of what book reviewers and other students have written about this book or film?

    ___ Yes ___ No

9. Do you have negative reviews of the book?
___ Yes ___ No

10. Where were they published?

_____

11. Would you be willing to provide summaries of the reviews you have collected?
___ Yes ___ No

12. What would you like your library/school to do about this work?
_____ Do not assign/lend it to my child.
_____ Return it to the staff selection committee/department for reevaluation.
_____ Other—Please explain

_____

_____

13. In its place, what work would you recommend that would convey as valuable a picture and perspective of the subject treated?

_____

_____

Signature _____

Date _____

At first, except for politely acknowledging the complaint and explaining the established procedures, the English teacher should do nothing. The success of much censorship depends upon frightening an unprepared school or English department into some precipitous action. A standardized procedure will take the sting from the first outburst of criticism. When the reasonable objector learns that he or she will be given a fair hearing through following the proper channels, he or she is more likely to be satisfied. The idle censor, on the other hand, may well be discouraged from taking further action. A number of advantages will be provided by the form, which will

- formalize the complaint,
- indicate specifically the work in question,
- identify the complainant,
- suggest how many others support the complaint,

- require the complainant to think through objections in order to make an intelligent statement on work (1, 2, and 3),
- cause the complainant to evaluate the work for other groups than merely the one he or she first had in mind (4),
- establish his or her familiarity with the work (5 and 6),
- give the complainant an opportunity to consider the criticism about the work and the teacher's purpose in using the work (7, 8, and 9), and
- give the complainant an opportunity to suggest alternative actions to be taken on the work (12 and 13).

The committee reviewing complaints should be available on short notice to consider the completed "Citizen's Request for Reconsideration of a Work" and to call in the complainant and the teacher involved for a conference. Members of the committee should have reevaluated the work in advance of the meeting, and the group should be prepared to explain its findings. Membership of the committee should ordinarily include an administrator, the English department chair, and at least two classroom teachers of English. But the department might consider the advisability of including members from the community and the local or state NCTE affiliate. As a matter of course, recommendations from the committee would be forwarded to the superintendent, who would in turn submit them to the board of education, the legally constituted authority in the school.

Teachers and administrators should recognize that the responsibility for selecting works for class study lies with classroom teachers and that the responsibility for reevaluating any work begins with the review committee. Both teachers and administrators should refrain from discussing the objection with the complainant, the press, or community groups. Once the complaint has been filed, the authority for handling the situation must ultimately rest with the administration and school board.

Freedom of inquiry is essential to education in a democracy. To establish conditions essential for freedom, teachers and administrators need to follow procedures similar to those recommended here. Where schools resist unreasonable pressures, the cases are seldom publicized and students continue to read works as they wish. The community that entrusts students to the care of an English teacher should also trust that teacher to exercise professional judgment in selecting or recommending books. The English teacher can be free to teach literature, and students can be free to read whatever they wish only if informed and vigilant groups, within the profession and without, unite in resisting unfair pressures.

(The current edition of The Students' Right to Read *is an adaptation and updating of the original Council Statement, including "Citizen's Request for Reconsideration of a Work," prepared by the Committee on the Right to Read of the National Council of Teachers of English (NCTE) and revised by Ken Donelson. Reprinted with permission of the NCTE.)*

National Council of Teachers of English Resolutions on Censorship

Recurring campaigns by individuals and groups advocating censorship of specific works of literature, restrictions on teaching materials, and limitations of teachers' academic freedom have prompted a series of resolutions by NCTE members. The Council has repeatedly warned other educators and the public of the dangers of restricting access to books and instructional materials. It has stressed the need for carefully spelled out book selection policies, and it has supplied teachers with information and suggestions for combatting attempts at censorship.

In a 1973 resolution prompted by Supreme Court actions of that year concerning obscenity, NCTE members expressed concern about possible results of the high court's placement of decision-making authority on questions of obscenity in the hands of local juries or judges who would apply contemporary community standards. The members said that while average lay persons would be aware of the moral and social climates of their communities, they might have little knowledge of how to evaluate whole works of literature for their artistic merit, and thus might make decisions violating the constitutional rights of authors, readers, students, and teachers. The resolution reads, in part:

> **Resolved**, that the National Council of Teachers of English affirm that all book-selection decisions be based upon soundly developed criteria and that the decisions be representative of a large segment of the community, rather than the vested interests of a few vocal members....

The need for an NCTE panel to monitor developments affecting freedom to read, teach, and learn was voiced in several resolutions in the early 1970s. Committees with temporary assignments involving academic freedom and censorship led in 1975 to formation of the Committee on Censorship, which in 1979 became the NCTE Standing Committee Against Censorship. *Dealing with Censorship*, a book developed by the committee, offers detailed advice on preventive measures teachers can take and community education efforts that can help the public understand the aims of English programs in their schools (NCTE, Stock No. 10622).

1. On Opposition to Censorship (1981)

Background: In the most recent of a series of general resolutions against censorship, NCTE members expressed concern that censorship attempts were increasing and showed evidence of being better organized than in previous decades.

Resolved, that in the face of increasing censorship the members of the National Council of Teachers of English reaffirm the student's right of access to a wide range of books and other learning materials under the guidance of qualified teachers and librarians; and

that all English teachers be urged to resist censorship by employing points of view and approaches recommended in *The Students' Right to Read* and other NCTE publications on censorship.

2. On Collecting Rationales for Defending Challenged Works (1984)

Background: This resolution stemmed from an awareness among NCTE members that the problem of dealing with advocates of censorship is a perennial challenge and that teachers must be poised at all times to mount a reasoned defense of the literary works and teaching materials in their schools—and on occasion, in colleges as well. They called on NCTE to make materials for such community education efforts widely accessible.

Resolved, that the National Council of Teachers of English Standing Committee Against Censorship collect or develop rationales for the defense of works that are challenged; and that the Committee use appropriate agencies and other resources for publication, storage, and dissemination of these materials.

Note: Two publications by NCTE affiliates, available nationally through NCTE, offer such rationales: *Celebrating Censored Books* (Wisconsin Council of Teachers of English, 1985, Stock No. 04835) and *Rationales for Commonly Challenged Taught Books* (Connecticut Council of Teachers of English, 1983, Stock No. 38241).

3. On Opposing Abridgment or Adaptation as a Form of Censorship (1984)

Background: This resolution was prompted by a trend among educational publishers to abridge works of literature such as plays of Shakespeare, intended for classroom use, in some cases without explaining the purposes of cuts. "Adaptation of a work, perhaps warranted in some cases, may also result in censorship," the proposers said. "Publishers have a responsibility to provide information about the extent and nature of any alterations so that, when selecting a text, teachers can make informed choices."

Resolved, that the National Council of Teachers of English recommend that publishers present the complete text or sections of works which they choose to print, whether in a single text or in an anthology; and that NCTE urge that if publishers do abridge or adapt a text, they clearly state in the text that these alterations have occurred, and explain the nature and extent of the abridgment or adaptation in promotional information, teachers' guides, and other support materials.

(Reprinted with permission of the National Council of Teachers of English.)

IRA Stands Against Censorship, *Reading Today*, March 1989

The International Reading Association has been concerned about the issue of censorship for many years. The Association's interest in fighting censorship is demonstrated by the adoption of the following two resolutions at the IRA Delegates Assembly in Toronto in 1988.

On Opposing Abridgment or Adaptation as a Form of Censorship

Background: This resolution reflects concerns among reading teachers about the publishing practice by which important works of literature are abridged and sometimes altered for use in textbooks without adequate explanation by the publisher. Teachers want to uphold the integrity of written materials as published by an author rather than use unapproved edited forms. In some instances, abridgment and adaptation may even constitute censorship. Moreover, teachers can make informed choices in the textbook selected only when full information is provided about changes in texts. Be it therefore

Resolved, that the International Reading Association join the National Council of Teachers of English in recommending that publishers present the complete text or sections of works which they choose to print, whether in a single text or in an anthology; and that IRA urge that if publishers do abridge, adapt, or edit a text in any manner, they clearly state in the textbook that these alterations have occurred, and explain the nature and extent of the abridgment or adaptation in promotional information, teachers' guides, and other support materials.

On Textbook and Reading Program Censorship

Background: The debate over the control of school programs has a long history. Occasionally, the debate erupts into conflict and even violence. School programs and materials may come under attack by individuals or groups with narrow interests.

Even though it is recognized that one purpose of reading is to learn about diversity in the world, these individuals or groups would at times deny students the right to read about other cultures, customs, and beliefs. Often materials and reading programs are eliminated or drastically modified as a result of non-instructional considerations. Be it therefore

Resolved, that the International Reading Association commend those state, provincial, and local educational agencies which support the professional judgment of reading and language arts teachers when self-appointed censors attempt to restrict the students' freedom to read, and be it further

Resolved that IRA condemn attempts by those with narrow interests to deprive students of quality reading programs;

that IRA condemn efforts by those with narrow interests to prevent or disrupt objective discussion of materials and school reading program issues; and

that IRA widely publish and disseminate this resolution and the 1986 resolution on textbook adoption to legislators, boards of education, professional organizations, chief state school officers, and school administrators.

References

Accelerated Reader [Computer software]. (2001). Wisconsin Rapids, WI: Advantage Learning Systems. Available: http://www.advlearn.com/ar

Alabama Department of Education's Office of Technology Initiatives. (2000). *Literacy partners—A principal's guide to an effective library media program for the 21st century*. Bulletin 2000, *46*. Montgomery, AL: Alabama Department of Education's Office of Technology Initiatives. Available: http://www.alsde.edu/26/librarians/LiteracyPartners.pdf

Alley, J. (1991, November 17). Christian Coalition spits election venom. *Virginia Beach Beacon*, p. 6.

Alliance for Childhood. (2000, September). *Fool's gold: A critical look at computers in childhood*. Washington, DC: The Alliance for Childhood. Available: http://www.allianceforchildhood.net/projects/computers/computers_reports_fools_gold_contents.htm

Ambach v. Norwick, 441 U.S. 68, 77 (1979).

American Association for School Librarians and the Association for Educational Communication and Technology. (1998). *Information power: Building partnerships for learning*. Chicago: American Library Association. Excerpts available: http://www.ala.org/aasl/ip_nine.html

American Civil Liberties Union, et al. v. Reno, et al. (II), United States Court of Appeals for the Third Circuit, No. 99-1324, (2000).

American Library Association. (1988). *Celebrating the freedom to read*. Chicago: Author.

American Library Association. (1996). Library Bill of Rights. In *Celebrating banned books* (pp. 16–19). Chicago: Author.

American Library Association Office of Intellectual Freedom. (2000). *The 100 most frequently challenged books of 1990–1999*. [News release]. Chicago: American Library Association. Available: http://www.ala.org/bbooks/top100bannedbooks.html

Anderson, L.H. (1999). *Speak*. New York: Farrar, Straus & Giroux.

Applebee, A.N. (1989). *A study of book-length works taught in high school English courses* (Report 1.2, Appendix A). Albany, NY: Center for the Learning and Teaching of Literature.

Aronson, M. (1995, March/April). A mess of stories. *The Horn Book Magazine*, p. 34.

Aronson, M. (1996, Fall). No renaissance without openness: A philosophy of American multiculturalism. *Bookbird*, *34*(4), 27–32.

Association for Library Service to Children. (2000). *Intellectual freedom for children: The censor is coming*. Chicago: American Library Association.

Bannerman, H. (1899). *The story of Little Black Sambo*. Philadelphia: Lippincott.

Bannerman, H. (1996). *The story of Little Babaji*. Ill. F. Marcellino. New York: Dial.

Barreras, R.B., Dressman, M., & Thompson, V.D. (1997). *Kaleidoscope: A multicultural booklist for grades K–8, covering books published 1993–95*. Urbana, IL: National Council Teachers of English.

Baskin, B.H., & Harris, K.A. (1977). *Notes from a different drummer: A guide to juvenile fiction portraying the handicapped.* New York: Bowker.

Baskin, B.H., & Harris, K.A. (1984). *More notes from a different drummer: A guide to juvenile fiction portraying the disabled.* New York: Bowker.

Bissinger, H.G. (1991). *Friday night lights.* New York: HarperCollins.

Blume, J. (1970). *Are you there God, it's me, Margaret?* New York: Bradbury.

Blume, J. (1982). *Forever.* New York: Simon & Schuster.

Board of Education, Island Trees Union Free School District v. Pico, 457 U.S. 853, 102 S. Ct. 2799 (1982). Available: http://www.fac.org/columns/970919b-s.asp

Boyers, S.J. (2000). *Teen power politic: Make yourself heard.* Brookfield, MA: Millbrook Press.

Bruchac, J. (1995, March/April). All our relations. *The Horn Book Magazine, 71*(2), 158–162.

Bruni, F. (2000, July 31). For Laura Bush, a direction she never dreamed of. *New York Times* [Online]. Available: http://www.nytimes.com/library/politics/camp/073100wh-bush-laura.html

Burress, L., & Jenkinson, E.B. (Eds.). (1982). *The Students' Right to Know.* Urbana, IL: National Council of Teachers of English.

Busha, C.H. (1972). *Freedom versus suppression and censorship: With a study of librarians' opinions and a bibliography of censorship.* Littleton, CO: Libraries Unlimited.

Cai, M. (1994, September). Images of Chinese and Chinese Americans mirrored in picture books. *Children's Literature in Education, 25*(3), 169–191.

Cai, M. (1995, Winter). Can we fly across cultural gaps on the wings of imagination? Ethnicity, experience, and cultural authenticity. *The New Advocate, (8)*1, 1–15.

Campbell, P. (1999, November/December). The sand in the oyster: Radical monster. *The Horn Book, LXXV,* 6, 769–773.

Carr, M., & Forchion, S. (1999). *Huck Finn in context: A teacher's guide.* Boston: WGBH Educational Foundation. Available: http://www.pbs.org/wgbh/cultureshock/teachers/huck/index.html

Carter, B. (1996, October). Hold the applause! Do Accelerated Reader & Electronic Bookshelf send the right message? *School Library Journal. 42*(10), 22–25.

Carter, B. (2000, July 1). Formula for failure. *School Library Journal* [Online]. Available: http://206.236.152.83/articles/articles/20000701_8332.asp

Carvin, A. (Ed.). (2000, February). *The e-rate in America: A tale of four cities.* The Benton Foundation & the EDC/Center for Children and Technology. Available: http://www.benton.org/e-rate/e-rate.4cities.pdf

Carvin, A. (2000, April 20). Student free speech rights on the Internet and the ghosts of Columbine. *The Digital Beat, 2,* 29. Available from: Benton-compolicy@cdinet.com

Child Online Protection Act, Sec. 1401-1406. Of the Omnibus Consolidated and Emergency Supplemental Appropriations Act of 1999 (P.L. 105-277).

Children's Internet Protection Act of 2000 [Online]. Available: http://www.cdt.org/legislation/106th/speech/001218cipa.pdf

Cleverly J., & Phillips, D.C. (1986). *Visions of childhood: Influential models from Locke to Spock* (Rev. ed.). New York: Teachers College Press.

Cormier, R. (1974). *The chocolate war.* New York: Pantheon.

Cormier, R. (1977). *I am the cheese.* New York: Knopf.

Cormier, R. (1992). A book is not a house: The human side of censorship. In D.R. Gallo (Ed.), *Authors' insights: Turning teenagers into readers & writers* (pp. 73–74). Portsmouth, NH: Heinemann.

Council on Interracial Books for Children. (1980). *Guidelines for selecting bias-free textbooks and storybooks.* New York: Author.

Council on Interracial Books for Children. (1981). *Unlearning Asian stereotypes.* New York: Author.

Davis, J.E. (Ed.). (1979). *Dealing with censorship.* Urbana, IL: National Council of Teachers of English.

Dewey, J. (1899). *The school and society.* Chicago: University of Chicago Press. (Reissued 1991)

Dewey, J. (1902). *The child and the curriculum.* Chicago: University of Chicago Press. (Reissued 1991)

Dewey, J. (1916). *Democracy and education: An introduction to the philosophy of education.* New York: Macmillan. (Reissued 1997, New York: Simon & Schuster)

Donelson, K.L. (Ed.). (1972). *Students' right to read.* Urbana, IL: National Council of Teachers of English. Available: http://www.ncte.org/censorship/right2read.shtml

Donelson, K.L., & Nilsen, A.P. (1996). *Literature for today's young adult* (5th ed.). Reading, MA: Addison-Wesley.

Dresang, E.T. (1997). *What is authenticity?* [Online]. Available: http://www.scils.rutgers.edu/special/kay/authentic.html

Dresang, E.T. (1999a). *Radical change: Books for youth in a digital age.* New York: H.W. Wilson.

Dresang, E.T. (1999b). Informal information-seeking behavior of youth on the internet. *Journal of the American Society for Information Science, 50*(12), 1123–1124.

Ebert, M. (1991, December 16). Liberals malign parents as 'censors.' *Citizen, 5*(2), 1–6.

Editorial. (1999, August 16). *The Washington Post,* p. A14.

Educational Leadership. (1983, January). Alexandria, VA: Association for Supervision and Curriculum Development, 46(1), 54.

FCC v. Pacifica Foundation, 438 U.S. 726 (1978).

Florian, J. (1999, December 15). *Teacher survey of standards-based instruction: Addressing time.* Aurora, CO: Mid-continent Research for Education and Learning. Available: http://www.mcrel.org/products/standards/addressingtime.asp

Gabler, M., & Gabler, N. (1985). *What are they teaching our children?* Wheaton, IL: Victor.

The Gablers fighting for purity. (1979, December 11). *Time Magazine,* 76.

Gann, L. (1998). School library media standards & guidelines: A review of their significance and impact. In K. Latrobe (Ed.), *The emerging school library media center* (pp. 153–194). Englewood, CA: Libraries Unlimited.

Garden, N. (1982). *Annie on my mind.* New York: Farrar, Strauss & Giroux.

Gardner, H. (1993). *Frames of mind: The theory of multiple intelligences* (10th Anniversary Edition). New York: Basic Books.

Gates, D. (1940). *Blue willow.* New York: Viking.

Gilligan, C. (1982). *In a different voice: Psychological theory and women's development.* Cambridge, MA: Harvard University Press.

Gingrich, N. (1994, October 5). [Speech given to the Heritage Foundation].

Gish, K.W. (2000, May/June). Hunting down Harry Potter: An exploration of religious concerns about children's literature. *The Horn Book Magazine*, 76(3), 262–271.

Glave, J. (1998, November 26). Teacher is threatened for using ethnic book. *Tallahassee Democrat*, p. A3.

Gold, J.C. (1995). *Board of Education v. Pico*. New York: Twentieth Century Books.

Gove, P. (Ed.). (1961). Introduction. *Webster's Third New International Dictionary*. Springfield, MA: G.C. Merriam Webster.

Gross, M. (1999, Winter). The imposed query and information services for children. *Journal of Youth Services in Libraries*, 13, 2.

Guernsey, L. (2000, January 9). O.K. Schools are wired, now what? *The New York Times* [Online]. Available: http://archives.nytimes.com/archives

Hamilton, V. (1982). *Sweet whispers, Brother Rush*. New York: Philomel.

Harris, R.H., & Emberley, M. (1999). *It's quite amazing: a book about eggs, sperm, birth, babies, and families*. New York: Candlewick Press.

Harris, V.J. (1996, Spring). Continuing dilemmas, debates, and delights in multicultural literature. *The New Advocate*, (9)2, 109–122.

Hart, T., & Dunnavant, S. (in press). *Electronic reading program manual*. Tallahassee, FL: State of Florida Department of Education.

Haselton, B. (2000, June 6). BAIR "image filtering" has 0% accuracy rate. *Peacefire: Open Access for the Net Generation* [Online]. Available: http://peacefire.org/censorware/BAIR/first-report.6-6-2000.html

Haselton, B. (2000, August 8). SurfWatch error rate for first 1,000 .com domains. *Peacefire: Open Access for the Net Generation* [Online]. Available: http://peace fire.org/censorware/SurfWatch/first-1000-com-domains.html

Hazelwood School District Vs. Kuhlmeier, 484 U.S. 260, 108 S. Ct. 562 (1988).

Healy, J. (1999). *Failure to connect: How computers affect children's minds and what we can do about it*. New York: Touchstone Books.

Hearne, B., & Jenkins, C. (1999, September/October). Sacred texts: What our foremothers left us in the way of psalms, proverbs, precepts, and practices. *The Horn Book Magazine*, 75(5), 536–558.

Hentoff, N. (1982). *The day they came to arrest the book*. New York: Dell.

Hentoff, N. (1992). *Free speech for me—but not for thee: How the American left and right relentlessly censor each other*. New York: HarperCollins.

Hentoff seeks the truth. (1999, February 20). Amazon.com reader reviews of *Free speech for me—but not nor thee: How the American left and right relentlessly censor each other* [Online]. Available: http://www.amazon.com/exec/obidos/ASIN/006019006X/qid=971878553/sr=1-1/002-9509043-7655245

Herring, H.B. (1999, March 14). Crayola changes stripes. *New York Times*. Section 4, p. 2.

Hewins, C. (1882). *Books for the young: A guide for parents and children*. [Pamphlet]. Hartford, CT: Author.

Hinton, S.E. (1967). *The outsiders*. New York: Viking.

Hipple, T. (1999, November). *The best YA novels of the 90s* [Survey]. University of Tennessee.

Hirsch, E.D. (1987). *Cultural literacy: What every American should know*. New York: Vintage Books.

Hopkins, D.M. (1992, Fall). Perspectives of secondary library media specialists about material challenges. *School Library Media Quarterly, 21*(1), 15–29.

Hopkins, D.M. (1993, January). Put it in writing: What you should know about challenges to school library materials. *School Library Journal, 39*(1), 26–30.

Hopkins, D.M. (1993). A conceptual model of factors influencing the outcome of challenges to library materials in secondary school settings. *Library Quarterly, 63*(1), 40–72.

Hopkins, D.M. (1996). *School library media centers and intellectual freedom: Intellectual freedom manual.* Chicago: American Library Association.

Hopkins, D.M. (1998). Toward a conceptual path of support for school library media specialists with material challenges. *School Library Media Quarterly Online* [Online]. Available: http://www.ala.org/aasl/SLMQ/support.html

Horning, K.T., Kruse, G.M., & Schliesman, M. (2000). *CCBC Choices 2000.* Madison, WI: Cooperative Children's Book Center, School of Education, University of Wisconsin–Madison.

Huck, C., & Hepler, S. (1996). *Children's books in the elementary school* (6th ed.). New York: McGraw-Hill.

Hulsizer, D. (1989). *Protecting the freedom to learn: A citizen's guide.* Washington, DC: People for the American Way.

In a high-profile censorship case, a federal judge in Kansas orders a school district to put *Annie on My Mind* back on the shelves. (1996). *School Library Journal, 42*(1), 13.

International Reading Association and National Council for Teachers of English. (1996). *Standards for the English Language Arts.* Newark, DE: International Reading Association; Urbana, IL: National Council of Teachers of English.

Jackson, J. (1940). *Call me Charley.* Eau Claire, WI: E.M. Hale.

Janows, J., & Lee, L. (2000). *Born to trouble: The Adventures of Huckleberry Finn* (J. Janows, Producer & Director). *Culture Shock.* Boston: PBS/WGHB. Available: http://www.pbs.org/wgbh/cultureshock/beyond/huck.html

Jenkins, C. (1993, Fall). Young adult novels with gay/lesbian characters and themes 1969–1992: A historical reading of content, gender, and narrative distance. *Journal of Youth Services in Libraries, 7,* 43–55.

Jenkins, C. (1998). From queer to gay and back again: Young adult novels with gay/lesbian/queer content, 1969–1997. *Library Quarterly, 68*(3), 298–334.

Jenkins, H. (Speaker). (2000, July 10). *It's our bill of rights, too!: Children, the First Amendment, and America's response to violence* (Cassette recording). Chicago: Program sponsored by the American Library Association Intellectual Freedom Committee, the America Association of Publishers Freedom to Read Committee, and the American Booksellers Foundation for Free Expression at the American Library Association Annual Conference.

Jesson, G.R. (1991, December 16). How parents can refute the "censor" label. *Citizen, 5*(2), 2–3.

Johnson, C. (1994). *Stifled laughter.* Golden, CO: Fulcrum.

Jones, B.M. (1999). *Libraries, access, and intellectual freedom.* Chicago: American Library Association.

Kaiser Family Foundation. (2000). *Kids and media@the new millenium.* Washington, DC: The Henry J. Kaiser Family Foundation. Available: http://www. childrens-media.org/medlit/m_rese8.html

Kendall, J., & Marzano, R. (1997). *Content knowledge: A compendium of standards and benchmarks for K–12 education* [Online]. Available: http://www.mcrel. org/standards-benchmarks/docs/chapter1.html See also: http://www.mcrel. org/compendium/Benchmark.asp?SubjectID=4&StandardID=4

Kristol, I. (1991, July 31). The tragedy of multiculturalism. *The Wall Street Journal* [Online]. Available: http://www.aidsinfobbs.org/articles/wallstj/91/201

Krug, J. (Ed.). (1995, November). *ALA Newsletter on Intellectual Freedom*. Chicago: American Library Association.

Krull, K. (1999). *A kids' guide to America's Bill of Rights: Curfews, censorship, and the 100-pound giant*. New York: Avon Books.

Kruse, G.M., Horning, K.T., & Schliesman, M., with T. Elias. (1997). *Multicultural literature for children and young adults*. Madison, WI: Cooperative Children's Book Center, Friends of the CCBC, Wisconsin Department of Public Instruction. Available from Friends of the CCBC, Inc., Box 5288, Madison, WI 53705.

Lance, K.C. (1993). *The impact of school library media centers on academic achievement*. Castle Rock, CO: Hi Willow Research and Publishing & Colorado Department of Education.

Lance, K.C. (1994, Spring). The impact of school library media centers on academic achievement. *School Library Media Quarterly*, *22*, 3. Available: http://www. ala.org/aasl/SLMR/slmr_resources/select_lance.html

Larrick, N. (1965, September 11). The all-white world of children's books. *Saturday Review*, *48*, 63–65.

Larrick, N., & Merriam, E. (1973). *Male and female under 18: Frank comments from young people about their sex roles today*. New York: Discus Books.

Leo, J. (1991, July 8). Multicultural follies. *U.S. News & World Report*, p. 12.

Lester, J. (1996). *Sam and the tigers*. Ill. Jerry Pinkney. New York: Dial.

Lewin, T. (2000, July 30). Tales of raw misery for ages 12 and up. *New York Times* [Online]. Available: http://nytimes.com/library

Lindsay, H., & Crouse, R. (1948). *Life with father*. New York: Dramatists' Play.

Lipsyte, R. (1967). *The contender*. New York: Harper & Row.

Lowry, L. (1993). *The giver*. Boston: Houghton Mifflin.

Macaulay, D. (1990). *Black and white*. Boston: Houghton Mifflin.

Macaulay, D. (1991, Summer). 1991 Caldecott Acceptance Speech. *Journal of Youth Services for Libraries*, *4*(4), 340–347.

Males, M.A. (1999). *Framing youth: Ten myths about the next generation*. Monroe, ME: Common Courage Press.

Marsh, D. (1991). *50 ways to fight censorship & important facts to know about the censors*. New York: Thunder's Mouth Press.

Marzano, R. (1994). Censorship and the "New Age." In J.S. Simmons (Ed.), *Censorship: A threat to reading, learning, thinking* (pp. 37–44). Newark, DE: International Reading Association.

Means, F.P. (1938). *Shuttered windows*. Boston: Houghton Mifflin.

Mertz, M., & England, D. (1983, October). The legitimacy of American adolescent fiction. *School Library Journal*, *30*(2), 119–123.

Meyer, R. (1996, April). *Annie's* day in court: The decision from the bench. *School Library Journal*, *42*(4), 22–25.

Miami Herald Publishing Co. v. Tornillo, 418 U.S. 241 (1974).

Miles, B. (1980). *Maudie and me and the dirty book*. New York: Knopf.

Miller v. California, 413 U.S. 15 (1973).

Minarcini v. Strongsville (Ohio) City School District, 541 F.2d 577, 6th Cir. (1976).

Minkel, W., & Feldman, R.H. (1999). *Delivering web reference services to young people*. Chicago: American Library Association.

Moffett, J. (1988). *Storm in the mountains: A case study of censorship, conflict, and consciousness*. Carbondale, IL: Southern Illinois University Press.

Monteiro vs. Tempe Union High School District, 97-15511, U.S. 9th Circuit Court of Appeals (1998).

Morrison, T. (1992). *Playing in the dark: Whiteness and the literary imagination*. Cambridge: Harvard University Press.

Muggles for Harry Potter. (2000a). *Banned Book Week heroes honored at Library of Congress* [Online]. Available: http://www.mugglesforharrypotter.org/potter4.htm

Muggles for Harry Potter. (2000b). *Zeeland schools rescind most Harry Potter restrictions* [Online]. Available: http://www.mugglesforharrypotter.org/zeeland.htm

Muller, A.P. (1973). *The currently popular adolescent novel as transitional literature*. Unpublished doctoral dissertation, Florida State University, Tallahassee Florida.

Muller, A.P. (1974, September). Thirty popular adolescent novels: A content analysis. *English Journal, 63*(6), 97–99.

Myers, W.D. (1999). *Monster*. New York: Scholastic.

Myers, W.D. (2000). *Malcolm X: A fire burning brightly*. Ill. L. Jenkins. New York: HarperCollins.

National Center for Educational Statistics. (2000a). *Internet access in U.S. public schools and classrooms: 1994–1999*. Washington, DC: U.S. Department of Education. Available: http://nces.ed.gov/pubsearch/pubsinfo.asp?pubid=2000086

National Center for Educational Statistics. (2000b). *Computer and internet access in private schools and classrooms: 1995 and 1998*. Washington, DC: U.S. Department of Education. Available: http://nces.ed.gov/pubsearch/pubsinfo.asp?pubid=2000044

National Coalition Against Censorship. (1985, Spring). *Censorship news*, 4–5.

National Council of Teachers of English. (1972). *Students' right to their own language*. Urbana, IL: National Council of Teachers of English. Available: http://www.ncte.org/ccc/12/sub/state1.html

National Telecommunications and Information Administration. (2000). *Closing the digital divide* [Online]. Available: http://www.digitaldivide.gov/

Newsletter on Intellectual Freedom. (1991, July). Chicago, IL: American Library Association, 108.

Newsletter on Intellectual Freedom. (1996, October). Chicago, IL: American Library Association, 11.

Nussbaum, D. (1998, October 22). Computer haves and have nots in the classroom. *The New York Times* [Online]. Available: http://archives.nytimes.com/archives

Odean, K. (1997). *Great books for girls: More than 600 books to inspire today's girls and tomorrow's women*. New York: Ballantine.

Odean, K. (1998). *Great books for boys: More than 600 books for boys 2–14*. New York: Ballantine.

Oglesby, J.R., & Shannon, T.A. (1989). Foreword. *Censorship: Managing the controversy* (p. i). Washington, DC: National School Board Association.

O'Hara, J. (1934). *Appointment in Samarra*. New York: New American Library.

O'Hara, M. (1941). *My friend Flicka*. New York: Lippincott.

O'Hara-Connell, H. (1994). *Gender bias in high school canon novels: A subversion of power.* Unpublished dissertation, Florida State University, Tallahassee.

Orwell, G. (1949). *1984.* New York: Harcourt Brace.

Ostling, R. (1995, November 8). Elections weaken strength of Religious Right. *Tallahassee Democrat,* p. A8.

Panel on Education Technology. (1997, March). *Report to the President on the use of technology to strengthen K–12 education in the United States.* Washington, DC: The White House. Available: http://www.whitehouse.gov/WH/EOP/OSTP/NSTC/PCAST/k-12ed.html#7.5

Papert, S. (1994). *The children's machine: Rethinking school in the age of the computer.* New York: Basic Books.

Paterson, K. (1978). *Bridge to Terabithia.* New York: HarperCollins.

Paterson, K. (1980). *Jacob have I loved.* New York: HarperCollins.

Paterson, K. (1999). Katherine Patterson on censorship. In J. Blume (Ed.), *Places I never meant to be: Original stories by censored writers* (p. 70). New York: Simon & Schuster.

Peck, R.S. (2000). *Libraries, the first amendment, and cyberspace.* Chicago: American Library Association.

People for the American Way. (1995). *Redondo Beach: A stand against censorship* [Video]. Washington, DC: People for the American Way.

People for the American Way. (1996). *Attacks on the freedom to learn.* Washington, DC: Author.

People for the American Way. (1997). *A right wing and a prayer.* Washington, DC: PFAW Foundation. Available: http://www.pfaw.org/issues/education/rwp97.summary.shtml

Petitt, D.G. (1961). *A study of the qualities of literary excellence which characterize selected fiction for younger adolescents.* Unpublished doctoral dissertation, University of Minnesota, Twin Cities.

Pfeffer, S.B. (1999). Susan Beth Pfeffer on censorship. In J. Blume (Ed.), *Places I never meant to be: Original stories by censored writers* (p. 126). New York: Simon & Schuster.

Piaget, J., & Inhelder, B. (1969). *The psychology of the child* (H. Weaver, Trans.). New York: Basic Books.

Piper, W. (1978). *The little engine that could.* New York: Grosset & Dunlap.

Protection of Pupil Rights Amendment (PPRA), 20 U.S.C. § 1232h; 34 CFR Part 98 (1994).

Rawlings, M.K. (1985). *The yearling.* New York: Atheneum. (Original work published 1938)

Red Lion Broadcasting Co. v. FCC, 395 U.S. 367, 386 (1969).

Reno, Attorney General of the United States, et al. v. American Civil Liberties Union, et al., Appeal from the United States District Court for the Eastern District of Pennsylvania, No. 96-511 (1997). [Online]. Available: http://caselaw.findlaw.com/scripts/getcase.pl?court=us&navby=case&vol=000&invol=96-511

Review of *Malcolm X: A fire burning brightly.* (2000). Quoted from *The Horn Book Magazine* [Online]. Available: http://www.amazon.com/exec/obidos/ASIN/0060277076/qid=971969763/sr=1-24/002-9509043-7655245

Right to Read Defense Committee v. School Committee of the City of Chelsea, 454 F. Supp. 703, D. Mass. (1978).

Robertson, P. (1984, October 2). *The 700 Club*. Virginia Beach, VA: Christian Broadcasting Network.

Rochman, H. (1993). *Against borders: Promoting books for a multicultural world*. Chicago: American Library Association.

Rochman, H. (1995, March/April). Against borders. *The Horn Book Magazine*, p. 148.

Rowling, J.K. (1998a). *Harry Potter and the sorcerer's stone*. New York: Scholastic.

Rowling, J.K. (1998b). *Harry Potter and the chamber of secrets*. New York: Scholastic.

Rowling, J.K. (1999). *Harry Potter and the prisoner of Azkaban*. New York: Scholastic.

Rowling, J.K. (2000). *Harry Potter and the goblet of fire*. New York: Scholastic.

Salinger, J.D. (1951). *Catcher in the rye*. Boston: Little, Brown.

Scales, P. (1995, September). Studying the First Amendment. *Book Links, 6*, 20–24.

Schacter, J., Chung, W.K., & Dorr, A. (1998). Children's internet searching on complex problems: Performance and process analyses. *Journal of the American Society for Information Science, 49*, 890–850.

Schlessinger, L. (2000, September 1). Is your library x-rated? *Family Circle Magazine*.

Schneider, K.G. (1997). Learning from TIFAP. *TIFAP: The Internet Filter Assessment Project* [Online]. Available: http://www.bluehighways.com/tifap/learn.htm

Sendak, M. (1963). *Where the wild things are*. New York: Harper & Row.

Sendak, M. (1970). *In the night kitchen*. New York: Harper & Row.

Serebnick, J. (1979, Summer). A review of research related to censorship in libraries. *Library Research, I*, 95–118.

Shafer, R.E. (1994). Censors and the new proposals for literacy. In J.S. Simmons (Ed.), *Censorship: A threat to reading, learning, thinking* (pp. 77–85). Newark, DE: International Reading Association.

Simmons, J.S. (1990). U.S. censorship: An increasing fact of life. In M. Hayhoe & S. Parker (Eds.), *Reading and response* (p. 119). Philadelphia: Open University Press.

Simmons, J.S. (1998, Winter). A bridge too far—but why? *ALAN Review, 25*(2), 21–23.

Simmons, J.S., & Deluzain, H.E. (1992). *Teaching literature in middle and secondary schools*. Boston: Allyn & Bacon.

Sims Bishop, R. (1992). *Shadow and substance: Afro-American experience in contemporary children's literature*. Urbana, IL: National Council of Teachers of English.

Singer, D.G., & Revenson, T.A. (1996). *A Piaget primer: How a child thinks* (Rev. ed.). New York: Plume.

Sites blocked by ClickSafe. (2000, July 18). *Peacefire: Open Access for the Net Generation* [Online]. Available: http://peacefire.org/censorware/ClickSafe/screenshots-copacommission.html

Skursynski, G. (1998). *Discover mars: Includes 3-D glasses*. Washington, DC: National Geographic Society.

Smolan, R. (1998). *One digital day: How the microchip is changing our world*. New York: Times Books.

Spencer, G. (1996, March 14). *The nation's fifty-something population projected to grow by 50 percent during next decade, Census Bureau reports*. Washington, DC: U.S. Census Bureau. Available: http://www.census.gov/Press-Release/cb96-36.html

Stacey, J., Bereaud, S., & Daniels, J. (1974). *And Jill came tumbling after: Sexism in American education*. New York: Dell.

Steinbeck, J. (1992). *The grapes of wrath* (Reissue edition). New York: Penguin. (Original work published 1939)

Steinbeck, J. (1993). *Of mice and men* (Reissue edition). New York: Penguin. (Original work published 1937)

Stevana Case v. Unified School Dist. No. 233, 908 F. Supp. 864 (D. Kan. 1995).

Supreme Court rejects e-rate appeal. (2000, June 5). *American Library Association* [Online]. Available: http://www.ala.org/alonline/news/2000/000605.html#rep

Sutherland, Z. (1996). *Children and books* (9th ed.). Ill. T.S. Hyman. Reading, MA: Addison-Wesley. (Original work by May Hill Arbuthnot)

Symons, A., & Harmon, C. (1995). *Protecting the right to read : A how-to-do-it manual for school and public librarians*. New York: Neal-Schuman.

Tapscott, D. (1998). *Growing up digital: The rise of the net generation*. New York: McGraw-Hill.

Taxel, J. (1994, Spring). Political correctness, cultural politics, and writing for young people. *The New Advocate, 7*(2), 93–108.

Telecommunications Act of 1996, Pub. LA. No. 104-104, 110 Stat. 56 (1996).

Tingle, M. (1958). *The image of the family in selected junior novels*. Unpublished doctoral dissertation, University of Minnesota, Twin Cities.

Tinker v. Des Moines Independent Community School District, 393 U.S. 503 (1969).

Tunis, J. (1989). *All-American*. New York: Harcourt Brace. (Original work published 1939)

Turkle, S. (1995). *Life on the screen: Identity in the age of the internet*. New York: Simon & Schuster.

Twain, M. (1999). *The adventures of Huckleberry Finn*. New York: Puffin. (Original work published 1884)

Tway, E. (Ed.). (1981). *Reading ladders for human relations* (6th ed.). Urbana, IL: National Council of Teachers of English.

United States Census Bureau. (2000, January 13). *Projections of the resident population by race, Hispanic origin, and nativity: Middle series, 1999 and 2000*. Population Projections Program. Washington, DC: U.S. Census Bureau. Available: http://www.census.gov/population/projections/nation/summary/np-t5-a.txt

United States Department of Education. (1996, June 29). *Getting America's students ready for the 21st century: meeting the technology literacy challenge: A report to the nation on technology and education*. Washington, DC: U.S. Department of Education. Available: http://www.ed.gov/Technology/Plan/NatTechPlan/priority.html

United States National Commission on Excellence in Education. (1983). *A nation at risk*. Cambridge, MA: USA Research.

Update. (1995, January). Alexandra, VA: Association for Supervision and Curriculum Development, *25*, 18–21.

Vail, R. (1999). Rachel Vail on censorship. In J. Blume (Ed.), *Places I never meant to be: Original stories by censored writers* (pp. 60–61). New York: Simon & Schuster.

Vygotsky, L.S. (1962). *Thought and language* (E. Haufmann & G. Vakar, Eds. & Trans.). Cambridge, MA: MIT Press.

Walsh, M. (1995, November 5). *San Francisco Examiner.* (Quoted in *Education Weekly, 16*(3), July 18, 1997, p. 10.)

Warner, M. (1994). *Six myths of our times.* New York: Vintage.

The Web-based Education Commission. (2000, December). *The power of the internet for learning: Moving from promise to practice* (Report of the Web-based Education Commission to the President and Congress of the United States). Washington, DC: The Web-based Education Commission. Available: http://interact.hpcnet.org/webcommission/text.htm

Weiner, N. (1991). National textbook: The McGuffey Reader. In *Background briefing* [Online]. Available: http://www.backgroundbriefing.com/mcguffee.html

West, M. (1997). *Trust your children: Voices against censorship in children's literature* (2nd ed.). New York: Neal Schuman.

Wiley, R. (1997). *Excerpts from* "Spike Lee's Huckeberry Finn" [Online]. Available: http://www.citadel.edu/faculty/leonard/wileyscenes.htm

Willhoite, M. (1990). *Daddy's roommate.* Boston: Alyson Publications.

Witt, M. (Ed.). (1980). *The humanities: Cultural roots and continuities.* Boston: Houghton Mifflin.

White, E.B. (1952). *Charlotte's web.* Ill. G. Williams. New York: HarperCollins.

Whitson, J.A. (1998, Winter). After Hazelwood: The role of school officials in conflicts over the curriculum. *The ALAN Review, 20*(2), 3–4.

Willard, N. (1996). *A legal and educational analysis of K–12 Internet acceptable use policies* [Online]. Available: http://www.erehwon.com/k12aup/legal_analysis.html

Woodard, E.H. (with N. Gridina). (2000). *Media in the home 2000: A fifth annual survey of parents and children.* Philadelphia: Annenberg Public Policy Center. Available: http://www.appcpenn.org/inhome.pdf

Woodworth, M.L. (1976). *Intellectual freedom, the young adult and schools* (Rev ed.). Madison, WI: Communication Programs, University of Wisconsin Extension.

Wordsworth, W. (1798). We are seven [Online]. Available: http://homepages.tesco.net/~andy.oddjob/word04.htm

X, M., & Haley, A. (1992). *The autobiography of Malcolm X.* New York: Ballantine. (Original work published 1965)

Yeats, W.B. (1989). The second coming. In R.J. Finneran (Ed.), *Collected poems of W.B. Yeats* (p. 187). New York: Macmillan. (Original work published 1921)

Yuill, P. (1976). *Little Black Sambo: A closer look—A history of Helen Bannerman's* The story of Little Black Sambo *and its popularity/controversy in the United States.* New York: Racism and Sexism Resource Center for Educators.

Zindel, P. (1968). *The pigman.* New York: Harper & Row.

Zwick, J. (1997). *Banned books and American culture* [Online]. Available: http://www.marktwain.about.com/arts/marktwain/library/weekly/aa092397.htm

Zwick, J. (1998a). *Civil rights or book banning? Three new approaches to* Huckleberry Finn [Online]. Available: http://marktwain.about.com/arts/marktwain/library/weekly/aa980922.htm

Zwick, J. (1998b). *Huckleberry Finn on trial* [Online]. Available: http://marktwain.about.com/arts/marktwain/library/weekly/aa981027.htm

Zwick, J. (2000). *Reading* "Spike Lee's Huckeberry Finn" [Online]. Available: http://marktwain.about.com/arts/marktwain/library/weekly/aa000222a.htm?terms=spike+lee

Index

Note: Page reference followed by *t* or *f* indicates table and figure.

A

BROWN V. BOARD OF EDUCATION OF TOPEKA, KANSAS, 25, 37
BRUCHAC, J., 98
BRUNI, F., 42
BURRESS, L., 173
BURT, DAVID, 137
BUSHA, C., 54
BUSH, LAURA, 42

C

CAI, MINGSHUI, 96–98
CAMPAIGN FOR WORKING FAMILIES, 188, 195
CAMPBELL, P., 101–104
CARLIN, GEORGE, 126
CARLSEN, G.R., 116
CARR, M., 93
CARTER, BETTY, 86
CARVIN, A., 121
CASE, STEVANA, 55
CATTON, BRUCE, 204
CELEBRATING THE FREEDOM TO READ (ALA), 171, 206–207
CENSORS: motives of, 111; organizations of, 152–161; use of Internet by, 137
CENSORSHIP: alliance against, 39–62; and future of education, 21–22; and Internet, 119–142; litigation on, 143–161; origins of, 25–38; prime targets of, 63–78, 111–114, 132; responses to, 162–181, 198–199; scorecard on, 71–73; societal factors affecting, 25–29; sources of, 54; spread of, 29–31; statistics on, 117–118; types of, 31–36; youth literature on, 56, 57f–59f
CENSORSHIP NEWS, 174
CENTER FOR DEMOCRACY AND TECHNOLOGY, 134, 136, 140, 180
CHALLENGED MATERIALS, 73–77; alternatives to, 169; growth of, 82–86; prime targets, 63–78, 111–114, 132; retention of, factors affecting, 54; topics and themes in, 64–71
CHAUCER, GEOFFREY, 36, 147
CHEATING, 29
CHILD ONLINE PROTECTION ACT/COMMISSION, 128, 130, 133–134
CHILD PROTECTION AND OBSCENITY ENFORCEMENT ACT, 156
CHILDREN'S CATALOG, 115
CHILDREN'S INTERNET PROTECTION ACT, 128–129
CHILDREN'S LITERATURE, 104–107; change in, 110
CHILDRESS, ALICE, 64, 70, 73; A Hero Ain't Nothin But a Sandwich, 65, 145
CHOICE, 151–152

GARDNER, H., 13

GATES, DORIS: *Blue Willow,* 108

GAY/LESBIAN ISSUES, 40–41, 84; inclusion of, 90–91

GILLIGAN, C., 13

GINGRICH, NEWT, 83, 158

GINSBERG V. NEW YORK, 126–127

GIPSON, FRED, 204

GISH, K.W., 113

GLAVE, J., 162–163

GLOBAL INTERNET LIBERTY CAMPAIGN, 141

GO ASK ALICE, 65, 72, 145

GOLD, JOHN COPPERSMITH: *The Board of Education vs. Pico,* 56–57*f*

GOLDING, WILLIAM: *The Lord of the Flies,* 70

GORDIMER, NADINE, 36

GORE, AL, 156

GORE, TIPPER, 153, 155

GOVE, PHILIP, 84

GRADE INFLATION, 29

GRAY, ELIZABETH J., 204

GREENBERG, KEITH: *Adolescent Rights: Are Young People Equal Under the Law,* 57

GRIFFIN, CAROL, 153

GROSS, M., 18

GUERNSEY, L., 120, 123

GUEST, JUDITH, 73; *Ordinary People,* 72

H

HALEY, A., 105

HAMILTON, VIRGINIA, 97; *Sweet Whispers, Brother Rush,* 94

HARRIS, K.A., 90

HARRIS, ROBIE, 110–111

HARRIS, VIOLET, 96–97

HARRY POTTER SERIES, 69, 99, 112–114

HART, T., 86

HASELTON, B., 135

HATCH AMENDMENT, 149–151

HATCH, ORRIN, 149

HATRED, 79–81

HAWTHORNE, NATHANIEL, 69; *The Scarlet Letter,* 70

HAZELWOOD SCHOOL DISTRICT V. KUHLMEIER, 34, 38, 61, 83, 146–149

HEAD, ANN, 205

HEALY, J., 123–124

I

MINKEL, W., 122

MINORITIES: backlash against, 26–27; condemnation of, 29; image of, 69–71; inclusion of, 87–91

MOFFETT, J., 65

MONTEIRO, KATHY, 92, 160

MONTEIRO V. TEMPE UNION HIGH SCHOOL DISTRICT, 160

MOORE, A.C., 114

MORAL MAJORITY, 79, 153

MORRIS, DESMOND: *The Naked Ape*, 145

MORRISON, TONI, 64, 70, 88, 157

MOWAT, FARLEY: *Never Cry Wolf*, 151

MUGGLES FOR HARRY POTTER, 112–113, 118

MULLER, A., 115–116, 205

MULTICULTURALISM: in challenged material, 83; and change in literature, 109–110; complexities of, 87–98; definition of, 87; emerging concerns about, 95–98; opposition to, 91–94

MUNSON, AMELIA, 114

MYERS, WALTER DEAN, 91, 96, 111–112; *Malcolm X: A Fire Burning Brightly*, 105–106; *Monster*, 101–104

N

NABOKOV, VLADIMIR, 156

NASA, 4, 23

NATIONAL ASSOCIATION FOR THE ADVANCEMENT OF COLORED PEOPLE, 93, 156–157, 161

NATIONAL ASSOCIATION OF CHRISTIAN EDUCATORS, 155

NATIONAL ASSOCIATION OF ELEMENTARY SCHOOL PRINCIPALS, 177, 180

NATIONAL ASSOCIATION OF SECONDARY SCHOOL PRINCIPALS, 177, 180

NATIONAL CAMPAIGN FOR FREE EXPRESSION, 142

NATIONAL CENTER FOR EDUCATION STATISTICS, 9, 17, 23, 120–121

NATIONAL COALITION AGAINST CENSORSHIP, 38, 174, 180, 195

NATIONAL COUNCIL OF TEACHERS OF ENGLISH, 33, 38, 48, 113, 151, 168, 172–174, 180; Resolutions on Censorship, 214–216; *Students' Right to Read*, 209–213

NATIONAL EDUCATION ASSOCIATION, 42

NATIONAL ENDOWMENT FOR THE ARTS, 83

NATIONAL ENDOWMENT FOR THE HUMANITIES, 83

NATIONAL INFORMATION INFRASTRUCTURE INITIATIVE, 120

NATIONAL LAW CENTER FOR CHILDREN AND FAMILIES, 134

NATIONAL LEGAL FOUNDATION, 153, 161

NATIONAL ORGANIZATION FOR WOMEN, 156, 161

NATIONAL RESEARCH COUNCILS, 130–131

34–35, 83; library media program and, 42–43; twenty-first century, characteristics of, 19–21